WITHDRAWN
NDSU

Joseph
HELLER

a reference guide

*A
Reference
Publication
in
Literature*

Jackson Bryer
Editor

Joseph HELLER
a reference guide

BRENDA M. KEEGAN

GEORGE PRIOR PUBLISHERS, LONDON, ENGLAND

G.K. HALL & CO.
70 LINCOLN STREET, BOSTON, MASS.

PS
3558
E476
Z785

Available for sale in the British Commonwealth from
George Prior Publishers, 2 Rugby St., London, England
ISBN (U.K.)   0-86043-241-6

Copyright © 1978 by Brenda Keegan

Library of Congress Cataloging in Publication Data
Keegan, Brenda, 1940-
   Joseph Heller: a reference guide.

   (Reference publications in literature)
   "Works by Joseph Heller": p.
   Includes index.
   1. Heller, Joseph — Bibliography.   I. Series.
Z8395.519.K43   [PS3558.E476]   016.813'5'4
ISBN 0-8161-8143-8   78-6853

This publication is printed on permanent/durable acid-free paper
MANUFACTURED IN THE UNITED STATES OF AMERICA

Contents

INTRODUCTION	vii
WRITINGS BY JOSEPH HELLER	xxxv
WRITINGS ABOUT JOSEPH HELLER, 1961–1977	1
INDEX	143

Introduction

Although Joseph Heller published several stories in national magazines in the 1940's, he received virtually no critical attention until Catch-22 was published in 1961. Even then, only a small review appeared on page 50 of the New York Times Book Review (1961.B64), and the Library Journal (1961.B4) advised only libraries with very large fiction collections to purchase this "tedious" novel. Fortunately, however, some reviewers and the general public were more enthusiastic. Over the years Catch-22 grew instead of diminishing in popularity until it replaced Catcher in the Rye and Lord of the Flies as college students' favorite contemporary classic. Many of its characters and phrases have "passed into folklore" (1973.A2) to become part of "the American idiom" (1974.B162); the title has become "an international synonym for any example of twisted logic" (1975.B9). By the time Something Happened was published in 1974, Heller's literary reputation had grown so remarkably that almost every major newspaper and magazine in the country carried reviews and feature articles about him. The New York Times Book Review then devoted its first three pages to commentary by Kurt Vonnegut and George Plimpton on the new novel (1974.B210 and 1974.B155). This bibliography traces the development of Heller's reputation through reviews and re-reviews of his work and through critical reconsideration as Catch-22 gained in popularity. It also describes reports on Heller's personal life and viewpoints, scholarly analyses of various aspects of his work, comparisons of Catch-22 and its film version, and assessments of Heller's place among modern writers.

Although Heller was not a known writer when Catch-22 was published, his editor, according to Kirkus (1961.B5), planned "considerable publicity" for the novel. That, along with some enthusiastic advance reviews (Calder-Marshall in Broadsheet [1961.B31] and Ludlow in Book Buyers Guide [1961.B48]) helped to bring the novel to the attention of the national press. Many reviewers enjoyed and recommended the book; but, overall, reaction was mixed. The New Mexico Quarterly reviewer, for example, called it "the funniest war novel since Journey to the End of the Night," but added, "Farce and fantasy, however, rob Catch-22 of reality and soften its impact" (1961.B4).

Introduction

Some reviewers found it brilliantly funny and meaningful. As a sampling of early enthusiastic notices, the Newsday reviewer described it as "crazy, wonderful, yet cruelly sane" (1961.B6); Arnold Rosenfeld of the Houston Post said it was "a tremendously funny tragic story" (1961.B57); Melvin Seiden in Nation found the book "fantastically inventive" (1961.B61); Orville Prescott, writing later than Stern in the New York Times, pronounced it "a dazzling performance that...will not be forgotten by those who can take it" (1961.B56); Ken Musson in the Tampa Tribune predicted it would give the reader "new laugh wrinkles and perhaps an occasional lift to an unexpected philosophical plane" (1961.B52); Bunny Honicker in the Nashville Tennessean saw it as "a perfect marriage of humor and horror" (1961.B43); and Roy Newquist in the Chicago Heights Star proclaimed it as "Ribald, outrageous, put together with conniving skills that never seem contrived, it is a stinging indictment of the military mind and committee judgement" (1961.B53).

Several reviewers were reminded of their own wartime experiences. Miles Smith in his syndicated review said that "anyone who has experienced the horror of military logic will recognize in this story the essential madness of war" (1961.B63). Bill Branche in the Niagara Falls Gazette, wrote, "Not since Stephen Crane has a writer seen war and the military more keenly" (1961.B27). However, others like Daniel Aherne of the Hartford Courant, "one long acquainted with the heroic work of the Air Force in World War II," violently disagreed and stated that such a squadron of men never existed (1961.B2).

Maurice Dolbier's prediction that Catch-22 would be "one of the most talked about books of the new season" (1961.B35) seemed correct as reviewers acclaimed Heller's inventive talent for comedy but expressed annoyance with or confusion about his innovative techniques. Jim Turner's Cleveland Press headline perhaps summarized the attitude best: Catch-22 "Mixes War, Humor--Not Well" (1961.B67). Walter Greenwood in the Buffalo News also questioned the "human decency involved in the technique of intertwining riotous farce with the agonies of death" (1961.B40). Granville Hicks in the Saturday Review admired Heller's satire but found his style "dizzying" (1961.B41). Similarly, Richard Stern in the New York Times Book Review acknowledged Heller's talent but condemned his "want of craft and sensibility" (1961.B64); Richard McLaughlin in the Springfield Republican found Catch-22 "savage and funny" but lacking "lucidity, perfect form, and characters who control one's interest" (1961.B49); and Spencer Klaw in the New York Herald Tribune also complained that Heller didn't develop sympathetic characters (1961.B47). Frank Hynes in Peninsula Living objected that Heller's writing lacked subtlety (1961.B44), while Douglas Posten in the Los Angeles Times (1961.B55) and John Thompson in the Chicago Tribune (1961.B66) both used the term "undisciplined" to describe the novel. The Time reviewer saw Heller's talent as "impressive" but complained of the novel's "boring repetition," "comic non sequitur," and "experimental formlessness" (1961.B12).

Introduction

Milton Bass in the Berkshire Eagle, however, saw past the annoying confusion ("an oddness to the people, a seeming disorganization to the plot and a weirdness to the atmosphere that makes you feel trapped in a mental institution") and found that, after further reading, "the pattern falls into place, and you realize that there is fantastic organization to the spider web of the plot and that the people are everybody you know carried to their logical extremes and the incidents are everything that has happened, is happening or will happen to you" (1961.B24). Roger Sale in The Hudson Review realized that the novel has artistic form, that after the "brittle undergraduate wisecracks," Heller "tells the same stories over and over, each time etching them a bit deeper..." (1962.B54).

Moreover, Robert Brustein in The New Republic saw purpose in Heller's strange characterization and began to explain how Catch-22 reveals that the most seemingly lunatic characters are actually the most sane and that it "is our conventional standards [in the whole society, not just the military] which lack any logical consistency" (1961.B28).

Others were even more excited about the value of the novel. Kenneth Tynan in the London Observer said it was the "most striking debut in American fiction since Catcher in the Rye" (1961.B68); Studs Terkel in the Chicago Times called it an "apocalyptic masterpiece" (1961.B65); in "Books and Authors" the Lewiston Sun reviewer speculated that it could well become one of the major works of the mid-century (1961.B10); Leonard Rowe in the Cincinnati Enquirer suggested it might be the greatest novel about World War II (1961.B58); Gladwin Hill in the Los Angeles Mirror foresaw that it might become a "classic of this era"(1961.B42); and, of great significance, the prominent critic Nelson Algren, writing in Nation, judged it "not merely the best American novel to come out of World War II...the best American novel that has come out of anywhere in years" (1961.B3).

By the end of 1961 Catch-22 had grown enough in popular stature to be recommended by Life (1961.B7), Saturday Review (1961.B20), Mademoiselle (1961.B15), the St. Louis Post-Dispatch (1961.B21), and the New York Herald Tribune (1961.B22) for Christmas giving. Don Bryant, of the Lincoln Journal Star (1961.B29) listed it as one of his favorite books of the year. Several articles indicated that it was a prime contender for the National Book Award in fiction; when it didn't win, Mary Snyder suggested that for many readers it was still "too wearing a novel in its shifting from hilarity to horror" (1962.B58).

In England, though, when it was first published by Jonathan Cape in June of 1962, the book became an immediate popular and critical success. Within one week of publication, it was first on the best seller lists; and the critics were uniformly positive in their responses, though two found it a bit too long. Andrew Leslie, the Guardian critic, called it "brilliantly comic" (1962.B41). Julian

Introduction

Mitchell in the Spectator said it was "a book of enormous richness and art, of deep thought and brilliant writing" (1962.B44); the Daily Express reviewer noted its "fierce and impressive satire" (1962.B9); Edna O'Brien in the Evening Standard named it as "a great, comic, and intricate fantasy" (1962.B47); and Bamber Gascoigne in the Sun Telegraph described it as "brilliantly constructed" (1962.B28). The Times critic went into the construction of the novel further, explaining Heller's "facility for playing tricks with time, for introducing incidents, then dropping them and allowing their full implications to become evident only very much later in the narrative" (1962.B10); Olivia Manning in the Sunday Times also saw purpose in Heller's catching "the confusion of a dream," returning to incidents over and over until they gained significance (1962.B42). Philip Toynbee in the London Observer Weekend Review lauded Catch-22 as "the greatest satirical work in the English language since 'Erewhon'" (1962.B61).

Inspired by the favorable response to the novel in England, the American publisher, Simon and Schuster, took out a full-page ad in the New York Times Book Review in late July, 1962, as part of a new publicity campaign for Catch-22. Perhaps because of this publicity, perhaps because of the Dell paperback version, or perhaps because of the book's growing number of enthusiasts, described in a Newsweek article called "The Heller Cult" (1962.B19) and a New York Times Book Review article called "Catch Cult" (1962.B65), a number of critics re-evaluated it. William Hogan still found it "overlong and immature" (1962.B35); Alan Cheuse in Studies on the Left objected that the non-comic passages were "overbearing sentimentality" (1963.B12); an anonymous Daedalus contributor took strong exception to the rave notices printed on the book's cover on the grounds that the book was badly written and immoral in its "mindless" attack on institutions and ideals (1963.B1); and George Woodbury in the Manchester News was stopped "in...[his] tracks" by the book's "total obscurity, non-sequitur, and incoherences...[and] complete absence of any kind of literary, or other, discipline" (1962.B68). Frederick Kiley clarified what the problem in appreciating Catch-22 was, perhaps without realizing it, when he protested that literary criticism had not yet devised the proper test to suit this novel (1968.B18). Douglas Day in The Carolina Quarterly also pointed up a problem for the "Establishment" with reading Catch-22 because the novel lacked "taste in the traditional sense with its mixture of humor and horror and because its hero is an unheroic satyr-like anarchist" (1963.B13). Allen Gilbert issued a worthwhile warning, too, in the Northwest Arkansas Times when he advised that the book required "careful reading" (1961.B38).

On a more positive note, A. C. Greene reported in the Dallas Times-Herald that, after trying to avoid the Catch-22 cult for a year, he finally had to acknowledge the book was "a delightful piece of reading for the irony and acid displayed throughout.... But...a tearjerker when you realize how true it is, how unlimited to time and place" (1962.B31). Shimon Wincelburg in The New Leader announced

Introduction

his judgment that Catch-22 lived up "almost completely to its rave notices" (1962.B67); Nelson Algren in the Chicago Daily News defended his earlier praise for Catch-22 and Heller's technique, calling the book "a classic because it employs fantasy to depict truths too devastating to tell by factual narration" (1962.B1); W. H. Scarborough in the Chapel Hill Weekly surmised that it might become "the legend of the age...[in its] magnification of every classic soldier's tale of mix-ups, chicanery, and top echelon fatuity" (1962.B55); Richard Starnes in the Cleveland Press predicted that it would become "one of the enduring monuments in our language...[for] we all have a share in Yossarian...none of us will ever be able to escape from Colonel Cathcart, Milo, or Snowden" (1962.B59); and James Garret in the Cleveland Press went so far as to advise that it be "compulsory reading for every world leader, for the citizens of all nations" (1962.B27).

By the spring of 1963 college students were wearing Army field jackets with Yossarian name tags. Newspaper and magazine articles, such as the "Currents" section of Publishers Weekly (1963.B8), were beginning to note the staying power of Catch-22, and Time magazine included Heller among novelists of "proven excellence" in an article about writing in the United States (1963.B5). Furthermore, the novel began to be mentioned in scholarly articles and books about war novels and trends in contemporary writing. Some such examples were Littlejohn's article in Daedalus on "anti-realist" writers (1963.B19); Hassan's articles in the Massachusetts Review on absurdity (1962.B34), in the English Journal on rebel-victim heroes (1962.B33), and in American Scholar on black humor (1963.B8); Black's article in Wisconsin Studies in Language and Literature on Thurber and other "tragic comedians" (1964.B2); in Alfred Kazin's The Great Ideas Today (1962.B38); in Frederick J. Hoffman's The Modern Novel in America (1963.B16); in Paul West's The Modern Novel (1963.B26); in Robert Detweiler's Four Spiritual Crises in Mid-Century American Fiction (1964.B3); in Leslie Fiedler's Waiting for the End (1964.B6); and in H. E. F. Donohue's Conversations with Nelson Algren (1964.B5).

John M. Muste in 1962 wrote an essay in Critique (1962.B46) about the emergence with Catch-22 and Ashmead's The Mountain and the Feather of a new kind of war novel that relied on stock characters of humorous novels like Mr. Roberts but involved them in the real horrors of war. Similarly, in 1964 in The Mortal No: Death and the Modern Imagination, Frederick J. Hoffman devoted several pages to Catch-22, "the most notorious of the war novels that make madness laughable without ignoring the realities of war" (1964.B9). In 1964, Heller's work was considered in two other serious literary commentaries as well. Henry T. Moore included in his Contemporary American Novelists Frederick R. Karl's essay "Joseph Heller's Catch-22: Only Fools Walk in Darkness," a tribute to the novel and a defense of Yossarian (1964.B10); and Joseph J. Waldmeir compared "Two Novelists of the Absurd: Heller and Kesey" in Wisconsin Studies in Language and Literature (1964.B16).

Introduction

Although Heller came out second-best in the Waldmeir analysis, and was mentioned only in passing in most of the scholarly works cited, he was coming to be recognized in the early 1960's as a writer who could not be ignored when contemporary literature was discussed.

In the mid and late sixties, Catch-22, already a favorite of students, came to be seen as a Bible of anti-military, anti-establishment groups. Bumper stickers that said "Better Yossarian than Rotarian" became popular, and a number of magazine articles commented on this special appeal the novel had for the young and disenchanted. Leslie Fiedler in an essay called "The New Mutants" in Partisan Review (1965.B11) named Catch-22 and A Mother's Kisses as two "fictional vaudevilles...that currently please the young...and suggest in their brutality and discontinuity, the politics of mockery, something in the spirit of the student demonstrations." More writers argued, though, that, as America was in another war, this time clearly an unpopular war, Heller's criticism of the military and establishment seemed apt. Stanley Kauffmann in The New Republic (1970.B32) wrote that while "Yossarian had to fly fifty missions before he saw that 'the enemy is anybody who is going to get you killed'.... Today's young men...know before they get into a uniform what Yossarian had to learn the hard way." Michael Kalter in a letter to the New York Times (1970.B31) expressed alarm that the novel had "proven such an accurate forecast of America." Heller himself remarked that "Vietnam is the war I was writing about all the time" (1970.B28). Paul Levine, writing about "The Politics of Alienation" in Mosaic (1967.B20), saw Catch-22 as turning the problem of "craziness" raised in Catcher in the Rye "upside down" so that "the hero's sanity is now questioned by his society but not by his creator." Josh Greenfeld wrote a feature article for page one of the New York Times Book Review (1968.B52) about the relevance of Catch-22 to the Vietnam War and resistance to it. He objected, however, to Yossarian's failure to rebel forcefully and called his personal, non-ideological opposition an example of the mentality of the fifties, not the sixties. Carl Oglesby, a revolutionist writer, also objected to the "privatistic" nature of Yossarian's rebellion in a Motive article (1968.B83). Although not all these writers admired Yossarian, they all clearly recognized his stature as a hero of the anti-establishment.

As this controversy continued, Heller published his first play, We Bombed in New Haven, clearly an anti-war tract. It was performed first at the Long Wharf Theater in New Haven, Connecticut, in December, 1967, and afterwards on Broadway in the fall of 1968. Students and others in the audience reportedly participated in the play, shouting support for its anti-war themes. Critical response was, as it had been for Catch-22, mixed. Most reviewers agreed with its "message," but some felt Heller relied too much on that. Harold Clurman in Nation (1968.B35), for example, said the play wakened little more than mild assent, and Gerald Weales in The Reporter (1968.B108), complained about the "obviousness" of the material, saying only viewers

Introduction

who thought all anti-war writing was good would enjoy We Bombed in New Haven. Theophilus Lewis in America (1968.B71) objected that the play suggested that "all who aren't burning draft cards are advocates of more and bloodier wars." The particular aspect of the play that led to this objection was Heller's involvement of the audience in the guilt of those who failed to stop young soldiers from being sent off to die. Other critics found this technique the strongest part of the play. Tom Prideaux of Life (1968.B85) judged We Bombed in New Haven "the best war play of our day" because of this "meshing" of the play and reality. Gerald Wade in the Beaumont Journal (1968.B103) warned that viewers might come away believing they were the enemy, and then he asked "Well?" Geoffrey Wolff of the Washington Post (1968.B111) felt Heller's involving the audience in responsibility made some uneasy and showed that Heller "continues to understand us better than we should want him to understand."

A major concern of the play's reviewers was whether it measured up to Catch-22 as a work of art. Mike Steele of the Minneapolis Tribune (1968.B98) claimed that drama was the "perfect outlet" for Heller, and H. Mitgang of the New York Times (1968.B78) found the play "more universal than Catch-22." On the other hand, Roy Finocchiaro of the Wilmington Morning News (1968.B47) called it Catch-22 "weakly reincarnated," and the Delaware State Library Book Selection (1968.B16) reviewer called it "warmed-over Heller," as did Publishers' Weekly (1968.B4). The Time (1967.B3) reviewer said it proved Heller was another good novelist who's a bad playwright. Henry Hewes of Saturday Review (1968.B56) wished for more of Heller's "special quality in writing" and less abstraction.

Several others made the same complaint. Just as Martin Gottfried objected to too much "preaching and sentiment" in his Womens Wear Daily review (1968.B51), Roderick Nordell in the Christian Science Monitor (1967.B24) said the characters lectured too much. Edith Oliver in the New Yorker (1968.B84) criticized the play for being "so intricate and self-conscious that it...engages our attention without engaging our hearts." Edward Hipp of the Newark Evening News (1968.B59) agreed, suggesting that Heller should have tried to move people against war by "touching hearts." Walter Shapiro of the Michigan Daily (1968.B93) admired greatly Heller's ambitions in trying to make people see the consequences of their apathy, but he found the characters "cardboard." Walter Kerr of the New York Times also praised the moral concern and attempt to involve most theatre goers in the experience, but thought the dramatic technique was "clumsy." Kerr argued that Heller didn't "dramatize" war; he only talked about it. The characters, he explained, weren't developed as believable human beings with an emotionally coherent story (1968.B66). Nonetheless, Clive Barnes, also of the New York Times (1968.B24), rated We Bombed in New Haven "a bad play any good playwright should be proud to have written and any good audience fascinated to see." Most of the reviewers, in spite of their reservations about the experimental technique and didactic nature of the play, probably would have agreed.

Introduction

The play was also performed in Berlin in 1968, at the Cockpit Theatre in London in 1971, and off Broadway in 1972; and it has been mentioned in several books and articles on theatre and contemporary literature. Few real studies of the play have been published; but Otis L. Guernsey, Jr., in The Best Plays of 1968-1969 (1969.B13) described the way the spectators are made to be the "fall guys" and concluded that the play was "one of the season's noteworthy events... because of its contemporary style and highly relevant subject matter." Gerald Weales in The Jumping Off Place (1969.B30) agreed with a number of the early reviewers in counting it an interesting experiment that didn't really work on stage. Catherine Hughes in Plays, Politics, and Polemics (1973.B9) devoted several pages to the play but decided Heller let a good idea erode into an "overwritten and overwrought example of message drama."

Catch-22, by comparison, continued to grow in literary stature during the late 1960's and early 1970's. This bibliography provides extensive evidence of the growing attention Heller's writing was receiving. The books listed here are surely but a sampling of the many books which mention Heller's work, as it would be impossible to find all such instances without reading the whole corpus of modern criticism.

More detailed studies of Heller's work have also increased over the years. Often inspired by negative reviews of Catch-22, they took up the much needed work of explaining Heller's revolutionary techniques to the literary establishment.

Naturally, one of the first concerns was to establish Catch-22's legitimacy as a war novel. Eric Solomon (1969.B27) traced the similarities between Catch-22 and earlier war novels such as War and Peace and A Farewell to Arms while noting the difference--its "coruscating humor"--and arguing that "paradoxically...this wild laughter" makes Heller's book "even more despairing than the work of his contemporaries who have written about war in our time." Solomon acknowledged that the novel "defies easy critical categories," but attempted to explain its use of humor in a Christian framework. Anthony Burgess (1967.B7) also recognized Heller's use of a "surrealistic, absurd, even lunatic" approach "to show the mess of war," and Leslie Fiedler (1966.B7) applauded Heller for rising above the slickness and stereotypes of most war novels by using "the techniques of the Black Vaudevillian to present...a vision of war as ultimate burlesque, an event too farcical for tears." Alfred Kazin, in his Saturday Review article "The War Novel: From Mailer to Vonnegut" (1971.B18), held that modern writers, having experienced the previously unimagined horrors of World War II, can no longer write in a logical way and that Heller was, therefore, wise to picture the insane, omnipresent danger of war by juxtaposing the "pseudo-rationality of Jewish humor" with the inescapable, violent horror of

Introduction

war. Wayne Charles Miller in his book <u>An Armed America: Its Face in Fiction</u> (1970.B36) devoted a chapter to explaining his theory that <u>Catch-22</u> "provides the meeting ground for almost all the themes and ideas...followed by novelists dealing with Americans at war and Americans within the military structure." Miller claimed that Heller had condemned the concepts of "honor, glory, and patriotism" as much as Hemingway and Dos Passos but with a new element--satire. However, Miller contended that Heller used the military setting mainly as a vehicle to satirize American life and culture which "Heller clearly regards as immoral and absurd." Miller later elaborated on this point further in his critique of the movie version of the novel written for <u>A 'Catch-22' Casebook</u> (1973.A1). Lucy Frost agreed that <u>Catch-22</u> was primarily a critique of American society in her <u>Meanjin</u> article (1971.B8). She went on to illustrate how Heller's picturing of the Army as enemy and of Rome as governed by "Catch-22" enabled him to expose the horror of modern American life.

Other critics expanded the view that Heller was writing about more than World War II by concentrating on his use of humor, satire, or a sense of the absurd. Scott Byrd, in a <u>Language Quarterly</u> essay entitled "A Separate War: Camp and Black Humor in Recent American Fiction" (1968.B32), commented on the value of <u>Catch-22</u> as a fantasy with "exuberance that may substitute...for despair," since "ideological dead horses" have not been destroyed by calm logic or invective. Richard Hauck in his book <u>A Cheerful Nihilism</u> (1971.B15) wrote of the effectiveness of absurdity in fiction (such as Milo's contract) to make readers consider the seemingly incredible things that do happen (like the Japanese Zeroes made out of United States scrap metal). Michael French, in his essay "The American Novel in the Sixties" in <u>Midwest Quarterly</u> (1968.B48) saw the surrealistic absurdity as a kind of "psychological realism," reflecting the "disarray" in the minds of the characters. Brian Way with "Formal Experiment and Social Discontent: Heller's <u>Catch-22</u>" in <u>Journal of American Studies</u> (1968.B107) emphasized, instead, Heller's use of absurdity as effective social protest because the absurd "vision and logic are more in harmony with what he sees around him." For example, Way explained that Heller used "Catch-22" to reveal the "infinite capacity of the absurd to mask itself in reason, and to institutionalize itself in bureaucracy." W. K. Thomas in "What Difference Does It Make? Logic in <u>Catch-22</u>" in <u>Dalhousie Review</u> (1970.B57) brought in extensive textual evidence to support his conclusion that the misuse of logic in the book forces one to look into the difference between the form and substance of things said and done in contemporary life. In a similar study, Robert Protherough in "The Sanity of <u>Catch-22</u>" in <u>The Human World</u> (1971.B28) examined four devices Heller used for satiric effect to show the absurdity of official attitudes and cliches. Jim Castelli in "<u>Catch-22</u> and the New Hero" in <u>Catholic World</u> (1970.B16) analyzed Heller's questioning of "the very nature of sanity" and "Yossarian's new heroism, refusing to obey an absurd system which acts contrary to his rationality and sense of humanity."

Introduction

Several other writers have taken the position, like Castelli, that Heller used absurdity, not just for social criticism, but to show a metaphysical absurdity: the meaninglessness of human existence. Richard Kostelanetz made this point in two articles, "The Point Is That Life Doesn't Have Any Point," in the New York Times Book Review (1965.B17) and "Dada and the Future of Fiction" in Works (1968.B67). In "The New American Fiction" in The New American Arts (1965.B16), he elaborated further on this point, comparing Heller's writing to the European absurd theatre in his use of a series of absurd events to show the meaninglessness that results when society distorts any relationship between intention and result or need and fulfillment. To the same end, Jean Kennard in her study "Joseph Heller: At War with Absurdity" in Mosaic (1971.B19) illustrated in considerable detail how Heller's experimental narrative techniques, characterization, and use of tone, reason, and language dramatized an Existentialist view of a world with "no meaning," where reason and language are useless. Jesse Ritter in an essay written for A 'Catch-22' Casebook (1973.A1) explored this idea further through an analysis of Heller's "surrealism" and "ironic radical juxtaposition." Characterizing the narrative method as "objectified stream-of-consciousness," Ritter pointed out how social satire gave way as the horror of war and Yossarian's growing awareness of the power of "Catch-22" increased ("the absurd gives way to the Absurd").

John Hunt in his essay "Comic Escape and Anti-Vision: The Novels of Joseph Heller and Thomas Pynchon" in Adversity and Grace: Studies in Recent American Literature (1968.B63) went even one step further philosophically, contending that Heller accepted absurdity as a premise, and went on to explore the "defeat of meaning by the strategies used to protect it" and the "unnecessary abandonment of reason in the human enterprise" in an attempt to find a meaningful way to live. Koji Numasawa in "Black Humor: An American Aspect" in Studies in English Literature (1968.B82) also argued that Heller sees beyond the paradox of "Catch-22," which demands that man be "simultaneously both mad and sane" and even beyond a God who is only subject to ridicule, to realize that one can achieve "a certain comic dignity." Paul Loukides in "The Radical Vision" in Michigan Academician (1973.B12) took a similar view, explaining that because of a modern crisis in belief in which science and reason are seen as "inadequate to reveal the truth," Heller and other contemporary novelists have presented a "radical vision," or alternative view of reality. Nonetheless, Loukides argued, Heller has not accepted absurdity as total though he has recognized its threat; instead, he shows through Snowden's revelation to Yossarian, that only belief in man is possible. Vance Ramsey in "From Here to Absurdity: Heller's Catch-22" in Seven Contemporary Authors (1966.B21) came to much the same conclusion after exploring the relationship of Catch-22 to literature of the absurd, Camus, and Hemingway, and giving special attention to the "nothingness" or denial of self that threatened Yossarian and his friends from all sides. Ramsey found "strength" in Yossarian's rejecting attempts to make him over and in the fact that he "consciously and

Introduction

resolutely is." Charles B. Harris in his Contemporary American Novelists of the Absurd (1971.B14) agreed that, while Heller pictured a cosmic absurdity, he did see hope for reform or escape. Thus, "the novel not only protests absurdity but rejects it as the ultimate reality." Harris went on to examine Heller's use of "absurdist" techniques, i.e. employing traditional novelistic devices ironically or farcically, burlesquing the pseudo-logic of the military and business with tautological dialogues, serious descriptions ending with trivial or ludicrous details, and comic reversals. However, Nathan Scott in an essay called "The 'Conscience' of the New Literature" in The Shaken Realist (1970.B49) warned against classifying Heller's technique as "absurdism" because it might link him too closely with European contemporaries. Scott felt "black humor" was a more appropriate term for Heller's "ironic preposterousness." He also argued that Heller and other black humorists have little patience with the "art of the novel and controlling forms," since they find the world itself "indeterminate"; thus, they choose an improvisational method "in order to be truly open to the turbulent incoherence of reality."

While many critics have felt comfortable with Scott's term "black humor," few would agree with him that Heller's writing lacks "controlling forms." In fact, a great many have argued to the contrary, that Heller's work is carefully controlled, even in his radical mixing of humor and horror. Louis Halsey, for one, in "Dramtic Tension in Catch-22" in Midwest Quarterly (1974.B93) pointed out the pattern Heller devised to make the responsive reader "walk a tight-rope" as he leans first to riotous humor and then tips to the side of black tragedy, as the bitter humor "flaunts" a resistance to the pain of life but never ignores it. Walter McDonald studied this pattern or technique of reversal to make even a "jaded audience recoil" in "Look Back in Horror: The Functional Comedy of Catch-22" in the CEA Critic (1973.B13). Donald Simmons observed the effect of this technique in a letter to the New York Times (1970.B53) expressing his disappointment in the film version of Catch-22 because the scenes which sought to provoke the audience's rage and indignation were not funny enough. He pointed out that in the book the reader "is seduced by his own laughter into a sort of complicity with the inhumanities," bringing him to the disturbing awareness that "to a great extent 'they' were 'us.'" John Muste, in his paper presented at the "Modern Satire: A Mini-Symposium" and published in Modern Satire (1969.B20), also noted Heller's playing on audience response through shock or reversal in much the same way in We Bombed in New Haven, to reveal that "our scorn has been directed at a human being that is not very much more ludicrous than ourselves."

Other scholars saw a more traditional concept of literary form underlying Heller's work. Constance Denniston's "The American Romance Parody: A Study of Purdy's Malcolm and Heller's Catch-22" in The Emporia State Research Studies (1965.B9) was one of the first major works of this nature. Responding to critics who had called Catch-22 formless and unrealistic, she pointed out that it had the

Introduction

strict form of the romance-parody, with archetypal characters and a complex, often repetitive plot in the form of a three-staged quest filled with conflicts and masked identities. By contrast, Arthur Mizener, writing about "The New Romance" in Southern Review (1972.B15) contended that Catch-22 could be seen in terms of old romances in themselves in that Heller represented "as reality the images in his mind...and relations among those images that satisfy him."

    Such conflicting views might suggest that various scholars have seen a limited aspect of Catch-22 in terms of their own academic interests rather than in terms of the novel as a whole; and, indeed, there is a degree of truth in this, particularly since the novel is such a large and complicated work to deal with. Norman Mailer acknowledged this difficulty when he remarked, "If I were a major critic, it would be a virtuoso performance to write a definitive piece on Catch-22. It would take ten thousand words or more" (1963.B20). To this date, no critic has attempted to do that sort of "definitive piece," but a number have done very careful and illuminating studies of various aspects of the book.

    Minna Doskow's "The Night Journal in Catch-22" in Twentieth Century Literature (1967.B10) was one of these, as she built a solid case for Yossarian's journey through the streets of Rome as being similar in language and image to the classical descents into hell. Thus, she pointed out, Yossarian could only achieve salvation by recognizing evil in the world and in himself and resisting it. Victor Milne in "Heller's 'Bologniad': A Theological Perspective on Catch-22" in Critique (1970.B37) was also instructive as to the notable parallels between Catch-22 and The Iliad. With this perspective, the comedy and horror mocking outworn values seem to take the form of mock-epic where "a modern Achilles says 'baloney' to the demands of a corrupt society with its iniquitous heroic code requiring the sacrifice of human lives." Caroline Gordon and Jeanne Richardson did a worthwhile comparison of Heller's fictional techniques with those of Lewis Carroll in "Flies in their Eyes? A Note on Joseph Heller's Catch-22" in The Southern Review (1967.B13). They illustrated how Heller, like Carroll, showed a character contrasting, with wonder and outrage, the way things were in his lunatic world with the way they "ought to be." Donald Monk in "An Experiment in Therapy" in The London Review (1967.B23) analyzed in some depth a number of aspects of Heller's style such as his syntax, his use of montage, his revelation of prejudice in direct speech, and his Dickens-like caricatures. Tony Tanner in his book City of Words (1971.B34) also analyzed Heller's "struggle with language and the existing conventions of the novel," finding that Yossarian's decision to leave was similar to the choice of many fictional American heroes "to redefine the direction in which true reality lies" and that both Heller and Yossarian had to "keep on spinning to avoid being trapped."

Introduction

While those studies, and to a lesser degree several others such as Douglas Day's "Catch-22: A Manifesto for Anarchists" in Carolina Quarterly (1963.B13) and G. B. McK. Henry's "Significant Corn: Catch-22" in Critical Review (1966.B14), were helpful in showing the traditional elements in Heller's writing, other critical works were equally revealing in their analyses of some of his experimental techniques.

Thomas A. Nelson, for instance, in "Theme and Structure in Catch-22" in Renascence (1971.B23) explained the way the novel was "meticulously constructed" with a first cycle where people and events were treated as glimpses, to be shown next as interrelated in an inescapable way, and finally, in the concluding cycle, their significance would become clear to Yossarian and the reader. James M. Mellard in "Catch-22: Deja vu and the Labyrinth of Memory" in Bucknell Review (1968.B77) also analyzed the use of repeated images (deja vu) and their relation to the rest of the novel, mainly to Yossarian's mythical journey to "the underworld, the labyrinth, the heart of darkness" in the process of being reborn out of American culture to a sense of responsibility and life. James L. MacDonald in "I See Everything Twice: The Structure of Joseph Heller's Catch-22" in University Review (1968.B75) did still another worthwhile study of deja vu and other formal aspects of the book as repetitions of and variations on Heller's theme, as did Thomas Blues in "The Moral Structure of Catch-22 in Studies in the Novel (1971.B3). Blues related the use of deja vu to the metaphor of seeing or imperfect vision in the novel. Harold Stark in "The Anatomy of Catch-22" written for A 'Catch-22' Casebook (1973.A1) did yet one more study of Heller's use of deja vu, presque vu, and jamais vu to illustrate how "incident by incident, image by image" Heller melded imagistic scenes into a "psychological continuum" with the horror under all of a world governed by irrationality. Most useful was Stark's explanation of Lt. Fortiori in terms of the term a fortiori in logic and its use to distort logic, climaxing with all the implications of "Catch-22" so that the absurdity "no longer seems illogical or abnormal." Stark did see hope, though, in Yossarian's realization of the situation and his determination to "break the lousy chain of habit that was imperiling them all."

A great many critics have dealt with the time sequence in Catch-22, but they have disagreed dramatically as to its purpose. Max F. Schulz in "Pop, Op, and Black Humor: The Aesthetics of Anxiety" in College English (1968.B91) called Heller's fixing of time an "endless circularity" and saw it as indicative of the temporality of the literary form. However, John Wain in "A New Novel About Old Troubles" in Critical Quarterly (1963.B25) defended the scrambled time-sequence as appropriate for bomber pilots who lived in circular time from mission to mission. Gabriel Chanan in "The Plight of the Novelist" in Cambridge Review (1968.B33) praised Heller for revealing an aspect of life which "has its existence laterally in a web of interrelations not dependent on time or consequence." And Charles B. Harris

Introduction

in <u>Contemporary American Novelists of the Absurd</u> (1971.B14) decided Heller confused the chronology of events to suggest the absurdity of existence. Moreover, John Colmer took a similar view in the introduction to his <u>Approaches to the Novel</u> (1966.B4), arguing that Heller deliberately invented situations to show "the absurdity of man's predicament" and destroyed any "ordinary time scheme." Colmer also went on to say that this chronology, especially its withholding of information, was "functional"; Yossarian's compassion for the dying Snowden was released at the "critical moment in the narrative" to enlist the readers' sympathies for Yossarian when he decided to leave.

Jan Solomon was the first to attempt a detailed study of the time sequence in "The Structure of Joseph Heller's <u>Catch-22</u>" in <u>Critique</u> (1967.B32). He found two independently valid time sequences: Yossarian's psychological time which goes backward and forward, developing events in order of their significance; and Milo's time, which moves directly forward. Since the two cannot mesh, they create another dimension of absurdity, enhancing Heller's theme. Doug Gaukroger responded to Solomon's article several years later with "Time Structure in <u>Catch-22</u>" in <u>Critique</u> (1970.B22). He presented a large body of evidence to show that Solomon's reading of the time sequence was incorrect and then described the "proper" order of events. A few years later in "Spindrift and the Sea: Structural Patterns and Unifying Elements in <u>Catch-22</u>" in <u>Twentieth Century Literature</u> (1973.B2), Clinton S. Burhans made still another attempt at elucidating the "apparent episodic chaos" of the novel. He worked out elaborate patterns of structure, chronology, and tonal changes with interesting descriptions of how the flashbacks function.

There have not been so many studies of Heller's characterization as of his structure, but a few are noteworthy. James Nagel's reproduction of Heller's early attempts at <u>Catch-22</u> and commentary on them in "Two Brief Manuscript Sketches" in <u>Modern Fiction Studies</u> (1974.B139) is especially interesting for what it shows of how Heller changed his characters from obvious ethnic types to another kind of caricature. Richard Orr gave literary perspective in relating Heller's characterization to E. M. Forester's definition of "flat characters." Orr's article titled "Flat Characters in <u>Catch-22</u>" appeared in <u>Notes on Contemporary Literature</u> (1971.B25). Charles Child Walcutt in his book <u>Man's Changing Mask</u> (1966.B26) commented on the same aspect, explaining that one cannot believe in the characters in Heller's "mad world," but adding, "Nor does the author expect us to do so. That's the point." Alan Greenberg in "Choice--Ironic Alternatives in the World of the Contemporary Novel" in <u>American Dreams, American Nightmares</u> (1970.B24) focused on the character of Orr. Greenberg saw Orr as embodying the alternative of withdrawal, which, in the end, gives "renewed meaning and new possibility" to Yossarian's "rapidly disintegrating world." Yossarian thinks of death as "irreversible," thinks that he is "going to lose" until he hears about Orr's reaching Sweden and realizes that Orr had been preparing for survival all along. Eric Solomon's essay (1969.B27) provided

Introduction

another way of seeing Orr (not as "or" but as "ore," "rock," hence "Peter") in a religious explanation of the novel. However, Howard Stark, in his essay "Catch-22: The Ultimate Irony" written for Critical Essays on Catch-22 (1973.A1), contended that Orr is a "gnome, dwarf" who can do almost anything and who speaks in circumlocutions, but who, in fact, is "only a myth...a satiric view of the American dream and adaptable pragmatism."

By far the greatest number of character studies centered on Yossarian, particularly on his final decision to leave his squadron. On this point, as on many others in Catch-22, critical opinion has been widely divided. David Galloway in "Clown and Saint: The Hero in Current American Fiction" in Critique (1965.B14) included Yossarian in his list of "saintly clowns" whose "role is to redeem in some measure the absurdity of life." Galloway contended that Yossarian shows that, while it might be impossible to change the world, one need not become its victim. Nelvin Vos took a similar view in his book, For God's Sake! Laugh! (1967.B33), seeing Yossarian as a "clown of conscience" who uses his antics to "arouse a surprise-proof public" and tries to avoid being made into a "thing." Tony Tanner (1971.B34) noted the same concern of Yossarian's about not becoming a "thing" in a world where the Air Force (or American society) has so structured life that identity becomes "a matter of papers rather than flesh and blood." Gerald B. Nelson in his Ten Versions of America (1972.B16) picked up this same concern, reading the message of Catch-22 as the loneliness of the modern man whose only responsibility is to save himself from a power system that would destroy him. But Stephen L. Sniderman took a radically different view in "'It Was All Yossarian's Fault': Power and Responsibility in Catch-22" in Twentieth Century Literature (1973.B18). He compiled long lists of examples to show that Yossarian can and does affect the lives of those around him. While admitting that a number of these cases are indirect or involuntary, Sniderman insisted that Yossarian is responsible--even for Nately's death and the deaths of others in his squadron because he lends "his presence and his tacit sanction to the system perpetrated by the U.S.A.F. and distorted by Cathcart and Korn." The burden of guilt is more on Yossarian than on the other men because he alone sees the absurdity and danger of flying more missions and because he is able to influence others. While Sniderman's essay may have been a bit too ingenious and optimistic about the changes Yossarian could effect, it is provocative in its view of Yossarian's role.

Much of the controversy over the ending of Catch-22 has been based on the question of what Yossarian's moral responsibility requires him to do--and whether he fulfills or avoids that responsibility by leaving. John Wain (1963.B25) complained that Heller does not face squarely the ethical questions about desertion in a just war, and Thomas Blues (1971.B3) objected to his "clouding our vision of the meaning of Yossarian's desertion...failing to make us utterly aware of the price man has to pay to make his best dreams come true."

Introduction

Norman Podhoretz in "The Best Catch There Is" in Show (1962.B49) took the position that the ending is "nonintegrated," reflecting a shift in tone and attitude from earlier parts of the novel. Podhoretz blamed Yossarian for "shrinking" in his desertion from the premise that the book was based on, that "nothing on this earth is worth dying for." He predicted that Yossarian would find nothing in Sweden worth dying for either; therefore, Podhoretz would like to have told Heller, "So you see, there are more clauses in Catch-22 than even you know about." Wayne Charles Miller (1970.B36) conceded that the ending might involve a shift in tone, but explained that Heller and Yossarian are aware that the desertion is not a completely positive choice. After Danby tells Yossarian his conscience will never let him rest, Yossarian replies that he wouldn't want to live "without strong misgivings." Miller suggested that neither Yossarian nor any other man could be totally satisfied with the human condition but that taking off "for the undiscovered country" might be the only way that "men and cultures survive."

A great many other critics saw Yossarian's move as definitely necessary and perhaps heroic. Thomas B. Whitbread in Seven Contemporary Authors (1966.B27) classified him as "a true anti-hero: a combination of the sane absurd." Robert Scotto in his "Introduction" to Catch-22: A Critical Edition (1973.A2) asserted that in an age "wherein heroism becomes ludicrous...the only courageous act left is desertion." John Hunt (1968.B63) took much the same position, supporting Yossarian's choice as one of reason, sanity, and responsibility as Heller seeks "some meaningful way whereby our fractured lives may be made whole." Jerry H. Bryant in The Open Decision-- The Contemporary American Novel and Its Intellectual Background (1970.B12) found Yossarian's desertion an excellent example of an "open decision," an authentic choice made with knowledge of all options open and what they involved. Yossarian realizes that there are more possibilities than "other system" offers. Frederick Karl also described Yossarian's choice as an acceptance of responsibility "in good faith" in his essay "Joseph Heller's Catch-22: Only Fools Walk in Darkness" (1964.B10). Victor Milne (1970.B37) also took this view, claiming that Yossarian's act is responsible and moral in that, since he can make no totally "good" choice, he resists the greatest evils: exploiting others and letting himself be exploited. Walter McDonald in "He Took Off: Yossarian and the Different Drummer" in CEA Critic (1973.B14), like Tanner (1971.B34), went even further to look at Yossarian as part of a cultural tradition of American heroes who "took off."

Donald Monk (1967.B23) and Constance Denniston (1965.B9) also commended the ending but for different reasons. Monk saw it as "fantastical," a kind of "therapy" often given to people to help them deal with "facts too terrible to face." Denniston saw it as being in keeping with the romance-parody form she postulated where the ending should be ironic with the naive hero thinking his defeat was a success. Howard Stark (1968.A1) also argued that Yossarian's

Introduction

choice is built on wish-fulfillment and the illusion that he can escape in a "fantastical" way, as Orr has done. But Stark found that Yossarian's choice is "not an involved commitment because he...has committed himself to a dream" where as the chaplain makes the only free and "true" choice: "to stay with spirit and live bravely and committedly in the face of absurdity."

When the film version of Catch-22 was released in the summer of 1970, it rekindled the controversy over the ending and over the book's meaning and merits. While most of the articles published at that time were primarily concerned with the film, a few made significant points about the book and gave a good indication of its esteem almost a decade after its publication.

The excitement about the film's production itself indicated something of Heller's popularity. The New York Times Magazine printed Nora Ephron's lengthy article on the making of the film (1967.B12); Newsweek included a three-page article on it by Raymond Sokolov (1969.B26); Look devoted four pages to Flagler's article (1970.B20); and Life carried a large spread of pictures and commentary under the headline "The Frantic Filming of a Crazy Classic" (1970.B5). Beverly Gross in Nation labeled it "a movie of the most acclaimed American novel of these times" (1970.B25).

When the film was released, many writers expressed disappointment. Grover Sales in an article called "Catch-$" in San Francisco (1970.B43) and Peter Schjeldahl in the New York Times (1970.B47) blamed the book for the failure of the movie. Sales called the book a "children's pop novel...a grandiose over-sold fake," objecting to the novel's repetitions, echolalia, verbosity, silly characterizations, and corny jokes, but especially to its lack of seriousness about the real World War II enemy. Schjeldahl saw the movie as "a remarkably faithful adaption" and therefore suffering the same faults as the novel, which is "riddled with cheap preciousness and sentimentality...a specimen of a particular intellectual and moral attitude born of the '50's...paranoid of the 'them-us' variety." Schjeldahl's article was attacked by many in letters to the Times. One of these writers, Lee Adams (1970.B1) was so annoyed that he accused Schjeldahl of attacking a work of "monumental worth" just to become known. Arvine Levine (1970.B34) claimed that Schjeldahl had never read the book, since he commented on the impropriety of Yossarian's escaping to Sweden on a rubber raft, a detail which was not in the book. Michael J. Kalter (1970.B31) said Schjeldahl's judgement was surely not valid since "the novel has...proven such an accurate forecast of America in the '70's." Edgar Dannenburg (1970.B19) agreed, suggesting that Schjeldahl, with his belief that "these days" one can change the world, had never served in the army or worked in a large business organization. Robert Capone (1970.B15) contended that Schjeldahl had missed the central thesis of Catch-22, which gives it "appeal for all decades," *i.e.* "man's battle against the absurd and his struggle to maintain an identity within a massive bureaucracy." Donald Simmons,

Introduction

(1970.B53) argued that Heller's main contribution was in bringing us, as we come to look on our laughter with horror, to an awareness that "to a great extent 'they' were 'us.'"

Other critics, besides Sales and Schjeldahl, expressed disappointment with the movie, but these critics objected because it failed to communicate all of the book's meaning, which they admired. For example, Andrew Sarris in his Village Voice review (1970.B45) complained that in dispensing with many characters and almost all the "obsessional power struggles of petty bureaucrats," the movie stripped away "every last vestige of Heller's satiric sociology." Wayne Charles Miller (1970.B36) also argued that the film missed the main thrust of Heller's attack on a misguided, "dangerous" American society.

Still others such as Richard Schickel in his Life review (1970.B46) and Winifrid Blevins in the Los Angeles Herald-Examiner review (1970.B10) were bothered by the loss of Heller's inventive verbal style and humor. Fred Marcus and Paul Zall, in their essay Film and Literature: Contrasts in Media (1971.B22), examined in more depth the effect of the loss of the book's "verbal emphasis" in the film. Judith Christ in New York (1970.B17), Joseph Morgenstern in Newsweek (1970.B38), and Beverly Gross in Nation (1970.B25) also saw this problem but reminded their readers of the difficulty of making Catch-22 into a film.

Several reviewers were more enthusiastic about the film version. Vincent Canby in his article "A Triumphant Catch" in the New York Times (1970.B14) declared that the movie's flashback that kept turning back on itself "was equivalent to Heller's verbal humor that depended on double negatives of reasoning." The Time reviewer (1970.B6) also appreciated the film's construction "like a spiral staircase set with mirrors" until Yossarian comes to "a landing of understanding." Les Staniford in "Novels into Film: Catch-22 as Watershed" in Southern Humanities Review (1974.B190) also admired the film's "tight progression of scenes which move Yossarian inexorably toward his enlightenment," a sequence in keeping with the book's "illogical concept of time."

Of special interest is Heller's own appreciation of the movie given in a talk at the Poetry Center of the Young Men's Hebrew Association in 1970 and printed in A 'Catch-22' Casebook (1973.A1).

As a matter of fact, from the time of his earliest success, Heller has made himself available to interviewers; thus, printed records of his own comments on his writing and the influence of events and earlier authors on it are readily available. One of the earliest of these was reported by W. J. Weatherby in The Guardian (1962.B66). In that interview Heller spoke of the inspirations he had for writing Catch-22 from Celine, Nabokov, and Evelyn Waugh, from two friends who were injured in World War II, and from the

Introduction

competitive atmosphere of New York City. About the same time, November, 1962, Paul Krassner related in The Realist (1962.B40) a conversation where Heller talked extensively about his aims and techniques in Catch-22 and about critical reaction to it. Richard Lehan and Jerry Patch in their article "Catch-22: The Making of a Novel" (1967.B18) also provided useful background for a biographical criticism of Heller's novel.

In later years, particularly at the time We Bombed in New Haven appeared on Broadway, when Catch-22 was released as a movie, and when Something Happened was published, Heller continued to comment on Catch-22 and the effect of his early life and readings on his other work. Susan Braudy cautioned in her interview-article in New York (1968.B28) that in conversations Heller "uses his humor to keep people from looking at him too closely"; nonetheless, Heller's interviews are always lively and interesting and often do provide additional insights into his work. His comments to Walter James Miller and Bonnie E. Nelson, reported in their Monarch Notes on Catch-22 (1975.A2) were particularly worthy of notice in that they brought up ideas not discussed elsewhere. This is also true of Al Dinhofer's interview-article in the San Juan Star (1964.B4), which gave Heller's views on movie scripts, and James Shapiro's interview report in Intellectual Digest (1971.B32), which presented Heller's views on Catch-22: A Dramatization (a work which was generally regarded as a rehash of Catch-22; see 1973.B4). The Barnard article in Detroit News (1970.B7), the New York Herald-Tribune feature "Writers at Work" (1962.B20), and Dale Gold's "Portrait of a Man Reading" from the Washington Post Book World (1969.B12) give additional looks at Heller as a writer and thinker, while the James Shapiro (1971.B32, Intellectual Digest), Alexis Gonzales (1971.B9, New Orleans Review), and Richard Sale (1972.B20, Studies in the Novel) interviews look forward to Heller's achievement in Something Happened and give perspective on his earlier career.

The flood of interview-articles on Something Happened around the time of its publication are interesting primarily for the insight they give into Heller's intentions in that work. In addition, though, they offer some worthwhile thinking on the relationship of Something Happened to Heller's earlier work. Newsweek's article "Heller Redux" (1974.B6), for example, relates Heller's observation that Catch-22 was "external" while Something Happened is "internal." The Harvard Crimson interview (1974.B10) also covers a number of points of similarity and contrast between the two books.

Many of these interview-articles are quite repetitious; in fact, it becomes apparent that a number are based on one question and answer session Heller held at Knopf with many critics. However, several articles report on particularly noteworthy points Heller made, which are not reported elsewhere. Mark Howat's article in The Record Lifestyle (1974.B102), for instance, records Heller's explanation of his deliberately repetitive style and his naming only Derek in the

Introduction

Slocum family in Something Happened. Robert Alan Arthur's piece in Esquire (1974.B25) explains Heller's decision to call his narrator Robert Slocum. Barbara Bannon's article in Publishers Weekly (1974.B29) points up Heller's view that Slocum sees his autistic son as a "reflection of himself, symbolically." Peter Gorner's notes in the Chicago Tribune (1974.B88) show how Heller sees Slocum in relation to himself and other people, and Robert Robinson in The Listener (1974.B162) reports similar discussions in Heller's interview on BBC. Jack Schnedler's article in the Chicago Daily News Panorama (1974.B172) includes Heller's reasons for writing Something Happened in the first person and a number of ideas he rejected for the book. George Plimpton's article in the New York Times Book Review (1974.B155) reveals a great deal about Heller's creative process. Articles in Forbes (1975.B3) and the Detroit Free Press (1974.B147) bring out Heller's own experiences in business and how those relate to Slocum's company.

The great number of interview-articles which appeared when Something Happened was published manifested the excitement with which it was greeted in literary circles and the popular press. Perhaps nothing reveals more clearly the growth in Heller's reputation by 1974 than the fact that his new novel was reviewed in no fewer than 160 publications.

Even before the book's actual publication, which Arnold Rosenfeld of the Dayton News called a "bona fide literary event" (1974.B166), early reviews and predictions of success began to appear. Kirkus (1974.B7) proclaimed that judging Something Happened was sure to be "the hottest game of Russian roulette in town this fall" and that the book would be "read, and read, and read." Publishers Weekly (1974.B8) didn't flinch at firing an early shot and judged the book "extraordinary...a work of genuine brilliance...a true novel of our times." But Rust Hills in Esquire (1974.B98) rejected the idea that Heller's work is major literature (because of its lack of compression) and suggested that readers would respond to it as they would to a Thematic Apperception Test.

Indeed, this seemed to be the case among early reviewers. Judson Hand in the New York News (1974.B94) saw Heller's book as "an authentic slice of hell in suburbia," while Robert Forsyth of the Sacramento Union (1974.B78) felt Heller's depiction of suburban life was not at all accurate. Furthermore, Forsyth objected to the novel's being "mostly boring, mostly trite, mostly depressing, and mostly sad." Eliot Fremont-Smith in New York (1974.B81) also noted the novel's sad qualities, but took a different perspective, praising Something Happened as a "very fine, wrenchingly depressing new novel."

The controversy about Something Happened in the months that followed also seemed to support Hills' contention that readers would respond to the novel very subjectively. Most of the later reviewers focused on the same aspects of the book as the early reviewers: its

Introduction

unhappy picture of life in America, Heller's repetitious rambling style, the nature and perception of the main character Slocum, and the dramatic ending; however, their reactions to these aspects of the novel differed profoundly.

Most reviewers felt keenly the depressing quality of the book. John Barkham of the Cincinnati Post (1974.B30) warned his readers that the book was a "study done in gray and black...in depth and with relentless realism." Walter Spearman of the Chapel Hill Newspaper (1974.B189) said the novel suffered from the same mishap as Slocum's son: "So much unadulterated joylessness actually suffocates the reader." Larry Swindell of the San Francisco Examiner (1974.B198) said no other novel he ever read had plunged him into such despair. But he added, "This is its power." Robert Sorensen of the Minneapolis Tribune (1974.B187) responded in much the same way: "Something Happened may be the most depressing book ever written. I couldn't put it down. Joseph Heller is a master." Ray Newquist in the Chicago Star (1974.B183) also explained the intense pain many readers felt in seeing so much of themselves in Slocum and judged Something Happened "the best single novel that agonizingly appraises life in our times." Harriet Door of the Charlotte Observer (1974.B68) stressed that even though the novel was depressing, one "must" read it. John Alexander of the Charlotte News (1974.B4) urged reading the novel in spite of its moroseness because of the character Slocum in whom "history and culture have been internalized." This insight is particularly interesting because Heller responded to it, noting that it made him aware of something he hadn't been conscious of.

Aside from the depressing tone, many reviewers felt the book was difficult to read because of Heller's style. Benjamin DeMott in Atlantic Monthly (1974.B66) was the first reviewer to criticize the style as having a "static and mechanical quality." However, Charles Stella of the Cleveland Press (1974.B193) defended Heller's style as a useful device to show that Slocum's "modest success" had only made him feel "trapped and defeated." Leonard Sanders of the Ft. Worth Morning Star-Telegram (1974.B170) suggested that the book's style be seen as "pointillism gradually building tiny dots and brush strokes into a total effect illuminating a basic vision." Similarly, Charles Truchart of the Greensboro News (1974.B205) praised Heller's "knack" for painting unhappiness and absurdity with the "conviction of experience." William Lupton of the Baltimore Sun (1974.B123) made the same point, asserting that, although the style of Something Happened might lose some readers, it gave "the raw feel of human life" and "a human image of the age." Milton Millhauser of the Bridgeport Post (1974.B135) particularly noted Heller's "carefully devised and meticulously controlled style," and Booklist (1974.B23) praised Heller's verbal "alchemy" in making Slocum's "numbing litany of self-pity and impotent humor into an arresting fabric of tensile strength." Kurt Vonnegut, writing in the New York Times Book Review (1974.B210), also defended Heller's use of hackneyed themes in new ways, describing the book as "splendidly put together."

Introduction

However convincing the apologies for Heller's style were, not all reviewers were impressed. Lois Timmick of the St. Louis Globe Democrat (1974.B204) called Something Happened "overlong, (intentionally) repetitious, trite, and tedious." Elliot Middleton of the Rocky Mountain News (1974.B134) claimed that Heller became boring when he meant only to depict boredom. Joseph Schwartz of the Milwaukee Journal (1974.B174) merely called it "a long, dull book." Both Douglas Buss of Spectator (1974.B51) and Robert Lasson of the West Side Literary Review (1974.B117) objected to the lack of editing in this "overindulgent, overwritten, overweight" book. However, Lasson went on to declare that the novel was "so incisive, so brilliant, so painful that it's a pity there isn't less of it."

Another controversy among reviewers revolved around the question of how successfully Heller had ended the book. Walter Clemons of Newsweek (1974.B58) felt it left "an aftertaste of contrivance"; Kenneth Tynan of the London Observer (1974.B206) saw it as a sentimental failure; and Francis King of the London Telegraph (1974.B112) thought it too clumsy in its symbolism. On the other hand, Roger Sale of Hudson Review (1975.B24) didn't like the book until the last fifty pages, which he felt were "moving, searing, and final."

Still another point of controversy among reviewers was the main character, Robert Slocum. Nelson Algren, one of Heller's earliest fans, writing in Critic (1974.B5), was the first reviewer to voice uneasiness because of disliking Slocum but never being sure if Heller rejected him too. Jack Scott of the Victoria Times (1974.B176) was firmer in his dislike; he simply called Slocum an "unbelievable jerk." Margaret Manning of the Boston Globe (1974.B127) was also strong in her dislike of Slocum: "a zombie, impossible to identify with." Caroline Blackwood of the London Times Literary Supplement (1974.B43) found him unbelievable as a narrator because he seemed too "commonplace and tiresome" to have the "superior insights" with which Heller endowed him. Albert Duhamel of the Boston Herald (1974.B71) argued that most people's motives are more complicated than Slocum acknowledges. On the other hand, Dave Jewett of the Vancouver Columbian (1974.B107) praised Slocum and Heller's other characters for being "so well drawn they nearly come to life on the pages." William Swanson, writing to the readers of Corporate Report (1975.B29) cited a number of incidents and quotations to show that Slocum's fear and "existential void" make him similar to "our real-life colleagues or...ourselves." Elsa Pendleton of Progressive (1975.B19) also saw Heller's scenes of office and home life as having "appalling familiarity."

Many other reviewers felt a universality in Slocum. Some of these were Anne C. Walsh of the Phoenix Gazette (1974.B211), Haywood Antone of the El Paso Times (1974.B24), Eddie Lopez of the Fresno Bee (1975.B14), Debbie Natanson of the Albany Times-Union (1974.B144). They said Heller had penetrated the consciousness of "the successful American everyman." James A. Phillips of Best Sellers (1974.B154)

Introduction

expressed hope for more books like <u>Something Happened</u> that "show us what man is like"; Don Romaniuk of the Edmonton <u>Journal</u> (1974.B164) called Slocum "Everyman" in the absurdity of contemporary society; and Bob Claypool of the Houston <u>Post</u> (1974.B57) explained that Heller had given Slocum "such convincing life and breath that even the stock situations emerge as Everyman's reality." Mark Howat of <u>The Record</u> (1974.B102) saw Slocum as, if not Everyman, at least representing "an entire generation of middle-class white males." John Thompson of <u>New York Review of Books</u> (1974.B202) felt Slocum could not bear the burden of being Everyman but that he did evoke an unpleasant personal recognition of the "elemental stink of life."

Some writers went so far as to urge reading the book for personal catharsis or moral improvement. Kevin Rudden of the <u>Brown Daily Herald</u> (1974.B168) emphasized the sexuality and preached, "...we should read this novel, we should be terrified--and perhaps we can find our way out of the suffocation." Paul Desruisseaux of the San Francisco <u>Examiner</u> (1974.B67) recommended <u>Something Happened</u> as "an important book, one that should make a difference, in the lives of its readers...a powerful indictment of the rotten, meaningless lives so very many people let themselves live, and a daring attempt to change them." Joan Bunke of the Des Moines <u>Register</u> (1974.B50) observed that the reason <u>Something Happened</u> is "hard medicine to swallow" is that there is some Slocum in all of us. Charles Shapiro of the Louisville <u>Courier-Journal and Times</u> (1974.B179) also saw the novel as being for "grownups" who would see a "good deal of themselves in Slocum;" Ralph Gleason, too, in the San Francisco <u>Examiner and Chronicle</u> (1974.B84) urged everyone to read the novel and see his "life in clearer and more devastating terms."

Naturally, many reviewers compared <u>Something Happened</u> to <u>Catch-22</u>. Christopher Lehman-Haupt of the New York <u>Times</u> (1974.B120) quickly pronounced the new book "a satisfying successor." Don Rose of the Chicago <u>Daily News</u> (1974.B165) predicted that it would not "captivate broad sections of the public as <u>Catch-22</u> had," but judged <u>Something Happened</u> a "superior" novel. Joel Conarroe of the Philadelphia <u>Evening Bulletin</u> (1974.B61) took the same position, exclaiming that <u>Something Happened</u> was "superior in every way to <u>Catch-22</u>...clearly written for grown-ups." Eve Sharbutt in her syndicated review (1974.B180) also judged <u>Something Happened</u> a book of "considerably more maturity than <u>Catch-22</u>." R. L. Schwartz of the Minnesota <u>Daily</u> (1974.B175) elaborated on this point, observing the circular motif in both novels and arguing that since Yossarian "jumped out of the circle" and Slocum does not, "Heller's work has matured beyoned myth, beyond childhood--and into truth." Geoffrey Wolff of <u>New Times</u> (1974.B218) saw the new book as "better made" in a style Heller learned from Faulkner.

Several reviewers saw Slocum, as Richard Benke of the Pasadena <u>Star-News</u> (1974.B38) did, as "Yossarian revisited." Clarence Olson

Introduction

of the St. Louis *Post-Dispatch* (1974.B149) extended this view to point out that Slocum in the end accepts the same kind of "deal" Yossarian rejected.

Melvin Maddocks of *Time* (1974.B125) also saw *Something Happened* as a "second installment of *Catch-22*" with Slocum "dying" in a "vile and muddy peace" but concluded that he was only a "tired retread of the anti-hero." The *Playboy* reviewer (1974.B17) was incensed that the "sole owner of the imagination that came up with Yossarian, Milo Minderbinder, Colonel Korn and all those others" would write this "novel in which nothing happens except that words accumulate page after page...ad nauseam." Helen Golay of *Viva* (1974.B87) contrasted *Catch-22* to *Something Happened* and labeled the new novel "overwritten and self-defeative." Edward Grossman in *Commentary* (1974.B89) also saw Slocum as Yossarian who has survived but feels as if he is "living in hell." Grossman found more integrity in the "dreary" vision of *Something Happened* but felt the novel sinking "under its weight."

Critics who took a more moderate stance included John Mellors of *The Listener* (1974.B132) who objected to the "dull" family sections although he admired the office sections, concluding, "Heller's great gifts shine fitfully through *Something Happened* where they blazed from the pages of *Catch-22*." Michael Ratcliffe of the London *Times* (1974.B157) made almost exactly the same criticism, praising Heller's "fluency matched by few novelists" in the office scenes, but complaining of the bathetic "sententiousness and sentimentality" of the scenes in the Slocum home. John B. Breslin of *America* (1974.B49) also felt an inconsistency in Heller's work, though for different reasons. He saw Heller's attempt to make the new novel a mirror image of *Catch-22* with the "complications, contradictions, and absurdities...generated from within" as a "fascinating tour de force, but ultimately an unsatisfying one" because Breslin eventually grew tired of Bob Slocum. Jeff Nathan of the Los Angeles *Free Press* (1974.B142) decided *Something Happened* was, in any case, the best novel he had read since *Catch-22*.

Yet one more controversy among reviewers involved *Something Happened* as an "American suburban novel." British reviewers, in particular, found fault with it as yet another example of this "genre." Ronald Blythe of the London *Times* (1974.B44) objected to the "familiar targets." Francis King of the London *Telegraph* (1974.B112) felt it was "too much like too many American novels." Michael Ratcliffe (1974.B157) considered Heller's choice of "territory" unfortunate because others like Updike, Cheever, and Vonnegut had, in his opinion, written about it better. Several American reviewers shared his view. Robert Evett of the Washington *Star-News* (1974.B73), for instance, listed many other authors who had written this sort of novel and complained that Heller had done "nothing better despite his book's appalling length." Edmund Fuller of the *Wall Street Journal* (1974.B82) was even stronger in his objection, saying, "We've walked this dreary route before ad nauseam" and calling it "a worked out vein of the novel" with "no new insight."

Introduction

John Berthelson of the Sacramento Bee (1974.B31) took exception to this view, however, arguing that Something Happened is not the "standard WASP suburban novel" but literature more akin to French existentialism "where man's only hope in an insane world is to examine himself, realize the hopelessness of his situation, and continue to exist and cope anyway." Pat Cecchini of Maroon (1974.B53) also contended that the novel is "more than a statement of contemporary urban angst"; it is a "serious consideration of the problems of growth and knowledge."

Other reviewers also reacted to the idea that Heller's novel was another tiresome example of the suburban novel, but for different reasons. Jeff Simon of the Buffalo Evening News (1974.B185) acknowledged that many writers had "examined the galling surfaces of middle-class angst" but argued that Heller "braves past the subcutaneous layers into the tender marrow." And Allen Mayer of the Riverside Press-Enterprise (1974.B131) admired Heller's "brilliant achievement" in "giving frightening specificity to our social and psychological entropy." Even one British writer, Walter J. K. Pickering of the London Free Press (1975.B21) praised Heller's "hand on the pulse of us all" as he asked the "meaning of success" and the "price the individual and society must pay to maintain the corporate mechanism." Martha Thomases of Win (1974.B201) explained that Slocum, never realizing the absurdity of his position, reveals "everything that is wrong with our patriarchal, capitalist society." Greg Lawless of the Harvard Crimson (1974.B118) recommended Something Happened mainly as "a study of the American ethic...the effects of the corporate state on individuals."

This interpretation of the book led some reviewers to see Slocum as a victim to be pitied. For example, John Clark of the Wichita Falls Times (1974.B56) viewed Slocum as "embarrassingly real...a product of the American system that requires domination as the key to strength and success and shuns any sign of emotion as a sign of weakness." Kildare Dobbs of the Toronto Globe and Mail (1974.B69) claimed Slocum was "becoming exactly the kind of person the American way of life demands." In fact, Jon Manchip White of the El Paso Herald-Post (1974.B214) admired Slocum, in spite of his faults, for struggling to "remain a responsible and loving human being," and Jerome Klinkowitz of the Richmond Times-Dispatch (1974.B115) saw Slocum's narrative as "a sensitive man's tale of a threatening and depressive world."

A few other reviews were worthy of special attention because they focused on a particular aspect of the novel and began the work of studying Something Happened as a piece of serious literature. These include Thomas LeClaire's look at the Slocum family as "the creative center of the book, a domestic Moby Dick" in the Cincinnati Enquirer (1974.B119), Pat Cecchini's explanation of Derek's importance in Maroon (1974.B53), Irving Malin's analysis of Slocum's obsession with doors in Commonweal (1974.B126), Tom Cervenak's evaluation of

Introduction

Something Happened as the "first pop art" novel in Pacific Sun (1975.B7), and Patricia Meyer Spacks' consideration in Yale Review (1975.B28) and Robert Scholes' in Chronicle of Higher Education Review (1974.B173), both on Heller's moral responsibility as an artist.

Ann Hyman in the Florida Times-Union (1974.B104) predicted that critics would argue for years over whether "what happens in the end is redemptive or damning," and several reviewers sparked that controversy which is, of course, of vital concern to understanding the book. Ken Musson, writing in the Tampa Tribune-Times (1974.B138) saw the end as positive in that when the boy dies, Slocum can "shuck the woes and fears of his own childhood" and become a man. William A. Silverman of the Detroit News (1974.B184) saw it, to the contrary, as proving that Slocum, when his son is injured, is "tragically unable to cope." Kathryn G. Boardman of the St. Paul Pioneer Press (1974.B45) also found the ending tragic but not because of the boy's accident. It is tragic because Slocum is able to go back to his job and carry on with preparations for the convention.

Finally, it must be noted that a significant number of reviewers praised Something Happened unequivocably as a superb piece of literature. To name just a few, James Childs of the New Haven Register (1974.B55) classified it as "masterful...perhaps the most significant novel of the decade"; Indra Kagis of the Montreal Star (1974.B109) also named it "possibly the most significant novel of the decade"; and John Aldridge in Saturday Review World (1974.B3) called the book "a major work of fiction, an abrasively brilliant commentary on American life that must be recognized as the most important novel to appear in this country in at least a decade." Edward Susman of the Hartford Times (1974.B195) was even more extravagant in claiming Heller had with this novel "proven his ranking as one of the foremost literary figures of our generation and generations to follow."

Several critics, such as Sidney Thomas of the Atlanta Journal Constitution (1974.B200), Robert Rifkin of Newsbeat (1974.B160), HPE of the Long Island Business Review (1974.B91), and Ralph J. Gleason of Rolling Stone (1974.B85) suggested Something Happened might be the "Great American Novel." William Starr of The State (1974.B191) and Michael Chessler of the Grinnell Scarlet and Black (1974.B54) rated the book "a classic."

At least some of this enthusiasm seemed justified as 1974 ended and Something Happened was placed on many critics' lists of books recommended for Christmas gifts and "best books" of the past year. Some of these included publications as diverse as the Washington Post (1974.B22), the Syracuse Times News (1974.B196), the Winnepeg Free Press (1974.B217), and Rolling Stone (1974.B163). The New York Times included it as one of seven "significant books of 1974" (1974.B21); Newsweek counted it among the "best of 1974" (1974.B59); Booklist named it one of the "notable books of 1974" (1975.B2); and Leo McConnell of the New England Business Journal called it "the most brilliant

Introduction

book of the year" (1975.B16). However, whether the book will be "critic-proof" and "time-proof," as William Parill of the Nashville Tenneseean predicted (1974.B152), or even whether it will be, as the Jersey City Journal reviewer predicted (1974.B27), "read and analyzed for years to come," is still uncertain. At least one scholarly essay assessing its literary value has appeared (1977.B4). Moreover, it is still selling well; and, perhaps significantly, the most recent paperback covers of Catch-22 list Joseph Heller as "the author of Something Happened."

Catch-22, which came to be known as a contemporary classic during the anti-establishment, anti-military fervor of the late 1960's and early 1970's, could seem less meaningful in a calmer America. Scholars will want to reassess whether its merit is temporary or timeless, just as they will continue to evaluate Something Happened. Certainly, whether regard for Heller's work grows or declines, he will continue to be interesting for his influence on other writers of the period.

In arranging this bibliography of Heller commentary to date, a chronological arrangement seemed most appropriate, particularly for those who might want to trace Heller's critical reputation. Therefore, I have arranged all books and articles by year of publication, then alphabetically by author within each year. Anonymous works are listed under "anon.," then chronologically. Books and graduate theses devoted solely to Heller's work are listed under "A Books" at the beginning of each year, while those which discuss Heller and other writers' works are listed under "B Shorter Writings."

For almost all listings (except some foreign works) I have provided annotations to give an idea of the content and scope of the work. A number of short checklists on Heller's work have been published, as well as one substantial bibliography of works about Catch-22 (1974.B213). I have included all works from these lists on my bibliography. In a few cases, when I was not able to verify or annotate such works, I marked them with an asterisk to the left of the listing. I have listed and annotated all published checklists and bibliographies as separate entries, but I have not listed each instance where Heller was mentioned in standard bibliographical sources such as the MLA Bibliography or Year's Work in English Studies.

I am grateful to Mr. Heller for responding to my letters and to his publishers, Simon and Schuster, Dell, and Knopf, for permitting me to use their clipping files of reviews and articles on Heller. John Beauchamp of Random House was particularly helpful. I have indicated with an (**) to the right of the entry listings from the clipping files which are incomplete because I was not able to find the missing information at the Library of Congress or by writing to local libraries where the newspapers were published.

My work would not have been possible without the encouragement and constructive criticism of Professor Jackson Bryer or without the

Introduction

copying and editing help, as well as the patience and support, of my parents and my husband.

    I cannot predict whether Heller's literary reputation will last as remarkably as it has grown, but I feel sure that the outcome will be influenced by the work of scholars in helping the reading public understand and evaluate it as literature. Hopefully, this bibliography will be of some use in that important work.

Writings by Joseph Heller

Books

Catch-22. New York: Simon and Schuster, 1961; London: Jonathan Cape, 1962; New York: Dell, 1962; New York: Modern Library, 1966; London: Corgi, 1964; New York: Delta, 1964; Large type edition--reprint of 1961 edition. New York: Simon and Schuster, 1969; New York: Dell, 1973; Critical edition, Robert M. Scotto, ed. New York: Dell, 1973.

>"Snowden" section reprinted in Jerome Charyn, ed. An Anthology of Contemporary Fiction: The Single Voice. London: Collier-MacMillan, 1969. Pp. 125-136.

>Chapter V reprinted in Louis Untermeyer, ed. Treasury of Great Humor. New York: McGraw-Hill, 1972. Pp. 654-660
>> Passage also reprinted as "Passages" in New York University Alumni News, March, 1962. (**)

We Bombed in New Haven. New York: Knopf, 1968; London: Jonathan Cape, 1969; New York: Dell, 1969; Library version, revised. New York: Dell, 1970.

Catch-22: A Dramatization. New York: Delacorte Press, 1973; New York: Samuel French, 1971; New York: Dell, 1973.

Something Happened. New York: Knopf, 1974; London: Jonathan Cape, 1974; New York: Ballantine, 1975.

Stories

"I Don't Love You Any More," Story, XXVII (September-October, 1945), 40-44.

"Castle of Snow," Atlantic Monthly, CLXXI (March, 1948), 52-55.
   Reprinted in Martha Foley, ed. The Best American Short Stories. Boston: Riverside Press, 1949. Pp. 127-134.

Writings by Joseph Heller

"Girl from Greenwich," Esquire, XXIX (June, 1948), 40-41, 142-143.

"A Man Called Flute," Atlantic Monthly, CLXXII (August, 1948), 66-70.

"Nothing to Be Done," Esquire, XXX (August, 1948), 73, 129-130.

"World Full of Great Cities." In Nelson Algren's Own Book of Lonesome Monsters. n.p.: Bernard Geis Associates, n.d. Pp. 7-19.

"Catch-18." In New World Writing. New York: New American Library, 1955. Pp. 204-214.
    First version of the first chapter of what was later to be Catch-22.

"McAdam's Log," Gentlemen's Quarterly, XXIX (December, 1959), 112, 166-176, 178.

"Love, Dad," Playboy, XVI (December, 1969), 181-182, 348.
    Reprinted in A 'Catch-22' Casebook (1973.A1) and Catch-22: A Critical Edition (1973.A2).

Miscellaneous

Reviews, Articles, Letters, and Humor in Periodicals and Anthologies

"Bookies, Beware!" Esquire, XXVII (May, 1947), 98.
    A "semi-fiction" about a student who uses purely scientific methods to pick a long-shot winner.

"Middle-Aged Innocence," The Nation, CXCIV (January 20, 1962), 62-63.
    A review of Evelyn Waugh's The End of the Battle.

"Coney Island: The Fun Is Over," Show, II (July, 1962), 50-54, 102-103.
    An essay about changes in the neighborhood where he grew up.

"Too Timid to Damn, Too Stingy To Applaud," New Republic, CXLVII (July 30, 1962), 23-24, 26.
    A review of Alfred Kazin's Contemporaries.

"Irving Is Everywhere," Show, III (April, 1963), 104-105, 126-127.
    Humorous article about an agent who had a part in the sale of the motion picture rights to Catch-22.

"Something Happened," Esquire, LXVI (September, 1966), 212-213.
    Condensation of unpublished novel.

New York Times, March 12, 1967, Sec. I, pp. 12, 22.
    Letter supporting Bertrand Russell's resistance to Vietnam War.

Writings by Joseph Heller

"'Catch-22' Revisited," Holiday, XLI (April, 1967), 44-61, 130, 141-142, 145.
    Travel article and commentary of Heller family's visit to Italy. Reprinted in A 'Catch-22' Casebook (1973.A1).

"The Critical Eye/Movies - How I Found James Bond, Lost My Self-Respect, and Almost Made $150,000 in My Spare Time," Holiday, XLI (June, 1967), 123-125, 128, 130.
    A humorous review of Casino Royale in the form of a tale of being offered $150,000 to rewrite the script.

"Not the Same Joseph Heller," New York Times, August 31, 1972, p. 32.
    Letter in which Heller stresses that he is not the same Joseph Heller who wrote two days before to say he was leaving the Democratic Party. Author Heller expresses enthusiasm for George McGovern.

"A Poet in Jail," New York Times, December 16, 1973, Sec. 4, p. 12.
    Letter by Heller, Jerzy Kosinsky, Dwight MacDonald, and 32 others protesting the imprisonment of Iranian poet and critic Reza Baraheni.

"On Translating 'Catch-22' into a Movie," In Frederick Kiley and Walter McDonald. A 'Catch-22' Casebook. New York: Thomas Y. Crowell, 1973. Pp. 346-362.
    An abridgement of remarks made by Heller at the Poetry Center, Young Men's Hebrew Center, New York City in December, 1970. See 1973.A1 for annotation.

NAGEL, J. "Two Brief Manuscript Sketches," Modern Fiction Studies, XX (Summer, 1974), 221-224.
    Reproduces two of Heller's early sketches for Catch-22. See 1974.B139 for annotation of Nagel's commentary.

"Letters to the Editor," Charlotte News. (**)
    Heller writes in appreciation for John Alexanders' review (1974.B4) of Something Happened which, he says, teaches him something new about his own work, notably that Slocum internalizes history and culture.

"From Sea to Shining Sea, Junk," New York Times, September 30, 1974, p. 35.
    Excerpt from Something Happened before publication.

"This Is Called National Defense," New York Times, November 24, 1975, p. 35.
    A previously unpublished fragment written in 1965 after Heller learned that Martin Luther King's telephone had been bugged.

Writings about Joseph Heller, 1961-1977

1961 A BOOKS - NONE

1961 B SHORTER WRITINGS

1. ADAMS, FRANK. "Comedy and Calamity--Unorthodox Novel of World War II," Norfolk *Virginian-Pilot*, October 22, Sec. F, p. 6.
   Sees *Catch-22* as "a modern tragicomedy...an unorthodox novel that mixes uproarious comedy with stark calamity to make a point about war: avoid it."

2. AHERNE, DANIEL E. "A Mythical Squadron," *Hartford* (Connecticut) *Courant Magazine*, November 5, p. 14.
   Had to "push" himself through *Catch-22* and, "as one long acquainted with the heroic work of the Air Force in World War II," states that such a squadron and men never existed. Goes on to describe disdainfully the activities of this "mythical squadron" as "dodging duty and pursuing prostitutes."

3. ALGREN, NELSON. "The Catch," *The Nation*, CXCIII (November 4), 357-358.
   Gives examples of some of the "formalized lunacy of the military mind" in *Catch-22*, then names it "not merely the best American novel to come out of World War II...the best American novel that has come out of anywhere in years." Reprinted: 1973.A1; 1974.A2.

4. ANON. Review of *Catch-22*, *New Mexico Quarterly*, XXXI (Autumn), 269.
   A short review which asserts that "*Catch-22* is the funniest war novel since *Journey to the End of the Night*. Compared to Celine, Heller is at once more logical and more fantastic in his treatment of the Man vs. War-Machine theme. Farce and fantasy, however, rob *Catch-22* of reality and soften its impact.... The only real, three-dimensional character in the novel is the Chaplain....perhaps the actual hero.... Yossarian is a comic-strip paper doll.... The real subject of this novel is paranoia."

Writings about Joseph Heller, 1961-1977

1961

5   ANON. Review of Catch-22, Kirkus, XXIX (September 1), 804-805.
    Reports that the publishers of Catch-22 "are planning considerable publicity" for this "wildly inventive comic novel." Tells about some characters and plot briefly.

6   ANON. Review of Catch-22, Newsday, October 9. (**)
    Brief squib which tells Yossarian's basic situation and calls the book a "crazy, wonderful, yet cruelly sane story, written with wit and wonder."

7   ANON. "Life Guide," Life, LI (October 13), 25.
    Lists Catch-22 as one of recommended books. Says it "traces the uproarious, surrealistic trials of a modern-day soldier Schweik...the book's unorthodox military moral: stay alive at all costs."

8   ANON. "War Is Wild," Lewiston (Idaho) Tribune, October 15. (**)
    Distinguishes between books like No Time for Sergeants, which use the war as a backdrop for situation comedy, and Catch-22, which "is actually ridiculing war itself...this is no stereotyped tale of war but rather a spoof on one."
    This syndicated review also appeared in other papers as follows:
        Tulsa (Oklahoma) Tribune, October 16, p. 32;
        Indiana (Pennsylvania) Gazette, October 19. (**);
        "Zany Tale of War Aviators," Philadelphia Evening Bulletin, November 19, Sec. 2, p. 3;
        J. B. "Heller Produces A Biting Satire Of Men At War," St. Petersburg (Florida) Times, January 28, 1962, p. 22.

9   ANON. "Lunacracy," Newsweek, LVIII (October 16), 116-118.
    Briefly summarizes the plot of Catch-22 and calls it "a first novel of great power and commanding skill."

10 ANON. "Books and Authors," Lewiston (Maine) Sun, October 17, p. 4.
    Speculates that "'Catch-22' could well become one of the major works of the mid-century," for it reveals "the secret citadels and ambitions of all types of men. There is...a certain identification for everyone."

11 ANON. Review of Catch-22, Mexico (Missouri) Ledger, October 24, p. 10.
    A cursory description of the book's plot and characters. At the end, declares, "Heller is a brilliant writer, with considerable talent as a satirist."

1961

This syndicated review also appeared in other papers as follows:
"New Books," Philadelphia Daily News, November 16. (**);
"Distorted View Of Air Force Given in Novel," Kingsport (Tennessee) Times News, November 19. (**);
"Daily-Times Book Reviews," Okmulgee (Oklahoma) Times, November 19, Sec. B, p. 5;
Tulare (California) Advance Register, November 21. (**);
New Haven (Connecticut) Journal-Courier, November 21, p. 8;
"War As Seen In Fun House," Houston Press, November 24, p. 11;
Bristol (Virginia) Herald-Courier, November 26, Sec. A, p. 4;
"Draws Grotesque Picture of War," Bloomington (Indiana) Pantagraph, November 26. (**);
"Book Report," Hanford (California) Sentinel, December 1, p. 6.

12   ANON. "Good Soldier Yossarian," Time, LXXVIII (October 27), 97-98.
A mixed review: "Heller is a superb describer of people and things...[his] talent is impressive, but it is also undisciplined, sometimes luring him into the bogs of boring repetition. Nearly every episode in Catch-22 is told and retold...an overdose of comic non sequitur and an almost experimental formlessness are not enough to extinguish the real fire of Catch-22."

13   ANON. "Action Novel," Pasadena (California) Independent Sun, October 29, p. 10.
Short review which calls Catch-22 "an interesting, offbeat novel."

14   ANON. "The Dispatch Tab--Side Looks at New Books," Columbus (Ohio) Dispatch TAB, October 29, p. 13.
Briefly describes the situation and "reasoning" of Catch-22.

15   ANON. "Christmas Classified," Mademoiselle, LIV (November), 103-109.
Recommends Catch-22 as a Christmas gift: "Could be Heller is our Swift."

Writings about Joseph Heller, 1961-1977

1961

16   ANON. Note on Catch-22, Long Beach (California) Independent, November 2. (**)
        Squib which tells Yossarian's situation and notes that reviewers are pledged not to reveal the climax, which comes in the last twelve words of the book.
        Printed the same day in the Long Beach, California Press-Telegram. (**)

17   ANON. "Humor Wins in Wild War," Lincoln (Nebraska) Sunday Journal and Star, November 5, Sec. C, p. 8.
        Doesn't quite know what to make of the book, feels guilty about laughing when the situation "undoubtedly isn't a bit humorous to the characters." Concludes that Catch-22 "will mean many things to many people, but it will certainly provide excellent reading entertainment for all."

18   ANON. "They've Just Been Published," Cleveland Plain Dealer, November 12, Sec. E, p. 29.
        Gives short rundown of story line in this "exceedingly verbose wartime novel." Decides many will be bored by it; others will be reminded of "their own wartime experiences and they'll love it."

19   ANON. Catch-22 Recommended, New York Herald Tribune Books, November 19, p. 5.
        Short blurb on Catch-22 as the novel "Our book editors suggest this week."

20   ANON. Catch-22 Recommended, "Christmas Books for Varied Tastes," Saturday Review, XLIV (December 2), 32.
        Recommends "this story of the good soldier Yossarian" as a Christmas gift.

21   ANON. Catch-22 Recommended, St. Louis Post-Dispatch, December 3, Sec. I, p. 6.
        Includes Catch-22 in list of Christmas gift recommendations.

22   ANON. "Outstanding Books of 1961 for Holiday Giving," New York Herald Tribune Christmas Books, December 3, pp. 6, 8, 10, 12, 14, 16, 20, 22, 24.
        Suggests Catch-22.

23   BALLIET, WHITNEY. Review of Catch-22, New Yorker, XXVII (December 9), 247-248.
        Reviewer dislikes Catch-22, "a manic travesty on the war and on all previous S.W.W. novels.... Heller wallows in his own laughter, and finally drowns in it."

Writings about Joseph Heller, 1961-1977

1961

24 BASS, MILTON R. "The Lively Arts," (Pittsfield, Massachusetts) Berkshire Eagle, October 31, p. 6.
Pronounces Heller a "genius," though only a small group of people will be able to appreciate his novel. "Catch-22 is one of those books that annoys you for the first 25 pages, mostly because you can't understand what the devil is going on..., there is an oddness to the people, a seeming disorganization to the plot and a weirdness to the atmosphere that makes you feel trapped in a mental institution...then...the pattern falls into place, and you realize that there is fantastic organization to the spider web of the plot and that the people are everybody you know carried to their logical extremes and the incidents are everything that has happened, is happening or will happen to you." Reprinted: 1973.A1.

25 BERNARD, KENNETH. "Nightmarish Satire," Louisville Courier-Journal, November 26, Sec. 4, p. 7.
Notes the difficulty of describing Catch-22, since "its approach is not representational.... [[Heller] uses the real details to build monstrous abstractions and weird interpolations of reality, which nevertheless are more felt than any grim documentary." Explains why "Heller is not a master of the absurd, but of the truth."

26 BOROFF, DAVID. "World War II: A New Look?" New York Post, December 10, Sec. II, p. 11.
Shows concern because "'Catch-22' subverts the great emotional investment many of us have in World War II," feels it must be viewed as "a tract for here and now. As such, it is magnificent." Elaborates on the novel's good qualities.

27 BRANCHE, BILL. "Nightmare of War Captured," Niagara Falls Gazette, October 15. (**)
Begins by saying, "Not since Stephen Crane has a writer seen war and the military more keenly than Joseph Heller." Goes on to argue that Heller goes further than Crane's realistic portrayal of war to penetrate "below events and emotions into a netherworld where small ambitions and large greeds, stupidity, arrogance and ignorance transform men at war into grotesque caricatures."

28 BRUSTEIN, ROBERT. "The Logic of Survival in a Lunatic World," New Republic, CXLV (November 13), 11-13.
Illustrates how Catch-22 persuades us that the most lunatic characters are the most logical and that "it is our conventional standards (in the whole society, not just the

1961

military) which lack any logical consistency." With examples of characters that "transcend caricature entirely and become vividly authentic" and of comedy, never for its own sake, but as "a prologue for some grotesque revelation," shows how the novel promotes "a new morality of refusal" in a world dominated by "cruelty, carnage, inhumanity, and a rage to destroy itself." Reprinted: 1973.A1; 1974.A2; 1972.B6.

29 BRYANT, DON. "Story of Ghetto, 'Mila 18' Is Favorite," Lincoln (Nebraska) Journal Star, December 31, Sec. C, p. 8.
    Includes Catch-22 among choices of "favorite reading in 1961"; calls it "humorous, grotesque, and good."

30 BUTLER, SHEPPARD, "Army System Ridiculed In A Dedicated Mission," Bridgeport (Connecticut) Sunday Post, December 15. (**)
    Objects to this "screwy...book in the 1961 manner," finds that "virtually nothing in it makes sense...what it has to do with war and the Army is the author's secret." Furthermore, "the text is painstakingly filled with lewd language."

31 CALDER-MARSHALL, ARTHUR. "Next Month's Choice--A Savage, hilarious, satirical novel about American airmen at war-- Catch-22 by Joseph Heller," Broadsheet (August). (**)
    Predicts that Catch-22 is the most likely of the many World War II novels to survive "for its high humor and its hatred of all forms of cruelty."

32 CARLSON, HARRY R. Review of Catch-22, Jamestown (New York) Post-Journal Saturday Magazine, November 25, p. 4.
    Describes the characters of Catch-22 at some length and pronounces the novel "fantastic."

33 COLLINGWOOD, LILLIAN. Review of Catch-22, El Paso (Texas) Herald Post, November 4, p. 4.
    Announces: "So great is Mr. Heller's skill at presenting paralyzing dilemma and hilarious paradox that you, like Yossarian, won't know whether you are mad, or the world is, or both are, or are not."

34 D. H. C. "Bitter-Sweet and Funny," Worcester (Massachusetts) Sunday Telegram, November 19, Sec. D. p. 11.
    Comments that the "ability to mix humor with bitterness is almost an innate talent, and [Heller]...was apparently born with all stars in juxtaposition."

Writings about Joseph Heller, 1961-1977

1961

35   DOLBIER, MAURICE. "Daily Book Review," New York Herald Tribune, October 10, p. 27.
     Describes Yossarian's situation in Catch-22 and a number of characters briefly; calls the novel "a wild, moving, shocking, hilarious, raging, exhilarating, giant rollercoaster of a book."
     This syndicated review also appeared in other papers as follows:
          "A Wild, Shocking, Hilarious, Rollercoaster of a Book," Baltimore News-Post, October 11, p. 39;
          "Shocking and Hilarious Tale of the Crazy World of War," Toledo (Ohio) Blade, October 15, Sec. 2, p. 6;
          "The Book Mark--Marx Brothers Script by Kafka," Oakland (California) Tribune, October 19, p. 23;
          "A Weird Crowd--Warriors Are Grotesque In 'Rollercoaster' Plot," Shreveport (Louisiana) Times, October 22, Sec. F, p. 4;
          "The Book Corner--A Zany Crew," San Francisco Examiner, November 6, p. 35.

36   _____. "About Books and Authors," New York Sunday Herald Tribune Books, October 15, p. 2.
     Predicts Catch-22 will be "one of the most talked-about books of the new season" and relates how its title was changed from Catch-18 because of possible confusion with Leon Uris' Mila 18.

37   FIDLER, DAVID. Review of Catch-22, Richmond (Virginia) Times Dispatch, October 22, p. 4F.
     Classes Catch-22 as "an absolutely original novel about war...a disturbing insight into the larger struggle of today--the survival of mankind."

38   GILBERT, ALLAN, JR. "Imperative Quality, Mad Logic Skillfully Woven Into Top Tale," (Fayetteville) Northwest Arkansas Times, November 10, p. 14.
     Interprets Heller's "changing from his illogic logic to normal logic" as a way of separating the crazy man from the normal one.

39   GOODSPEED, JOHN. "Comedy and Satire," Baltimore Sunday Sun, November 5, Sec. A, p. 5.
     Disapproves of Heller's "somewhat nihilistic" philosophy; assumes the theme of the novel is "that God doesn't care what happens to man" and Snowden's "secret" is "that a man's soul is destroyed along with his body."

7

Writings about Joseph Heller, 1961-1977

1961

40 GREENWOOD, WALTER R. "Pacing Is Uneven In Tale About War And Its Victims," Buffalo (New York) News, November 18, Sec. B, p. 8.
    Questions the "human decency involved in the technique of intertwining riotous farce with the agonies of death." Feels the paradoxes and logical absurdities are overworked; with so many "zany characters...the normal is lost from sight and with it any hope for great meaning in the book."

41 HICKS, GRANVILLE. "Medals for Madness," Saturday Review, XLIV (October 14), 32.
    Tells what the basic situations and Catch-22 are and describes a few characters, then gives a generally enthusiastic assessment of the satire in spite of finding the many characters and kinds of style somewhat dizzying. Reprinted: 1970.B28; 1974.A2.

42 HILL, GLADWIN. "Newcomer Author of Remarkable War Novel," Los Angeles Mirror, October 23, Sec. 3, p. 1.
    Extols Catch-22 as "one of the most remarkable books in a long time" and predicts it may "become a classic of this era." Heller "displays...the expository talents of a whole gallery of masters of literature, caricature, and satire, from Lewis Carroll to Franz Kafka."

43 HONICKER, BUNNY D. "Critic Goes Overboard on Catch-22," Nashville Tennessean, November 22. (**)
    A rave review: "Here is something Lewis Carroll might have done if he had ever penned a war novel.... Rarely has there been such an original novel, such a perfect marriage of humor and horror."

44 HYNES, FRANK. "Bombs Away," (Burlingame, California) Peninsula Living, October 22. (**)
    Feels that the novel lacks subtlety; Heller "fails to understand that satire is exaggeration to the point of absurdity, not insanity." However, it "has the making of a riotous Hollywood movie."

45 JOHNSON, LUCY. Review of Catch-22, Book-of-the-Month-Club News (October), p. 14. (**)
    Gives brief plot summary and classes Catch-22 as "an effective and savagely funny diatribe against man's inhumanity to man."

46 KEMPTON, MURRAY. "A Literary Act of Faith," New York Post, December 26, p. 33.
    A commentary praising Heller for qualities not often noticed by the reviewers, such as his "tender" moments,

Writings about Joseph Heller, 1961-1977

1961

the "endearing" character of the chaplain, and Yossarian's concern for his fellow victims. Calls <u>Catch-22</u> "the most satisfactory act of the imagination to become available this year...a work of great complexity."

47   KLAW, SPENCER. "Airman's Wacky War," New York <u>Herald Tribune</u>, October 15, Sec. 6, p. 8.
     Feels the book is ambitious but disappointing, since Heller does not develop his sympathetic characters, strains for satire with unsympathetic ones, and has little to say that is "new and fresh" about men at war.

48   LUDLOW, FRANCES. "The Editor's Choice of the Month," <u>Book Buyers Guide</u>, LXIV (October), 43.
     Describes "wonderful" book, <u>Catch-22</u>, to be published October 10, 1961, by Simon and Schuster.

49   McLAUGHLIN, RICHARD. Review of <u>Catch-22</u>, Springfield (Massachusetts) <u>Republican</u>, November 12, Sec. D, p. 2.
     Thinks <u>Catch-22</u> "savage and funny enough" but lacking "lucidity, perfect form, and characters who control one's interest."

50   MOORE, HENRY T. "Good Comedy About Air Force In World War II," Boston <u>Sunday Herald</u>, November 5, Sec. III, p. 2.
     A short, but complimentary review. Feels Heller has "caught some of the Kafka-esque meaning" of fliers' situations in World War II.

51   MURRAY, JOHN J. Review of <u>Catch-22</u>, <u>Best Sellers</u>, XXI (November 15), 345.
     Short review with explanation and enumeration of characters in this "good comic novel." Regrets that Heller chose to "give us a message...the now old existential one" in the end. Reprinted: 1973.A1.

52   MUSSON, KEN. "Here's Effervescent Originality," Tampa (Florida) <u>Tribune</u>, December 3, Sec. G, p. 13.
     Relates Yossarian's basic problems and urges reading the end first. Says <u>Catch-22</u> will give the reader "new laugh wrinkles and perhaps an occasional lift to an unexpected philosophical plane."

53   NEWQUIST, ROY. "Books of the Week--Most Original Novel May Be The Funniest," Chicago Heights <u>Star</u>, November 2. (**)
     Considers <u>Catch-22</u> an exceptional novel: "Skimming off the wildest elements of fantasy, satire, and reality,

Writings about Joseph Heller, 1961-1977

1961

'Catch-22' rollicks along with hilarity, occasionally pausing for a moment of pure poignancy. Ribald, outrageous, put together with conniving skill that never seems contrived, it is a stinging indictment of the military mind and committee judgment."

54 PINE, JOHN C. Review of Catch-22, Library Journal, LXXXVI (November 1), 3805.
    Recommends this "tedious" novel only to libraries with large fiction collections.

55 POSTEN, DOUGLAS. "'Catch-22' Fumbles Literary Ball," Los Angeles Times Calendar, October 29, p. 17.
    Mentions several examples of the "excellent writing Heller can produce," particularly "The Eternal City" chapter; but criticizes Heller for being "a compulsively clever writer who can't let his characters speak for themselves and who is sometimes given to an undisciplined originality."

56 PRESCOTT, ORVILLE. "Books of the Times," New York Times, October 23, p. 27.
    Predicts the success of Catch-22, "not a good novel by conventional standards...the strangest novel yet written about the United States Air Force in World War II. Wildly original, brilliantly comic, brutally gruesome, it is a dazzling performance that...will not be forgotten by those who can take it."

57 ROSENFELD, ARNOLD. "Quit or Stay, You're Crazy," Houston Post Houston Now, October 15, p. 37.
    Describes Catch-22 "the central theme of this tremendously comic, tragic World War II novel, the struggle of the individual to survive in a conflict that has lost all its sense and meaning," and several main characters who make up a remarkable group and a remarkable novel."

58 ROWE, LEONARD. Review of Catch-22, Cincinnati Enquirer, October 22, Sec. H, p. 8.
    Suggests this may be the greatest novel of World War II, while it is certainly the "most comic and satiric." Explains, "True, everything is savagely caricatured, and the insanities of army life are exaggerated to the nth power, but enough of the blinding light of truth is focused thereon to sting and pain the reader and...make him laugh aloud."

59 RUMLEY, LARRY. "Morning Advocate Books--A Disturbing Book--Heller's 'Catch-22' Pungent, Tough and at Times Brutal," Baton Rouge (Louisiana) Sunday Advocate, November 26, Sec. E, p. 2.

Writings about Joseph Heller, 1961-1977

1961

Emphasizes the "savage satire," commenting that Heller "recognizes the invalidity of sentimentality in situations where only venality exists."

60   SCHWEITZ, BOB. "War Book Is Funny Nightmare," <u>Army Times</u> (October 28), 27. (**)

Without passing judgment, describes the book as "opposed to war, military officers...and military life in general... also against patriotism and pomposity." Explains Catch-22 and asks, "How can you beat logic like that?"

61   SEIDEN, MELVIN. "The Hero and His War," <u>The Nation</u>, CXCIII (November 18), 408-412.

Reviews <u>Catch-22</u> along with four other war novels, finding its comedy "fantastically inventive, controlled, patterned and structured...dedicated to the Falstaffian proposition that it's better to be a live coward than a dead hero."

62   SLATER, LEONARD. "Sight and Sound," <u>McCall's</u>, LXXXVIII (September), 12-14.

Applauds Heller's effort in writing <u>Catch-22</u> during his spare time. Reports novel is causing "much" advance excitement in publishing circles.

63   SMITH, MILES. "Reader's Rare," Troy (New York) <u>Times Record</u>, October 7, Sec. B, p. 4.

Reports, "Death and human greed are the essential elements of this surrealistic nightmare...anyone who has experienced the horror of military logic will recognize in this story the essential madness of war."

This syndicated review also appeared in other papers as follows:

"Surrealist Nightmare In The Sky," San Jose (California) <u>Mercury News</u>, October 8. (**);

"Military Idiot Gambles Life of Bombardier," Vallejo (California) <u>Times Herald</u>, October 8. (**);

"Surrealistic War Novel," Fresno (California) <u>Bee</u>, October 8, Sec. F, p. 28;

"'Logic' of War," High Point (North Carolina) <u>Enterprise</u>, October 13. (**):

_____. Lancaster (Pennsylvania) <u>News</u>, October 15. (**);

"New War Novel by Heller Called Surrealist Nightmare," Hammond (Indiana) <u>Times Every Week</u>, October 15, p. 2;

Writings about Joseph Heller, 1961-1977

1961

"Greed Also Went To The Front," Miami (Florida) <u>Sunday News</u>, October 29, Sec. B., p. 6;
"Bound To Be Read - Sunday News Book Reviews," Manchester (New Hampshire) <u>Sunday News</u>, October 29, p. 17;
"<u>Catch-22</u>, A Weird, Strange Sort of Tale," Anniston (Alabama) <u>Star</u>, December 3, Sec. B, p. 11;
"Catch-22: A Madness Delineated," Miami (Florida) <u>Herald</u>, December 10, Sec. G, p. 7.

64 STERN, RICHARD G. "Bombers Away," <u>New York Times Books Review</u>, October 22, p. 50.
   Often referred to by later reviewers of <u>Catch-22</u> in the <u>Times</u>, this first review acknowledges Heller's talent but condemns the novel "for want of craft and sensibility." Claims it has no sustained mood or controlling interest. Reprinted: 1974.A2.

65 TERKEL, STUDS. "There's Always A Catch, Especially 22," Chicago <u>Sunday Sun Times</u>, November 26, Sec. III, p. 2.
   Sums up the book as an "apocalyptic masterpiece" after introducing a number of the characters, "madmen of every rank," and musing over whether it is funny or not, surrealistic or not.

66 THOMPSON, JOHN H. "An Antic Microcosm Alive With GI Flyers," Chicago <u>Sunday Tribune</u>, November 26, Sec. 4, p. 3.
   Depicts Heller as "undisciplined...in the abundance of his creation" yet decides he has "gut-catching power."

67 TURNER, JIM. "Mixes War, Humor--Not Well," Cleveland <u>Press</u>, October 10, Sec. A, p. 6.
   Admits there are "some genuinely funny episodes" in <u>Catch-22</u>, but thinks the book a failure: "little more than a lame attempt at playing funnyman."

68 TYNAN, KENNETH. Note on <u>Catch-22</u>, London <u>Observer</u>, December 17, p. 22.
   Comments briefly on the merits of <u>Catch-22</u>. Calls the novel "the most striking debut in American fiction since 'The [sic] Catcher in the Rye.'"

69 W. H. R. "The Regimented Man Who Wouldn't Play," Springfield (Massachusetts) <u>Daily News,</u> November 8, p. 34.
   Explains the "moral" of <u>Catch-22</u>, then compliments Heller, who "leads you to where he wants you to go; adroitly, astutely and so cleverly you hardly know you are being led."

Writings about Joseph Heller, 1961-1977

1962

70 WYATT, BOB. "Wartime Grotesques," <u>Tulsa</u> (Oklahoma) <u>World--</u>
<u>Your World</u>, November 19, p. 17.
Says that Heller "takes that thin line between sanity and insanity and kneads and pummels it completely out of shape," also that the characters are "amazing creations... that...never existed.... But...their kind do exist in the backwaters of nightmare life."

1962 A BOOKS - NONE

1962 B SHORTER WRITINGS

1 ALGREN, NELSON. "'Catch-22': A Happy Reappraisal," Chicago <u>Daily News</u>, June 23, p. 18.
Reviews some of the history of criticism of <u>Catch-22</u> and defends his early enthusiasm about it: "'Catch' is a classic because it employs fantasy to depict truth too devastating to tell by factual narration."

2 ANGALL, JAMES G. "<u>Catch-22</u> Explains All," Kansas City <u>Star</u>, October 14, Sec. E, p. 12.
A "re-review" of an older book "currently under discussion." Says Heller, like "Shakespeare's fool in 'King Lear',...writes with humor about situations in which suffering, grief and calamity are very explicit."

3 ANON. "Notes on Current Books," <u>Virginia Quarterly Review</u>, XXXVIII (Winter), x.
Short review which calls the book "preposterous, boisterous, occassionally humorous, sometimes macabre, often repetitious."

*4 ANON. Review of <u>Catch-22</u>, Playboy, IX (January), 20.
Cited in Weixlman bibliography (1974.B213).

5 ANON. Note on Heller, Decatur (Illinois) <u>Daily</u>, February 25. (**)
Recalls meeting with "dynamic" Joseph Heller in New York.

6 ANON. "Advertising: Agency People Turn Literary," New York <u>Times</u>, March 13, p. 44.
Mentions Heller as one of two advertising men whose novels were nominated for the National Book Award in 1962.

7 ANON. "Book Awards Announced," Oklahoma City <u>Oklahoman</u>, May 27, Sec. D, p. 19.
Observes that four candidates for the 1961 National Book

1962

Awards have been purchased for paperback reprint; Catch-22 is one of these.

8   ANON. Summary of Reviews, Book Find Club News (Summer). (**)
    Provides brief summary of enthusiastic reviews of Catch-22.

9   ANON. "Fiery, Fierce, and Funny," London Daily Express, Juen 14, p. 6.
    Judges the book to be "an original...funny and sad. It evokes symbols and cocks a snook at symbolism. It is a fierce and impressive satire."

10 ANON. "New Novels," London Times, June 14, p. 15.
    Praises Heller's "facility for playing tricks with time, for introducing episodes, then dropping them and allowing their full implications to become evident only very much later in the narrative." Cautions the reader that while it is funny, it contains very convincing passages of horror and is a protest against war.

11 ANON. "Fiction--Battle and the Bomb," The (London) Times Literary Supplement, June 15, p. 441.
    Gives basic summary of the book and adds that Heller "writes well, but what he has to say is spread very thinly over a great many pages."

12 ANON. "Men Who Wage War," (London) Times Weekly Review, June 21, p. 10.
    Explains that Heller's "rushing to and fro" in Catch-22 allows him to attach greater significance to the events and assesses the novel as "one that should be acclaimed and read."

13 ANON. "What London Is Reading," London Evening Standard, June 26, p. 14.
    Announces that Catch-22 has taken first place within one week of publication.

14 ANON. Review of Catch-22, Psychiatric Quarterly, (July), 575. (**)
    While viewing Catch-22 as "superficially...a satire directed at the military mind," probes "deeper" to see it as an attack on "the bizarre...all-consuming and all-obliterating...after 50 pages...boring."

15 ANON. "Currents," Publishers' Weekly, CLXXXII (July 30), 21.
    Reports that Catch-22 became the best seller in London within a week of its publication there. Consequently,

Writings about Joseph Heller, 1961-1977

1962

Simon and Schuster started a campaign to increase its sales in New York, including a full page ad in the New York Times Book Review on July 29.

16   ANON. Review of Catch-22, Renton (Washington) Record Chronicle, August 19. (**)
     Brief summary of the plot.

17   ANON. "Best-Selling 'Catch' Bought for Filming," Dallas (Texas) Times-Herald, August 29, p. 57A.
     Reports that Columbia Pictures has bought motion picture rights to Catch-22.

18   ANON. "David Merrick Options Best Seller 'Catch-22,'" Show Business (September 15). (**)
     Merrick Production Office confirms report that Merrick has an option to film Catch-22. Denies report that Sophia Loren will star in it.

19   ANON. "The Heller Cult," Newsweek, LX (October 1), 82-83.
     Article filled with interesting trivia about Heller's admirers. Also includes comments by Heller on a variety of subjects, most notably the influence of Celine and Nabokov on his work. Reprinted: 1973.A1.

20   ANON. "Writers at Work--Joseph Heller," New York Herald Tribune Books, October 7, p. 3.
     Tells of Heller's background and the success of Catch-22. Includes drawings of Heller and his children by Richard Waring Rockwell.

21   ANON. "Chodorov Signed to do Screenplay," Santa Ana, California Register, October 20, p. A13.
     Announces that Heller and Chodorov have been signed to write an original screenplay "based on a contemporary theme with an international background" for Columbia Pictures.

22   ANON. "Studio Buys Best-Seller," Syracuse (New York) Herald-Journal, December 4, p. D6.
     Gives brief review of Heller's career and success of Catch-22 in report on Columbia Pictures' buying motion picture rights to the book.

23   ARCHER, EUGENE. "'Catch-22' Movie Set by Columbia," New York Times, August 22, p. 27.
     News item about sale of motion picture rights to Catch-22.

1962

24 BARRETT, WILLIAM. "Reader's Choice--Two Newcomers," *Atlantic Monthly*, CCIX (January), 98.
    Objects that Heller stretches his good comedy until it becomes mechanical; feels he has "enough nerve not to have to try so hard to be funny."

25 BASS, MILTON R. "The Lively Arts," (Pittsfield, Massachusetts) *Berkshire Eagle*, September 27, p. 4.
    Explains why writer counts himself one of the *Catch-22* cult. Reprinted: 1973.A1.

26 BRADY, SUSAN. "Biting Humor," *Progressive*, XXVI (January), 50-51.
    Another favorable review which compares the battles of Yossarian to those of the Marx Brothers and sees the novel as, not about war, but about an "individual struggling to survive in an insane, hostile world [mid-century America] which Heller satirizes mercilessly."

27 GARRETT, JAMES. "Why 'Catch-22'?" Cleveland *Press*, October 19, p. 12.
    Another recounting of the growing success of *Catch-22*, particularly on the campuses. Suggests that it be "compulsory reading for every world leader, for the citizens of all the nations."

28 GASCOIGNE, BAMBER. "Mixed-Up Bunch," London *Sunday Telegraph*, June 17, p. 7.
    Discussing the "novelists of the absurd," classifies Heller as "a brilliant new acolyte of this ancient order." Points out that, in spite of Heller's "anarchistic" philosophy and style, the book is "brilliantly constructed" as seemingly random events "return to tie up a mystery or to achieve a completely unexpected comic effect."

29 GILBERT, ALLAN, JR. "The Record Book--Ah, There's the Catch," (Fayetteville) *Northwest Arkansas Times*, September 24, p. 12.
    Recounts the "ecstatic" reviews but lack of commercial success *Catch-22* had in its first year. Notes that the book "requires close, careful reading" and is even "funnier and more fascinating" on a second reading.

30 GLEASON, RALPH J. "Catch This Crazy World," San Francisco *Chronicle*, August 27, p. 45.
    Recommends *Catch-22* because of its relevancy to the modern world.

Writings about Joseph Heller, 1961-1977

1962

31   GREENE, A. C. "The Printed Page--The Book They're Cult-ivating," Dallas <u>Times-Herald</u>, December 30. (**)
     Although reviewer tried to avoid <u>Catch-22</u> cult for a year, finally acknowledges it is "a delightful piece of reading for the irony and acid displayed throughout. But it can amount to a tearjerker as you realize how true it is, how unlimited to time and place it is...." Also reports Steinbeck included Heller in group of American writers he considers worthy of Nobel Award.

32   HARDY, H. FORSYTH, "Truth Enlarged by Satire," (Edinburgh) <u>The Scotsman Week-End Magazine</u>, June 23, p. 6.
     Gives enthusiastic praise for <u>Catch-22</u>: "If Mr. Heller writes nothing more he has produced a novel to stand comparison with the most memorable works in satire."

33   HASSAN, IHAB H. "The Character of Post-War Fiction in America," <u>English Journal</u>, LI (January), 1-8.
     In list of "remarkable works of the last two decades" with rebel-victim heroes, mentions <u>Catch-22</u> as having a "comic picaro, traveling through a crowded life with nerve, and sustained by a gift of hope, but never finding for himself a home, except in the mythical territory ahead." Reprinted: 1963.B15.

34   _____. "Symposium: Fiction Today--The Existential Novel," <u>Massachusetts Review</u>, III (Summer), 784-797.
     Includes <u>Catch-22</u> in list of novels that indicate a modern trend toward "ironic catharsis...the recognition not only of irreconcilable conflicts but actually of <u>absurdity</u>."

35   HOGAN, WILLIAM. "'Catch-22'--A Sleeper That's Catching On," San Francisco <u>Chronicle</u>, May 3, p. 39.
     Relates the growing popularity of Catch-22 but agrees with its early mixed reviews: it has "wacky freshness... macabre satire" but is "overlong and immature."
     This syndicated article also appeared in other papers as follows:
        "Bookman--'Catch-22' A Matter of Taste," Las Vegas (Nevada) <u>Review-Journal</u>, May 19, p. 33;
        "'Catch-22' Catches on in Young Set," Syracuse <u>Herald American Magazine</u>, May 20, p. 4.

36   HOLLOWAY, DAVID. "Recent Fiction--Nightmare Fantasy of War," London <u>Daily Telegraph and Morning Post</u>, June 22, p. 19.
     Judges and speculates: "Everything is bound together into one big, vulgar vital book that expresses a resentment against war that may well be read and understood in a hundred years."

1962

37   HORAN, TIM. "Wide, Wide World of Books--James Jones Treads on All Too Familiar Ground," National Observer, September 24, p. 17.
   Gives renewed attention to the "delicious madness" of Catch-22 because Dell has just distributed 300,000 copies and a number of noted critics praised the book. Determines that while "denouncing the folly of war, author Heller aims his shafts at a broader target, at the corrupt standards and practices of our entire society.... Along with the shocking comedy runs a counterpoint of sadness and deep feeling."

38   KAZIN, ALFRED. "Literature" in "The Year's Developments in the Arts and Sciences." In The Great Ideas Today. Chicago: Encyclopedia Britannica, Inc. Pp. 115-161.
   Places Catch-22 in "the new category of studiously funny war books." Kazin sees it as only "an entertainment," though, simulating "serious" ideas.

39   KEMPTON, MURRAY. "Medical Report," New York Post, January 17, p. 43.
   Quotes section on Doc Daneeka from Catch-22 as introduction to commentary on medical abuses of public money.

40   KRASSNER, PAUL. "An Impolite Interview with Joseph Heller," The Realist, XXXIX (November), 18-31.
   An interview where Heller talks extensively about his techniques and aims in writing Catch-22 and about critical reaction to it. Reprinted: 1973.A1-A2.

41   LESLIE, ANDREW. "A Comedy of Horrors," (Manchester, England) Guardian, June 15, p. 5.
   Describes the situation in Catch-22: "The fliers are afraid of death; the staff colonels terrified of missing promotion. It is a taut network of anxiety from which there is no escape." Thinks the book rather long to sustain itself without a firmer story line, yet it is often "brilliantly comic." Reprinted: 1973.A1.

42   MANNING, OLIVIA. "Flight into Nightmare," London Sunday Times Magazine, June 17, p. 30.
   Praises Catch-22 as "an anti-war novel, as good as they come," later explaining, "At first 'Catch-22' seems a piece of prolix buffoonery. Most of the characters are flat and the manner is tediously repetitive. Then we return again and again over incidents seeing them waver, swell, change

1962

shape, and gain significance, we realize that Joseph Heller is deliberately setting out to catch the confusion of a dream.... Yossarian, the dreamer, is the only reality... the dream changes to nightmare."

43 MARTIN, JACK. "Paperback Parade--Just What's the Catch in 'Catch-22'?" Detroit Free Press, October 14, Sec. B, p. 5.
    Reviews Catch-22 briefly ("Catch-22 is wildly satirical --but there is bitter realism in it."), as its paperback version "is now catching on belatedly around the country."

44 MITCHELL, JULIAN. "Under Mad Gods," Spectator, CCVIII (June 15), 801.
    Calls Catch-22 "a surrealist Iliad, with a lunatic High Command instead of gods, and a coward for a hero." It creates "legend out of the wildest farce and the most painful realism.... [It is] a book of enormous richness and art, of deep thought and brilliant writing." Reprinted: 1973.A1.

45 MORRISSEY, JIM. "The Book Scene--A Gripping Novel of World War II," Louisville Times, March 7, Sec. 1, p. 11.
    Uses the colloquial term "something else" to define Catch-22: "Through the outrage, the hilarity, and the horror of this compelling novel is Heller's ringing indictment of man's inhumanity to man. Through exaggeration of character--which at times is almost grotesque in its concept--Heller strips away pompous veneer and exposes universal faults."

46 MUSTE, JOHN M. "Better to Die Laughing: The War Novels of Joseph Heller and John Ashmead," Critique, V (Fall), 16-27.
    Points out with Catch-22 and The Mountain and the Feather the emergence of a new kind of war novel, relying on the stock characters of humorous novels like Mr. Roberts but involving them in all the real horrors of war. Gives particular attention to Aarfy.

47 O'BRIEN, EDNA. "No Hero This--he just wanted to stay alive," London Evening Standard, June 19, p. 14.
    Lauds Catch-22 as "a great, comic, and intricate fantasy woven out of a real and feverish experience"; also compares Heller to Salinger, briefly explaining why Heller is "the greater writer."

1962

48 PERKIN, ROBERT L. "One Man's Pegasus--The NBA's for '62," (Denver, Colorado) Rocky Mountain News, March 11, Sec. A, p. 22.
    Lists Catch-22 among the leading contenders in the fiction category for the National Book Award.

49 PODHORETZ, NORMAN. "The Best Catch There Is," Show, II (April), 117-119.
    Praises Heller's gift for caricature which "has made it possible for him to achieve a very credible description indeed of the incredible reality around us," then recalls a number of events in Catch-22 to support this point and to show that the basic premise of the book is that "nothing on this earth is worth dying for." Finally objects to the ending for "shrinking" from this premise, feels Yossarian will find nothing in Sweden worth dying for either--wants to say to Heller: "so you see, there are more clauses in Catch-22 than even you knew about." Reprinted: 1966.B20; 1973.A1.

50 PRICE, R. G. G. "New Novels," Punch, CCXLII (June 20), 953-954.
    Review that decides Catch-22's "wild jokes, the choplogic dialogue, the feeling of organization as MENACE, the shifting realities, make it both very funny and very horrible."

51 PRUSAK, LAURENCE. "Book Review--Heller's 'Catch-22' Fires Bomb at Army with Classic Portrayal," Seawanhaka (Long Island University), September 26. (**)
    A positive review, unfortunately marred by recounting of inaccurate details from the book.

52 ROUBY, JASON. "'Catch-22'--The Air Force's Turn to Protest," (Little Rock) Arkansas Gazette, January 14, Sec. D, p. 8.
    Decides Heller deserves an Air Medal.

53 SAINER, ARTHUR. "Grotesques--Funny and Not," (New York) Village Voice, April 19. (**)
    Article which concerns itself mainly with the reviewers who "grasp...[Catch-22] to themselves" as symptomatic of a kind of self-hatred that could destroy America.

54 SALE, ROGER. "Novels, and Being a Novelist," Hudson Review, XV (Spring), 134-142.
    Commends Heller's "thoroughly American" satire: "and.... [He] begins with brittle undergraduate wise cracks and then,

Writings about Joseph Heller, 1961-1977

1962

wildy and patiently, he tells the same stories over and over, each time etching them a bit deeper until...the irony disappears, the savagery is subdued, and only cynicism and compassion remain."

55 SCARBOROUGH, W. H. "In the Margin," Chapel Hill Weekly (North Carolina), October 21. (**)
   A review-article on Catch-22 at the time of the Dell paperback publication. Predicts "it may become the legend of the age...the book has the glint of pure lunacy in the magnification of every classic soldier's tale of mixups, chicanery, and top echelon fatuity ever brought home from any war. Heller has an eerie knack for taking a cliche, turning it inside out and giving it a cutting edge that slices through idiot glee to sober and often terrifying observations of the horror and senseless waste of war."

56 SCHAAB, W. C. "Book Reviews," Albuquerque Review, (February 1), 6.
   Provides a spectrum of the characters in Catch-22 to show the tone of the book; summarizes, "It all seems wise and pertinent. It may not really be wise and pertinent, but it sure is fun."

57 SHARE, BERNARD. "Alfred Neuman's War," Irish Times, June 30, p. 8.
   Likens Heller's satiric technique to that of Mad magazine. Feels Heller is creating his "own category" and "it will be a long time before anybody climbs up to join him."

58 SNYDER, MARY RENNEIS. "Behind the Backs of Books and Authors," Gary (Indiana) Post Tribune, March 18. (**)
   Expresses disappointment that Heller didn't win National Book Award for fiction; decides "perhaps Catch-22 was too wearing a novel in its shifting from hilarity to horror."

59 STARNES, RICHARD. "Labels 'Catch-22' as An Enduring Novel," Cleveland Press, February 28, Sec. G, p. 12.
   Notes the success of Catch-22 and predicts it will be "one of the enduring monuments in our language" and that Yossarian will "live a very long time," for "we all have a share in Yossarian.... none of us will ever be able to escape from Colonel Cathcart, or Milo, or Snowden."
   This syndicated review also appeared in other papers as follows:
      "Long Life Ahead--Yossarian, 'Catch-22' Praised as Outstanding Among New Books," Fullerton (California) Tribune Daily News, March 1, p. 24;

1962

"Review of 'Catch-22,'" Washington Daily News, March 1, p. 25;
"Forceful Novel," (Tucson) Arizona Star, March 2, Sec. D, p. 12. Reprinted: 1973.A1.

60 TAUBMAN, ROBERT. "Objectivity," New Statesman, LXIII (June 15), 871.
    Repeats some of what other reviewers have said and rates this "one of the war books that deserves to last."

61 TOYNBEE, PHILIP. "Here's Greatness--in Satire," (London) Observer Weekend Review, June 17, p. 26.
    A frequently quoted review which calls Catch-22 "the greatest satirical work in the English language since 'Erewhon.'" Observes that evils being satirized must be felt by the reader to actually exist if the satire is to be successful, then gives several actual events and characters of World War II similar to those in the novel. Explains how the book rages at life in the U.S. Air Force, at modern warfare, at social organization and anyone who derives power from it, and finally at the human condition itself. Concludes that "Catch-22 is a book which should help us to feel more clearly." Reprinted: 1973.A1.

62 VINCENT, CLINTON. "Parade of Books: Puzzling and Prolix Novel Is Also Bitter Fun," Seattle (Washington) Post-Intelligencer, January 27, p. 9.
    Advises, "Read Catch-22 for fun but prepare to be outraged, too.... Taste and restraint are qualities Heller waives, but exuberance and riotous imagination he has in prodigal measure."

63 VOSS, ARTHUR W. M. Review of Catch-22, Books Abroad, XXXVI (Winter), 78.
    A very brief review which calls the novel a "tour de force."

64 W. T. C. "'Voice of Sanity' Comes From Novel," Durham (North Carolina) Morning Herald, June 10, Sec. D, p. 5.
    Reports "Here is a book...while employing a technique of floor-rolling hilarity, Mr. Heller slips up and quietly smashes into our consciousness with a painful and generative awareness of life, death, and war, and gives us a devastating insight into our times, our foibles."

1962

65   WALTERS, RAYMOND. "Catch Cult," New York Times Book Review, September 9, p. 8.
     Discusses growing popularity in America of Catch-22, especially in New York City area and among "people who take their reading seriously." Also describes efforts of Robert Gottlieb and N. Bourne of Simon and Schuster to make it a success.

66   WEATHERBY, W. J. "The Joy Catcher." The Guardian (Manchester, England), November 20, p. 7.
     Interview-article where Heller tells of his inspirations for writing Catch-22: Celine, Nabokov, and Evelyn Waugh, two friends who were injured in World War II, and the competitive atmosphere of New York City.

67   WINCELBERG, SHIMON. "A Deadly Serious Lunacy," New Leader, XLV (May 14), 26-27.
     A review which finds that Catch-22 "lives up almost completely to its ecstatic notices," although "most of his characters can be summed up in terms of a joke." Reprinted: 1969.B19; 1973.A1.

68   WOODBURY, GEORGE. "'Catch-22' Called 'Boozy' Triumph of Obscurity," Manchester (New Hampshire) Sunday News, September 23, p. 17.
     Discovers Catch-22 among books piled up on review desk as it "stops [him] in [his] tracks." Desides it is "a triumph of total obscurity, non-sequitur and incoherence, written with a complete absence of any kind of literary, or other, discipline.... If the reader wants to 'interpret' such delirium he can read into it anything he wants."

69   WYNDHAM, FRANCIS. "Novels," Encounter, XIX (September), 74-77.
     Dislikes the technique of Catch-22 ("Marx Brothers' script written by Franz Kafka"), "tiresome" dialogue in which speakers invariably end up where they began, although it makes an effective comment on military ritual.

70   YORICK. "Out of My Mind," The Reporter (Passaic County Bar Association), C (March), 2.
     Tells about Catch-22 in this publication for lawyers because book "should be read by every lawyer (and every doctor, plumber, Indian chief).... It is not only one of the funniest books ever written, but also one of the most tragic, most gruesome, and most perceptive."

1963

1963 A BOOKS - NONE

1963 B SHORTER WRITINGS

1 ANON. Article on Catch-22, Daedalus, XCII (Winter), 155-165.
Objects to the rave notices quoted on the cover of Catch-22 on the grounds that the book is poorly written (full of clichés and drawn out bad jokes, carelessly inaccurate in use of words, with no plot and only stereotyped characters, and lacking in form and decorem) and immoral in its mindless attack on all institutions' ideals. Critic particularly objects to Heller's suggestion that the only "sane" view is "live-and-let-live." Reprinted: 1963.B2; 1963.B6; 1973.A1; 1974.A1. See also 1963.B7, B21.

2 ANON. "A review: Catch-22." In Roger H. Smith, ed. The American Reading Public. New York: R. R. Bowker. Pp. 234-247.
Reprint of 1963.B1.

3 ANON. "The New Veers," Vogue, CXLI (January), 112.
A pithy blurb on Heller and Catch-22, a "laughing, hoaxy book...[which] veer[s] away from the mass horror war book towards a mathematician's logical destruction of the solemn absurdities in the Service...absurdities...even more true in civilian life."

4 ANON. "Catch-22," New Left Review, XVIII (January-February), 87-92.
Warns against analyzing Catch-22 in terms of plot and observes Heller's ability to fix characters in the reader's mind so their effect will not be lost if they reappear later. Finds fault with the book, though, for its lack of clarity about whether it is satirizing the army or parodying war novels and for its omission of discussion about why the soldiers were fighting at all.

5 ANON. "Sustaining Stream," Time, LXXXI (February 1), 82, M23.
A paragraph on Heller and Catch-22 (a "jabberwock of a book...a wild war satire") in this article about novelists of proven excellence in the United States.

6 ANON. "After Acclaim, a Dissenting Voice--A Look at Catch-22 and a Judgment: Pretentious, Immoral, and Poorly Written," National Observer, February 18, p. 14.
Reprint of 1963.B1.

Writings about Joseph Heller, 1961-1977

1963

7   ANON. "Letters to the Editor--A Review, Like 'Catch-22,' Sparks Controversy," National Observer, February 25, p. 10.
    Prints a sampling of the responses National Observer got to the Daedalus review reprinted in February 18 issue (1963.B6). Editor notes that Heller was invited to write a rebuttal but declined.

8   ANON. "Currents--Yossarian Lives On," Publishers' Weekly, CLXXXIII (April 8), 13.
    A blurb reporting that Catch-22 has become a Bible of college students. Many are wearing Army field jackets with Yossarian name tags. Also reports on publishers' estimates of hardcover and paperback editions sold.

9   ANON. "Honors Bestowed by Arts Academy," New York Times, May 23, p. 34.
    Reports Heller was one of several artists who received award of $2500 from National Institute of Arts and Letters.

10 ANON. "So They Say," Mademoiselle, LVII (August), 234-235.
    An interview in which Heller mentions the influence of Jones' and Mailer's writing on Catch-22 and discusses its humor and shifted time scenes.

11 BRADLEY, VAN ALLEN. "Bookman's Week--A Novel with Staying Power," Chicago Daily News Panorama, April 13, p. 11.
    Comments on the staying power of Catch-22 and some of its other merits.

12 CHEUSE, ALAN. "Laughing on the Outside," Studies on the Left, III (Fall), 81-87.
    In rereading Catch-22, decides Heller's non-comic writing is dull, "overbearing sentimentality." Reprinted: 1973.A1.

13 DAY, DOUGLAS. "Catch-22: A Manifesto for Anarchists," The Carolina Quarterly, XV (Summer), 86-92.
    Predicts that a large audience, or the Establishment, will not appreciate Catch-22 because it lacks taste in the traditional sense with its mixture of humor and horror and because its hero is an "unheroic satyr-like anarchist.... Natural Man trying to live the Simple Life in the midst of a world driven mad by the complexities of its systems." Reprinted: 1973.A1.

1963

14 GUERARD, ALBERT J. "Introduction to the Issue 'Perspectives on the Novel,'" Daedalus, XCII (Spring), 197-205.
    Introduces the Littlejohn article (1963.B19), mentioning Heller as one of the "anti-realists" to be considered.

15 HASSAN, IHAB. "The Character of Post-War Fiction in America." In Joseph J. Waldmeir, ed. Recent American Fiction. Boston: Houghton Mifflin. Pp. 27-35.
    Reprint of 1962.B33.

16 HOFFMAN, FREDERICK J. The Modern Novel in America. Chicago: Henry Regnery. Pp. 228, 231.
    Speculates on the direction World War II fiction will take, toward nihilism or toward the "horrible joke" approach of Catch-22. Objects to the latter for being "wearisomely 'funny'" and leaving little room for "defining or explaining or committing."

17 HYMAN, STANLEY EDGAR. "The Goddess and the Schlemihl," New Leader, XLVI (March 18), 22-23.
    Notes two similarities between Pynchon's V and Catch-22: characters' names that are "juvenile" and a return to the literary style of Tristram Shandy. Reprinted: 1966.B15; (slightly revised) 1969.B19.

18 KILEY, FREDERICK S. "Catch-All," Clearing House, XXXVII (January), 319.
    Predicts that Catch-22 will not stand the test of literary criticism because it is "a junk heap of worn-out comic devices" and because literary criticism has not yet devised the proper test to suit this novel.

19 LITTLEJOHN, DAVID. "The Anti-Realists," Daedalus, XCII (Spring), 250-264.
    Includes Heller in his group of little-known but important "anti-realistic" novelists who abandon expected elements and recognizable characters to re-create the "revealing life of the dreaming, subconscious self." Argues that Catch-22 is not a "war novel" except insofar as the war and army life accentuate basic human characteristics, mainly "anti-humanity, the quenching of one human soul by another, the refusal of each imprisoned ego to acknowledge even the identity of another."

20 MAILER, NORMAN. "Some Children of the Goddess--Norman Mailer vs. Nine Writers," Esquire, LX (July), 63-69, 105.
    Mailer's assessment of Catch-22 as "maddening" and "original"--"two thousand variations of the same good joke."

Writings about Joseph Heller, 1961-1977

1963

Claims Heller carries his reader on "a more consistent voyage through Hell than any American writer before him" but only showing an inferior aspect of Hell (frustration). Reprinted: 1964.B11. See also 1966.B22; 1967.B27.

21   NEWBERRY, MIKE. "Anger and Laughter in 'Catch-22' Rip Morality Mask Off 'Free World,'" The Worker (New York), March 5, pp. 5-6.
     Focuses primarily on Catch-22's indictment of Capitalistic society and replies to Daedalus review (1963.B1) with an apology for Heller's satiric technique.

22   R. C. "Best of the Paperbacks," Trenton (New Jersey) Sunday Times-Advertiser, February 17, Sec. IV, p. 4.
     Expresses hope that with the publication of the 75-cent Dell paperback Catch-22, which "never really caught on here" in spite of its success in England, will get "the mass readership it deserves."" Goes on to give the novel brief but enthusiastic praise.

23   ROSS, T. J. Article on Catch-22, Chicago Jewish Forum, XXI (Summer), 334-335.
     Agrees with the critics who have given Catch-22 "a standing ovation" because it shows the triumph of the human spirit in the "stupefied, conscienceless world" of the '40's and '50's "gracefully and shockingly."

24   SCAMMELL, W. "Correspondence," Critical Quarterly, V (Autumn), 273-274.
     Disputes Wain's evaluation of Catch-22 as a book of lasting worth. Laments Heller's inability to sustain the "fantastic" mode, which allows "talking meaningful nonsense." When Heller laspes into naturalism, he has to resort to "crude and vapid moralizing" to get his message across. Reprinted: 1973.A1. See also Wain (1963.B25).

25   WAIN, JOHN. "A New Novel about Old Troubles," Critical Quarterly, V (Summer), 168-173.
     Defends the scrambled time-sequence as appropriate for bomber-pilots who live in circular time from mission to mission and Yossarian as "loser"-hero, the victim of "phonies, liars, and exploiters" who lie between him and his ideals. Predicts that, in spite of "one serious flaw," not facing squarely the ethical questions about desertion in a just war, Catch-22 will "pass into literature." Reprinted: 1973.A1. See also Scammel (1963.B24).

1963

26 WEST, PAUL. The Modern Novel. London: Hutchinson. P. 314.
    In list of modern Americans prompted by the Cold War situation to write novels of "twin extremes of scathing documentary and escapist fantasy," Catch-22 mentioned as "a shambling, apocalyptic war satire about an Air Force captain persecuted because he is sane."

1964 A BOOKS - NONE

1964 B SHORTER WRITINGS

1 ANON. "It's a Paperback World," London Times, December 17, p. 13.
   Listing of new paperbacks. Observes that Catch-22, issued by Corgi, is one of the "few works to outlast the great satire year."

2 BLACK, STEPHEN A. "The Claw of the Sea-Puss: James Thurber's Sense of Experience," Wisconsin Studies in Contemporary Literature, V (Autumn), 222-236.
   Compares Thurber to Heller and other "tragic comedians" in an introductory statement to the article.

3 DETWEILER, ROBERT. Four Spiritual Crises in Mid-century American Fiction. Gainesville, Florida: University of Florida Press. Pp. 1-5.
   In writing about a new awareness of religion in postwar American fiction, acknowledges that "the novelists of war" (James Jones, Norman Mailer, and Heller) have excluded religion--"have depicted the soldier's and the flyer's hell of Europe and of the Pacific without the relief of a saving vision."

4 DINHOFER, AL. "'Catch-22' Author Now Has To Catch 10," San Juan Star Magazine, April 19, p. 5.
   Interview-article which focuses mainly on Heller's work on scripts for Sex and the Single Girl and How to Murder Your Wife.

5 DONOHUE, H. E. F. Conversations with Nelson Algren. New York: Hill and Wang, Pp. 226-228, 289.
   Includes gossip and comment on Heller.

6 FIEDLER, LESLIE. Waiting for the End. New York: Stein and Day. P. 29.
   Comments that recent writers such as Heller have felt obliged to tell the world that the Hero is dead.

1964

7 HASSAN, IHAB. "The Dismemberment of Orpheus: Notes on Form and Antiform in Contemporary Literature." In Robert Scholes, ed. <u>Learners and Discerners: Newer Criticism</u>. Charlottesville: The University Press of Virginia. Pp. 135-165.
   Observes "the clownish element" in <u>Catch-22</u> adding that the "new comedy, which combines boisterousness and bitterness, is really an attempt to restore sanity through madness or buffoonery."

8 _____. "Laughter in the Dark," <u>American Scholar</u>, XXXIII (Autumn), 236-240.
   Refers to Heller several times in this essay on the life-affirming aspect of gallows humor in modern literature. <u>Catch-22</u>'s "buffoonery...settles for nothing less than sanity and freedom. The sense of release, of possibility, is very large...."

9 HOFFMAN, FREDERICK J. <u>The Mortal No: Death and the Modern Imagination</u>. Princeton: Princeton University Press. Pp. 261-264.
   Discusses <u>Catch-22</u> as "the most notorious" of the war novels that make madness laughable without ignoring the reality of war. Argues that Heller is saying war is "stupid and run by idiots, and the best one can do is to stay alive while it is going on"; in fact, one should try to take advantage of "its stupidities to preserve oneself... and to make life as tolerable as possible."

10 KARL, FREDERICK R. "Joseph Heller's <u>Catch-22</u>: Only Fools Walk in Darkness." In Henry T. Moore, ed. <u>Contemporary American Novelists</u>. Carbondale: Southern Illinois University Press. Pp. 134-142.
   Largely a tribute to <u>Catch-22</u> as a novel which speaks to everyone in this age and a defense of Yossarian. Explains Yossarian's view that his life is as important as anyone's, Yossarian's acceptance of absolute responsibility for himself "in good faith," and his ideal of life in Sweden. Reprinted: 1973.A1-A2. See also 1964.B11.

11 MAILER, NORMAN. In Henry T. Moore, ed. <u>Contemporary American Novelists</u>. Carbondale: Southern Illinois University Press. Pp. 13-31.
   Reprint of 1963.B20. See also 1964.B10.

12 PINSKER, SANFORD. "Heller's <u>Catch-22</u>: The Protest of a <u>Puer Eternis</u>," <u>Critique</u>, VII (Winter 1964-1965), 150-162.
   Suggests that <u>Catch-22</u> begins where World War I novels ended: "the loss of values suffered by the 'lost generation'

1964

>   now becomes a black-and-white faith that institutions are
>   'bad' and individualism is 'good.'" Yossarian refuses
>   the traditional journey of learning in manhood, adopting
>   the attitude of a perennial innocent. Also, predicts that
>   Catch-22 will foreshadow the development of a novel of the
>   absurd, as it shows throughout a breakdown of communica-
>   tion, symbolized most dramatically by the soldier in white
>   who has merely "a frayed black hole" for a mouth.

*13   SMITH, MARCUS AYRES JOSEPH, JR. "The Art and Influence of
      Nathaneal West." Ph.D. dissertation, University of Wiscon-
      sin. Cited and abstracted in Dissertation Abstracts, XXV
      (January, 1965), 4155-4156.

14   THOMPSON, HOWARD. Review of Sex and the Single Girl, New York
      Times, December 26, p. 9.
         Review of Sex and the Single Girl which observes that
      the two scenarists, J. Heller and R. Schwartz, "supplied
      some genuinely amusing, peppery dialogue and incidents."
      Gives two examples.

15   TRACHTENBERG, STANLEY. "The Hero in Stasis," Critique, VII
      (Winter, 1964-65), 5-17.
         An essay on the new "novel of compromise" which stands
      between the "compulsive affirmation" of Bellow, Malamud,
      and Gold, and the "surrealistic agony" of Heller, Hawkes,
      and Pynchon.

16   WALDMEIR, JOSEPH J. "Two Novelists of the Absurd: Heller and
      Kesey," Wisconsin Studies in Contemporary Literature, V
      (Autumn), 192-204.
         Characterizes Catch-22 as a "conscious effort to trans-
      port the novel into the realm of the absurd" but a failure
      in that "it does not go anywhere that it has not already
      been in its first few pages," that it provides no "aware-
      ness of what things could or should be in order to be aware
      of the absurdity of things as they are," and that it has a
      sudden, non-integrated ending. One Flew over the Cuckoo's
      Nest, in contrast, is hailed as "the first truly successful
      American novel of the absurd since World War II." Re-
      printed as "Joseph Heller: A Novelist of the Absurd," in
      1974.A2.

17   WINCELBERG, SHIMON. "A Deadly Serious Lunacy." In Richard
      Kostelanetz, ed. On Contemporary Literature. Freeport,
      New York: Avon Books. Pp. 388-391.
         Reprint of 1964.B67.

Writings about Joseph Heller, 1961-1977

1965

1965 A BOOKS - NONE

1965 B SHORTER WRITINGS

1   ANON. "Joseph Heller." In <u>Who's Who in the East</u>, 10th Edition. Chicago: Marquis, 1965-66. P. 438.
    Brief listing of biographical details.

2   ANON. "The Black Humorists," <u>Time</u>, LXXXV (February 12), 94-96.
    Includes Heller in this group that "mock with a cleansing mirth" and devotes two paragraphs to <u>Catch-22</u> and Heller's future as a writer.

3   ANON. "American Fiction: The Postwar Years, 1945-65," <u>New York Herald-Tribune Book Week</u>, September 26, pp. 1-3, 5-7, 18, 20, 23-25.
    Lists <u>Catch-22</u> as eleventh of "Twenty Best Books" in order of frequency cited. Heller's work is mentioned by several of the contributors (of which Heller is one). He expresses the belief that Steinbeck and Faulkner "have a better chance of enduring than the other writers and deserve to."

4   BAUMBACH, JONATHAN. <u>The Landscape of Nightmare: Studies in the Contemporary American Novel</u>. New York: New York University Press. P. 6.
    Mentions <u>Catch-22</u> as a recent novel concerned with social wrongs even if the question of repairing these wrongs seems "nightmarishly beside the point."

5   BURGESS, ANTHONY. "The Postwar American Novel: A View from the Periphery," <u>American Scholar</u>, XXXV (Winter, 1965-66), 150-156.
    Alludes to <u>Catch-22</u> several times in this essay which compares the work of British and American novelists since World War II, but complains that such satire is "too muscle-bound to move quickly."

6   DAVIS, DOUGLAS M. "'The New Mood': An Obsession with the Absurd," <u>National Observer</u>, February 15, p. 22.
    Notes that Heller has been able to hold his reputation based on just one novel, Catch-22, considered a "modern 'classic' of its kind." Relates that college students are sporting automobile stickers that say "Better Yossarian than Rotarian."

1965

7   DeMOTT, BENJAMIN. "Dirty Words?" In his You Don't Say. New York: Harcourt, Brace and World. Pp. 54-74.
    Reprint of 1965.B8. See also 1969.B7.

8   _____. "Dirty Words?" Hudson Review, XVIII (Spring), 31-44.
    Complains that critics pair literary men, such as Coleridge and Heller, in ways that add up to chaos. Reprinted: 1965.B7; 1969.B7.

9   DENNISTON, CONSTANCE. "The American Novel: Two Studies--The American Romance Parody: A Study of Purdy's Malcolm and Heller's Catch-22," Emporia State Research Studies, XIV (December), 42-47, 52-59, 63-64.
    A response to critics who called Catch-22 formless and unrealistic. Points out how it has a strict form, fitting the category of romance-parody with archetypal characters and a complex, often repetitive, plot in the form of a three-staged quest filled with conflicts and masked identities. In this ironic form of parody "the only release is death, for social tyranny is inescapable," though the naive hero may think his defeat a success. Reprinted: 1973.A1 (portions); 1974.A2.

10 ENCK, JOHN J. "John Barth: An Interview." Wisconsin Studies in Contemporary Literature, VI (Winter-Spring), 3-14.
    Barth comments very briefly on Catch-22 as a "funny" book with new kinds of comic elements.

11 FIEDLER, LESLIE. "The New Mutants," Partisan Review, XXXII (Fall), 505-525.
    Names Catch-22 and A Mother's Kisses as two "fictional vaudevilles...that currently please the young...[and] suggest in their brutality and discontinuity, their politics of mockery, something of the spirit of the student demonstrations." Reprinted: 1971.B7.

12 FRIEDMAN, BRUCE JAY. Black Humor. New York: Bantam Books. Pp. vii-ix.
    In attempt to define Black Humor, observes that it is "in the prose style of Joe Heller and Terry Southern." Reprinted: 1968.B87.

13 _____. "Those Clowns of Conscience." New York Herald-Tribune Book Week, July 18, pp. 2, 7.
    Article on new anthology Black Humor (1965.B12) which includes work by Heller, briefly alludes to the "style of Joe Heller."

Writings about Joseph Heller, 1961-1977

1965

14   GALLOWAY, DAVID D. "Clown and Saint: The Hero in Current American Fiction," <u>Critique</u>, VII (Spring-Summer), 46-65.
        Yossarian noted as one example of the "saintly clown" in modern American fiction "whose role is to redeem in some measure the absurdity of life." While "Catch-22" is the "conditional phrase which sends man off in a Kafkaesque shuffle from one bureaucratic backroom to another, cancelling expectation and frustrating imagination," Yossarian shows that it may be impossible to change the world, but one need not become its victim.

15   HART, JAMES D. "Heller, Joseph." In <u>The Oxford Companion to American Literature</u>, 4th Edition. New York: Oxford University Press. P. 364.
        Lists Heller as author of Catch-22, "a success," and briefly describes the novel.

16   KOSTELANETZ, RICHARD. "The New American Fiction." In <u>The New American Arts</u>. New York: Horizon Press. Pp. 194-236.
        Contends that <u>Catch-22</u> resembles the absurd theatre of Europe in its depiction of a series of absurd events to reveal the ultimate absurdity (meaninglessness). Explains how Heller shows that society has so distorted any relation between intention and result, or need and fulfillment, that life has become absurd. Objects to Heller's use of many different styles of representation in the course of the novel yet sees him as having a "rich talent for comic invention."

17   _____. "The Point Is That Life Doesn't Have Any Point," <u>New York Times Book Review</u>, June 6, pp. 3, 28, 30.
        Commends <u>Catch-22,</u> along with the <u>Sot-weed Factor</u>, for "reaffirm[ing] the possibility of creating novels that are, in the contemporary sense, crucially new, and in the traditional sense, realized achievements." They present the ultimate absurdity, the meaninglessness of human existence, in a carefully preplanned work, using stylized human situations as effective symbols for metaphysical absurdity.
        The same essay appeared as "The Search for the Incongruities of Life" in <u>Chicago Tribune Books Today</u>, June 6, p. 8. Reprinted as "The American Absurd Novel (1965)" in 1967.B9.

18   _____. "Notes on the American Short Story Today," <u>Minnesota Review</u>, V (October-December), 214-221.
        Names Heller as an absurd writer who can show that history is absurd.

1965

19 _____. "Militant Minorities," Hudson Review, XVII (Autumn), 472-480.
    Heller listed as one of the Jewish writers Podhoretz praises in Doings and Undoings (1966.B20).

20 LEWIS, R. W. B. Trials of the Word. New Haven: Yale University Press. Pp. 185, 226-227.
    Identifies Heller as one of a group of novelists who have made "the day of doom the great saturnalia of our time," then goes on to describe "the locale of fictional apocalypse" where survival is "predicated upon a talent for clowning."

21 SCHROTH, RAYMOND A. "Catch Peace," America, CXIII (November 6), 527.
    Considers the "new humor," most notably of Catch-22, which exposes "the logic in man that can rationalize his own self-destruction" and "the moral pygmies who saw life as a parade and war as a game."

22 YATES, NORRIS W. "The Doubt and Faith of John Updike." College English, XXVI (March), 469-474.
    At the end of article, makes the point that Updike "unlike such post-war exponents of negation" as Heller and others, "refuses to admit that the search for God is hopeless or unnecessary."

1966 A BOOKS - NONE

1966 B SHORTER WRITINGS

1 ALTER, ROBERT. "The Apocalyptic Temper," Commentary, XLI (June), 61-66.
    Counts Heller as one of a group of writers in the tradition of "a picaresque vision of the apocalypse." Alter argues against such a view of life.

2 ANON. "Joseph Heller." In Who's Who in America, Vol. 34. Chicago: Marquis. P. 936.
    Brief listing of salient biographical details. Same as in Who's Who in the East, 1965-66 (1965.B1).

*3 BARKSDALE, RICHARD K. "Alienation and the Anti-Hero in Recent American Fiction," CLA Journal, X (September), 1-10.
    Cited by Weixlmann (1974.B213).

1966

4   COLMER, JOHN. "Introduction." In his Approaches to the Novel, Adelaide, Australia: Rigby. Pp. 6-8.
    In making the point that readers must discover the form or pattern which gives meaning to a novel, uses as example Catch-22 where "Heller deliberately invented situations to suggest the absurdity of man's predicament...ordinary time scheme [is] destroyed since such chronology implies purpose and progress...withholding of information is functional...information about what happened in the plane--that Yossarian felt such compassion for the dying Snowden--is finally released at the critical moment in the narrative to enlist our sympathies for Yossarian when he decides to opt out of the war." Thus, Heller uses his design to control the reader's response and to establish the value of "moral choice in an absurd universe." See also 1966.B6.

5   DIGGINS, JOHN P. "The American Writer, Fascism and the Liberation of Italy," American Quarterly, XVIII (Winter), 599-614.
    In an article examining the attitudes of American writers towards Mussolini and the liberation of Italy at the time and later, Catch-22 is briefly mentioned to show that after two decades the "horrors of the Italian campaign could so fade from memory that the war against Fascism itself becomes the setting for a Rabelaisian satire on human frailty and pretense."

6   DODD, BURWELL. "Social Commentary and Narrative Technique--Joseph Heller's Catch-22." In John Colmer, ed. Approaches to the Novel. Adelaide, Australia: Rigby. Pp. 71-78.
    Explains how Heller purposely confuses structure, plot incidents, and language to show that the world has become a "nightmare of chaos." See 1966.B4.

7   FIEDLER, LESLIE. Love and Death in the American Novel, Revised Edition. New York: Stein and Day. P. 480.
    Footnotes his argument that few war novels have risen above slickness and sterotype to mention Catch-22 as a "recent exception--rendering with the techniques of the Black Vaudevillian a vision of war as ultimate burlesque, an event too farcical for tears."

8   FRENCH, WARREN. The Social Novel at the End of an Era. Carbondale: Southern Illinois University Press. P. 119.
    Claims Catch-22 is a collection of brilliant fragments rather than a unified presentation of a consistent theme because Heller had to cope with fixing responsibilities on a military hierarchy.

1966

9   GLANVILLE, BRIAN. "Speaking of Books: Anglo-Jewish Writers," New York Times Book Review, April 17, pp. 2, 40.
    Complains that American-Jewish writing has been too narrowly channelled into one kind of novel; cites Heller's Catch-22 as an example of what else can be done.

10 GREENBERG, ALVIN. "The Novel of Disintegration: Paradoxical Impossibility in Contemporary Fiction, Wisconsin Studies in Contemporary Literature, VII (Winter-Spring), 103-124.
    Observes that in Catch-22 "with each movement forward in the military action...the world disintegrates a little more," but that "any effort needed to sustain life is worthwhile: 'what else is there?'"

11 GREENE, GAEL. "Similes and Metaphors--Labor-saving Vices," New York Herald-Tribune Book Week, February 6, p. 6.
    Asks various writers about their procrastinations. Heller lists quite a few, including getting angry at his publishers.

12 HASSAN, IHAB. "The Dial and Recent American Fiction," CEA Critic, XXIX (October), 1, 3.
    Paper on post-war fiction comments on the "new spirit of comedy" in Catch-22 with its "absurd or comical sense of life."

13 HAWKES, JOHN. "On His Novels," Massachusetts Review, VII (Summer), 449-461.
    In interview with John Graham, Hawkes compares his comedy with that of Heller, West, and Flannery O'Conner; he sees through its violence a "saving attitude," for if "something is pathetically humorous or grotesquely humorous, it seems to pull us back into the realm, not of mere conventional values, but of the lasting values (the need for idealism, innocence, purity, truth, and strength)."

14 HENRY G. B. McK. "Significant Corn: Catch-22," Critical Review, IX, 133-144.
    Sees Catch-22 as a development from the conventions of popular literature and the cinema, using "intensity" of experience to satirize the "meaningless savagery of contemporary civilization." Unfortunately, the power and logic of the book are dissipated in the "best-seller ending." Reprinted: 1973.A1.

15 HYMAN, STANLEY EDGAR. In Standards: A Chronicle of Books for Our Time. New York: Horizon Press. Pp. 138-142.
    Reprint of 1963.B17.

1966

16   KAZIN, ALFRED. "The Jew as Modern American Writer," Commentary, XLI (April), 37-41.
     Concludes article with statment that "the Jewish writer, with his natural interest in social fact, has been particularly quick to show the lunacy and hollowness of so many present symbols of authority" and includes Heller in a list of such Jewish writers.
     Also published as "The Jew as Modern American Writer" in Quadrant, X (July-August), 60-66.

17   KOSTELANETZ, RICHARD. "Le Roman Américain 'Absurde,'" Les Temps Modernes, XXI (April), 1856-1866.
     Counts Heller as one of a group of novelists who depict the absurdity of human existence, while others like Nabokov and Percy depict a more penetrating universal experience.

18   MAILER, NORMAN. Cannibals and Christians. New York: Dial Press. Pp. 85, 105-106, 117-119, 128.
     Some analysis and general comments on Catch-22's merits. Calls Heller "a writer with merry gifts" but feels he has "only grasped the inferior aspect of hell."

19   NEW, WILLIAM H. "The Island and the Madman: Recurrent Imagery in the Major Novelists of the Fifties," Arizona Quarterly, XXII (Winter), 328-337.
     Counts Catch-22 as one of several recent works which show that through madness a sustaining order can be found; to be exempted from society's insanities one must claim insanity.

20   PODHORETZ, NORMAN. "The Best Catch There Is." In his Doings and Undoings. New York: Farrar, Straus, and Giroux. Pp. 228-235.
     Reprint of 1962.B49. Reprinted: 1973.A1.

21   RAMSEY, VANCE. "From Here to Absurdity: Heller's Catch-22." In Thomas B. Whitbread, ed. Seven Contemporary Authors. Austin: University of Texas Press. Pp. 97-118.
     Responds to the various criticisms of Catch-22, explaining its relationship to literature of the absurd and Camus and Hemingway, particularly with regard to the "nothingness" or denial of self which threatens Yossarian and his friends from all sides. Also explains the reasons for the time-sequence being as it is. But complains of two major flaws in the book: some episodes simply don't fit in and the discursive quality of the ending and the change in Yossarian are not so successful as the early parts.

1966

Nonetheless, "Yossarian's strength is not only that he consciously and resolutely is, but that he constantly rejects attempts to make him over in terms of any ideal. He is a compelling creation and probably the shape of many heroes to come." Reprinted: 1973.A1. See also 1966.B27.

22 RUBIN, LOUIS D., JR. "The Curious Death of the Novel: or, What To Do About Tired Literary Critics," Kenyon Review, XXVIII (June), 305-325.

Comments that "Norman Mailer vs. William Styron, James Jones, James Baldwin, Saul Bellow, Joseph Heller, John Updike, William Burroughs, J. D. Salinger, Philip Roth," (1963.B20) proves more about Mailer's fiction than the condition of the contemporary novel. Reprinted: 1967.B27.

23 SCHOLES, ROBERT. "'Mithridates, he died old': Black Humor and Kurt Vonnegut, Jr.," Hollins Critic, III (October), 1-12.

Heller mentioned several times in this article as one of the "best young novelists in this country" and as a Black Humorist. Reprinted: 1971.B30.

24 STUBBS, JOHN C. "John Barth As a Novelist of Ideas: The Themes of Value and Identity," Critique, VIII (Winter), 101-116.

Explains how Barth, like Donleavy, Heller, and Hawkes, forces his heroes to see a world without absolute value, to see it as comically absurd.

25 TANNER, TONY. "The Great American Nightmare," Spectator, CXVI (April 29), 530-531.

Compares the nightmarish narrative technique of Stephen Schneck in The Nightclerk with that of Heller and other American writers who seem to feel that "old ways of constructing a novel cannot get at the real horrors and actual dreads of modern life."

26 WALCUTT, CHARLES CHILD. Man's Changing Mask. Minneapolis: University of Minnesota Press. P. 296.

In a chapter showing that many of the modern ideas that control novels have the effect of limiting characterization, Walcutt comments briefly that in the "mad world" Heller depicts in Catch-22, Milo's "crazy extravaganza makes the whole business unreal, and one cannot of course believe in the characters involved. Nor does the author expect us to do so. That's the point."

1967

27 WHITBREAD, THOMAS B. "Introduction." In his Seven Contemporary Authors. Austin, Texas: University of Texas Press. Pp. vii, xii, xiv.
    Classifies Yossarian "a true antihero, exemplifying the sane absurd: a combination of laughter with horror" and says that in Catch-22 "modern evil exists...in the guise of Horatio Alger dutifully climbing to success over the bleeding forms of his fellows." See also Ramsey (1966.B21).

28 YATES, NORRIS. "What Makes the American Novel Modern?" Jahrbuch Für Amerikastudien, II, 59-68.
    Asks at the end of his essay, whether the "comic and fantastic anti-heroes" of Heller, Bellow, and others represent the end of "modernity."

1967 A BOOKS - NONE

1967 B SHORTER WRITINGS

1 ANON. "Joseph Heller." In Who's Who in the East, 11th Edition. Chicago: Marquis. P. 471.
    Essentially the same biographical information as in previous volume (1966.B2). Changes Heller's address to Dell.

2 ANON. "Stock Review," Variety, December 13, p. 58.
    Considers the play We Bombed in New Haven "terribly overwritten...most of the first half and perhaps half of the second are more or less extraneous."

3 ANON. "Catchall-22," Time, XC (December 15), 87.
    Calls the play We Bombed in New Haven "a wastebasket version of anti-war clichés"--Heller belongs to an "honorable tradition" of good novelists who have been poor playwrights.

4 BARNES, CLIVE. "Theater: 'We Bombed in New Haven,'" New York Times, December 7, p. 58.
    Analyzes New Haven production, concluding that a lot of the play is extremely funny "but its aftertaste of pain is too conscientiously striven for."

5 BREWER, JOSEPH E. "The Anti-Hero in Contemporary Literature," Iowa English Yearbook, XII, 55-60.
    Includes Catch-22 as one of novels in a modern movement in which anti-heroes are protagonists.

1967

6   BUCKEYE, ROBERT. "The Anatomy of the Psychic Novel," *Critique*, IX (Number 2), 33-45.
    Argues that novels of Heller and others are fiction as "anti-reason," recognizing the limits of language and art to order psychic materials."

7   BURGESS, ANTHONY (WILSON, JOHN ANTHONY BURGESS). *The Novel Now....* New York: Norton. Pp. 53, 58.
    In a chapter entitled "War's Sour Fruits," calls *Catch-22* "America's most recent major contribution to war fiction." Comments on the "surrealistic, absurd, even lunatic" approach and its aim "to show the mess of the war, the victimization of the conscripts, the monstrous egotism of the top brass."

8   COOPERMAN, STANLEY. *World War II and the American Novel*. Baltimore: Johns Hopkins Press. P. 230.
    In making the point that World War II novelists reacted "savagely" to any hint of the "proving ground" of combat, states that this concept was indeed a target for Heller's comic anti-heroism.

*9 DAVIS, DOUGLAS M. "Introduction: Notes on Black Humor." In *The World of Black Humor: An Introductory Anthology of Selections and Criticism*. New York: E. P. Dutton, Pp. 13-26.
    Cited by Weixlmann (1974.B213). See 1967.B16.

10 DOSKOW, MINNA. "The Night Journey in *Catch-22*," *Twentieth Century Literature*, XII (January), 186-193.
    Makes a solid case for Yossarian's journey through the streets of Rome being similar in language and image to the classical descents into hell. He can only achieve salvation by recognizing evil in the world and in himself and resisting it. Reprinted: 1973.A1-A2; 1974.A2.

11 DOUGHERTY, RICHARD. "Joseph Heller Play Premieres at Yale," Los Angeles *Times*, December 8, Sec. IV, p. 23.
    Criticizes play for lack of clear point of view: "Nothing comes into focus until very near the end...at which time the monkeyshines, the muddled metaphors and the too-cute directional bits give way to some intensely moving moments." Does feel, however, that its "motives are trustworthy and its passions honest."

1967

12 EPHRON, NORA. "Yossarian Is Alive and Well in the Mexican Desert," *New York Times Magazine*, March 16, p. 30.
    Article mostly on making of the film. Reports "Help Save Joe Heller" graffiti on portable men's room wall and efforts to capture dream-like or remembered quality of the book.

13 GORDON, CAROLINE and JEANNE RICHARDSON. "Flies in Their Eyes? A Note on Joseph Heller's *Catch-22*," *Southern Review*, III (Winter), 96-105.
    Compares Heller's fictional techniques to Lewis Carroll's in *Alice in Wonderland*, mainly the technique of having the main character contrast, with wonder and outrage, the way things are in this lunatic world with the way they "ought to be." Reprinted: 1974.A2.

14 GUERARD, ALBERT J. "Saul Bellow and the Activists: On *The Adventures of Augie March*," Southern Review, III (Summer), 582-596.
    Classifies *The Adventures of Augie March* as a new "activist" kind of novel, like *Catch-22* and others, where the "novelists work in full conscious reaction to themes of defeat, apathy, acquiescence."

15 HIRSCH, SAMUEL. "Hirsch on Theater—Yale Play Takes New Look at War," Boston *Herald-Traveler*, December 13, p. 67.
    Objects to the switch in tone at the end of *We Bombed in New Haven*, yet finds that the play "insinuates itself into your mind and behind its satirical voice rides the remote rumble of Vietnam.... Its flaws show, but so do its fangs."

*16 KOSTELANETZ, RICHARD. "The American Absurd Novel (1965)." In Douglas M. Davis, ed. *The World of Black Humor: An Introductory Anthology of Selections and Criticism*. New York: E. P. Dutton. Pp. 306-313.
    Cited by Weixlmann (1974.B213). Reprint of 1965.B17. See also 1967.B9.

17 KROLL, JACK. "War Games," *Newsweek*, LXX (December 18), 96.
    Lauds *We Bombed in New Haven* as "very likely the most powerful play about contemporary irrationality an American has written...challenges the audience to rethink their own 'roles' in a tragic and absurd reality."

18 LEHAN, RICHARD and JERRY PATCH. "Catch-22: The Making of a Novel," *Minnesota Review*, VII (Number 3), 238-244.
    Provides background material from Heller's life and reading which influenced *Catch-22*. Also comments on the

1967

merits and flaws of the novel and on Heller's new book, which, like Catch-22, shows that "in the very center of the American nightmare is the American dream." Reprinted: 1973.B11; 1974.A2.

19 LESTER, ELENORE. "Playwright-in-Anguish," New York Times, December 3, Sec. II, pp. 1, 19.
Based on an interview with Heller during rehearsals for Yale Repertory Theater production of We Bombed in New Haven. Heller discusses, among other things, how he came to write the play and how he feels about the theatre. The director, Larry Arrick, also discusses the play.

20 LEVINE, PAUL. "The Intemperate Zone: The Climate of Contemporary American Fiction," Massachusetts Review, VIII (Summer), 505-523.
In this essay on writers in today's anxious world, Catch-22 cited as one example of modern novels which are organized by "the irrational logic of the dream" and which use insanity as the method for comprehending reality.

21 McDONALD, DANIEL. "Science, Literature, and Absurdity," South Atlantic Quarterly, LXVI (Winter), 42-49.
Includes Heller in a list of modern fiction writers who depict a "strange and confusing reality."

22 MILLER, JAMES E., JR. Quests Surd and Absurd: Essays in American Literature. Chicago: University of Chicago Press. Pp. 12-13, 15-17, 24-25.
Describes Catch-22 as a war novel where "the nightmare achieves an extra dimension" with its images of senseless brutality from which Yossarian (similar in his reactions to other modern protagonists) recoils "with sickening recognition." Also notes that the novel, like several others, still sees a "thin, frail line of hope" in the "assertion of one's humanity in the face of overwhelming forces that dehumanize and destroy." Predicts Heller's work will have a permanent impact on American fiction.

23 MONK, DONALD. "An Experiment in Therapy," London Review, II (Autumn), 12-19.
Illustrates and judges various aspects of Heller's style, comparing and contrasting it to the styles of other writers--simple syntax like Hemingway's but with tenuous adjectives, "sur-real montage" juxtaposing "things-as-they-are" with "things-as-society-disguises-them," prejudice as it appears in direct speech, and Dickens-like caricature with a tendency toward allegory. Finally, comments at

1967

at length on the strength and weakness of the ending, contending that Orr and Yossarian's escape can only be seen as "fantastical," a kind of "therapy" Heller offers the reader for "facts too terrible to be faced." Reprinted: 1973.A1.

24 NORDELL, RODERICK. "Premier of 'We Bombed in New Haven,'" Christian Science Monitor, December 8, p. 14.
    Calls play "a blend of satire, comedy, and tragedy that cuts to the quick" even though Heller can't always resist an irrelevant gag and lets his characters lecture the audience too often.

*25 RICE, JOSEPH A. "Flash of Darkness: Black Humor in the Contemporary American Novel." Ph.D. dissertation, Florida State University. Cited and abstracted in Dissertation Abstracts, XXVIII (June, 1968), 5067-5068.

*26 RITTER, JESSE P. "Fearful Comedy: The Fiction of Joseph Heller, Günter Grass, and the Social Surrealist Genre." Ph.D. dissertation, University of Arkansas. Cited and abstracted in Dissertation Abstracts, XXVIII (October, 1968), 1447.

27 RUBIN, LOUIS D., JR. The Curious Death of the American Novel: Essays in American Literature. Baton Rouge: Louisiana State University Press. P. 21.
    Reprint of 1966.B22.

*28 SANGER, MARSHALL. "The Image of Modern Generalship in the United States, 1940-1965: An Examination of the Contemporary Literature." Ph.D. dissertation, Columbia University. Cited and abstracted in Dissertation Abstracts, XXVIII (October, 1968), 1447-1448.

29 SCHOLES, ROBERT. The Fabulators. New York: Oxford University Press. Pp. 37, 38, 46, 59, 61.
    Heller mentioned several times with regard to trends in contemporary fiction, most notably in John Hawkes' description of an "avant-garde" quality he and Heller share with Celine, Purdy, and others: "a quality of coldness, detachment, ruthless determination to face up to the enormities of ugliness and potential failure within ourselves and in the world around us, and to bring to this exposure a savage or saving comic spirit and the saving beauties of language...."

1967

30 SKERETT, JOSEPH TAYLOR, JR. "Dostoievsky, Nathanael West, and Some Contemporary American Fiction," University of Dayton Review, IV (Winter), 23-35.
    Argues that Black Humor of Heller and others originates in Stern, Fielding, Dostoievsky, and the pessimism of Mark Twain and Nathanael West. Also sets out the basic characteristics of these "Black Humorists": the Americanization of nausea, discursiveness and intellectuality in the novel, and stylized and mannered form.

31 SKLAR, ROBERT. "The New Novel, USA: Thomas Pynchon," The Nation, CCV (September 25), 277-280.
    Gives passing attention to Heller in article on Pynchon. Refers to Catch-22 as "the first American novel truly to have attained a Cubist form in its treatment of space and time" but offers no further explanation.

32 SOLOMON, JAN. "The Structure of Joseph Heller's Catch-22," Critique, IX (Number 2), 46-57.
    A response to the criticisms of formlessness in Catch-22. Argues that it has two independently valid systems of time sequence: (1) Yossarian's psychological time, which moves forward and backward in actual time but develops events in order of their significance to Yossarian, and (2) Milo Minderbinder's time, which moves directly forward. The fact that these two time-sequences cannot possibly mesh creates its own dimension of absurdity, enhancing Heller's pervasive theme. Reprinted: 1973.A1-A2; 1974.A2. See also 1970.B22.

33 VOS, NELVIN. "The Angel, the Beast, and the Machine." In his For God's Sake Laugh! Richmond, Virginia: John Knox Press. Pp. 53-62.
    Characterizes Heller as a "clown of conscience" who uses his antics to "arouse a surprise proof public" and explains how Yossarian, like other contemporary heroes, tries to avoid being made into "a thing." Reprinted: 1973.A1.

34 WITKIN, RICHARD. "Antiwar Slate to Oppose Johnson in State Primary," New York Times, September 21, pp. 1, 32.
    Heller reported willing to run as anti-Johnson delegate.

Writings about Joseph Heller, 1961-1977

1968

1968 A BOOKS

*1 STARK, HOWARD J. "<u>Catch-22</u>: The Anatomy of a Novel." Ph.D. dissertation, University of New Mexico. Cited and abstracted in <u>Dissertation Abstracts</u>, XXIX (June, 1969), 4506.

1968 B SHORTER WRITINGS

1 ALDRIDGE, JOHN. "Contemporary Fiction and Mass Culture," <u>New Orleans Review</u>, I (Fall), 4-9.
   An article which traces some developments in contemporary fiction, particularly a "strong counter-movement... toward surrealism and Black Humor...anti-novelistic experiment and a new mode of novelistic self-burlesque and parody." <u>Catch-22</u>, one example, referred to as "the Sick Joke extended to book length and turned ultimately into the most deadly satirical commentary on some of our most cherished hypocrises...."

2 ANON. "Joseph Heller." <u>Who's Who in America</u>, Vol. 35. Chicago: Marquis. P. 995.
   Same listing of biographical details as in 1966 (1966.B2).

3 ANON. "Robards Will Star in Heller Comedy," New York <u>Post</u>, May 14, p. 66.
   Reports on the star, producers, and Broadway opening date of <u>We Bombed in New Haven</u>, "described by the author as a surrealist comedy, anti-war."

4 ANON. Review of Book <u>We Bombed in New Haven</u>, <u>Publishers' Weekly</u>, CXCIV (July 8), 162.
   Short review calls the book "fine, fast entertainment... effective theater but warmed-over Heller."

5 ANON. Review of Book <u>We Bombed in New Haven</u>, <u>The American News of Books</u>, (August). (**)
   Capsule summation of the play.

6 ANON. "Financial Aid Due for Heller Play," New York <u>Times</u>, August 7, p. 38.
   Reports that newly formed Theatre Development Fund chose <u>We Bombed in New Haven</u> as first play to receive its assistance, feeling that "it would appeal to new theatre audiences as well as theatregoers looking for plays of contemporary concern."

Writings about Joseph Heller, 1961-1977

1968

7   ANON. "534 Writers Bid U.S. End Bombing; Urge Cease-Fire," New York <u>Times</u>, August 12, p. 53.
     Lists <u>Heller</u> as one of prominent group of writers who sent petitions urging international cooperation to end the war.

8   ANON. "War Made Real," Wichita Falls (Texas) <u>Times</u>, August 25. **
     Announces the publication of the book <u>We Bombed in New Haven</u> and the two productions of the play.

9   ANON. "This Week," <u>Christian Century</u>, LXXXV (August 28), 1082.
     A one sentence review which calls the play "a compelling black-humor indictment of the war."

10   ANON. "Sked 'We Bombed' As London Entry," <u>Variety</u>, September 4, p. 49.
     Reports the play will be staged at the Royal Court Theatre in England.

11   ANON. Review of Book <u>We Bombed in New Haven</u>, <u>Newsday</u>, September 7. **
     A brief notice which suggests the play will come across better on stage, though "the irrationality and horror of our actions and attitudes today come across in a reading."

12   ANON. "Sell 'Bombed' Paperback Rights to Dell for 100G," <u>Variety</u>, September 11, p. 103.
     Reports this "believed record price" for paperback rights to an unproduced play.

13   ANON. "Releases with..." Phoenix (Arizona) <u>Gazette</u>, September 12, p. A16.
     Relates the basic story line of this "unsettling comedy."

14   ANON. Note on <u>We Bombed in New Haven</u>, New York <u>Daily Column</u>, September 25. (**)
     Reports Heller wrote the words for "Bomb, Bomb, Bombing Along," theme song of <u>We Bombed in New Haven</u>.

15   ANON. "Mixed Views Greet U.S. Play in Berlin," New York <u>Times</u>, September 26, p. 64.
     Reports on the European premiere of <u>We Bombed in New Haven</u>: "Persons old enough to have sent sons and husbands off to war were moved. The younger generation, though, was embarrassed by a thesis play that wore its emotion so nakedly on its sleeve, a trait held here to be too American."

Writings about Joseph Heller, 1961-1977

1968

16   ANON. Review of Book <u>We Bombed in New Haven</u>, <u>Delaware State Library Book Selection</u> (October). (**)
     Determines play is "effective theatre but warmed-over Heller."

17   ANON. "Scheduled B'way Preems," <u>Variety</u>, October 16, p. 70.
     Lists <u>We Bombed in New Haven</u> to open at Ambassador Theatre on October 16, 1968.

18   ANON. Summary of <u>We Bombed in New Haven Reviews</u>, <u>Variety</u>, October 23, (**)
     Summarizes press reviews of <u>We Bombed in New Haven</u> as "two favorable (Gaver, UPI; Watts, <u>Post</u>), two unfavorable (Chapman, <u>News</u>; Winchell, <u>Column</u>), and two mixed opinions (Barnes, <u>Times</u>; Glover, A.P.) and broadcast reviews as "Seven favorable...two unfavorable...and one no opinion."

19   ANON. "Indiscriminate Bombing," <u>Time</u>, XCII (October 25), 69.
     In spite of Heller's rewriting since New Haven, Broadway reviewer says the play is still "an anemic polemic against the war in Viet Nam."

20   ANON. "New Arrivals in the Theater," New York <u>Times</u>, October 27, Sec. D, p. 20.
     Summarizes reviews of <u>We Bombed in New Haven</u>.

21   ANON. Note on <u>We Bombed in New Haven</u>, <u>Variety</u>, October 30.   **
     Reports students and others of the audience have directly participated in <u>We Bombed in New Haven</u>, often shouting support for its antiwar theme or questioning actors.

22   ANON. "<u>We Bombed</u> Quits December 29 After Its 86th Performance," New York <u>Times</u>, December 3, p. 55.
     Announces close of Broadway run.

23   ARNON, JUDY BAILY. "Drama Mailbag--Aboard for 'New Haven,'" New York <u>Times</u>, November 10, Sec. D, p. 8.
     A letter about how deeply moved the writer was by <u>We Bombed in New Haven</u>.

24   BARNES, CLIVE. "Heller's 'We Bombed in New Haven' Opens," New York <u>Times</u>, October 17, p. 51.
     Confesses to confusion about the play and finally calls it "a bad play any good playwright should be proud to have written and any audience fascinated to see." Praises the moral concern and the ambitiousness (trying to "extend the

1968

theatrical experience of most Broadway playgoers"), the dialogue, and the atmosphere; but finds the fantasy unbelievable and the dramatic technique clumsy.

25 BIER, JESSE. The Rise and Fall of American Humor. New York: Holt, Rinehart, and Winston. Pp. xi, 308, 346-347, 354, 417.
   Objects to Heller's combination of realism and sense with his Marx Brothers' zaniness; feels this contributes to the "too muchness" of Catch-22.

26 BOLTON, WHITNEY. "Heller's 'We Bombed'...Inept," New York Morning Telegraph, October 18, p. 3.
   Reacts positively to the contention and some of the humor in the play but feels it "comes close to being no play at all."

27 _____. "Controversy Boils Over 2 New Plays," New York Morning Telegraph, October 28, p. 3.
   Speaks against people who think a play is great just because it is anti-war; has many objections to We Bombed in New Haven, including its seeming "to talk down to its audience."

28 BRAUDY, SUSAN. "Laughing All the Way to the Truth," New York, I (October 14), 42-45.
   An interview-article which discusses Heller's life and feelings about his work. Observes that "Heller uses humor to lure his audience into unexpected confrontations with a tragic truth. But in real life Heller uses his humor to keep people from looking too closely at him."

29 BROBERG, AV JAN. "Skrivmaskinens Pricks Kyttar," (Malmo, Sweden), Kvällsposten, November 5. (**)
   An announcement of the publication of the book version of We Bombed in New Haven.

30 BROWN, ADGER. "Man at War," (Columbia, South Carolina) The State and Columbia Record, August 25, p. 6B.
   Reports the publication in the coming week of the book version of We Bombed in New Haven, in which Heller "extends his vision of men in war, with a sympathetic but honest eye for the reality of military death."

1968

31 BUNCE, ALAN N. "Broadway: protests and musicals," <u>Christian Science Monitor</u>, October 26, p. 10.
    Claims "'We Bombed in New Haven' overworks its ideas and stretches some of its points outrageously. But much of it succeeds...."

32 BYRD, SCOTT. "A Separate War: Camp and Black Humor in Recent American Fiction," <u>Language Quarterly</u>, VII (Fall-Winter), 7-10.
    Comments briefly on <u>Catch-22</u> as an example of the work of modern writers who write fantasies with "an exuberance that may substitute...for despair" because "ideological dead horses" have not been destroyed by calm logic or invective.

33 CHANAN, GABRIEL. "The Plight of the Novelist," <u>Cambridge Review</u>, LXXXIX (April 26), 399-401.
    Praises Heller for helping us "to revise the pervasive metaphors of progress and time" enabling us to conceive "that other, vast aspect of our individual lives which has its existence laterally in a web of interrelations not dependent on time or consequence."

34 CHAPMAN, JOHN. "Heller's 'Bombed in New Haven' Is an Elusive Fantasy About War," New York <u>Daily News</u>, October 17, p. 81.
    Describes the main action of the play, concluding that "except for a few spots, the humor of <u>Catch-22</u> is lacking, and so is its bitter cynicism."

35 CLURMAN, HAROLD. "Theatre," <u>The Nation</u>, CCVI (January 1), 26-27.
    Classifies the play as "young generation Americana, flippantly derisive and at times quite funny," yet not really subversive, painful satire in that it awakens nothing in us "beyond a mild assent which is little more than complacency at our own inept liberalism."

36 COFFEY, JERRY. "Heller Bombs Own Troupes in Stage Bid," Fort Worth <u>Star Telegram</u>, September 8. (**)
    Predicts that readers expecting another <u>Catch-22</u> will be disappointed in "this heavy-handed antiwar tract" even though it is "a clever and audacious contrivance with brilliant bits of dark comedy and bitter satire and a powerful climax."

1968

37   COHEN, NATHAN. "This Would Bomb in New Haven if It Ever Got There," Toronto Daily Star, October 17, p. 26.
     Characterizes We Bombed in New Haven as "a very wet, wornout fuse."

38   COLBY, ETHEL. "Entertainment on Broadway--Robards and Sands Star in Hit at Ambassador," Journal of Commerce, October 18, p. 5.
     A very enthusiastic review which extols Heller's "dramatic skills and comic wrappings" as "this deadly serious play comes across with its pummeling message intact.

39   COOKE, RICHARD P. "Heller on War," Wall Street Journal, October 18, p. 16.
     Finds the play "noisy and preachy and not very convincing," and feels compelled to warn Heller that "nations which become defenseless don't usually live long enough to enjoy the pleasures of revolt against authority."

40   DIESEL, LEOTA. "The Theatre," Villager, October 24. (**)
     Feels that the effect of the play "stays with you long after the ending: It is absolutely scathing in its scorn of the stupidities of soldering [sic] and war, and it says so with a bitter, black humor."

41   DRIVER, TOM. "Curtains in Connecticut," Saturday Review, LI (August 31), 22-24.
     A review-article on We Bombed in New Haven where Driver explains why he feels the play has no "theatrical substance" equivalent to the "verbal substance" of Catch-22 and urges Heller to "go on talking."

42   DUNCAN, CHARLES. "Absurdity of War Probed in a Play," Atlanta Journal and Constitution, September 8, Sec. D, p. 4.
     Analyzes in more depth than most reviews the way the play "explores ever-present tensions between role-playing and essential identity which become excruciating in the experiences of war."

43   EARNEY, ALAN. "Catch-22," New York Times Book Review, April 28, p. 49.
     Man responsible for publication of Catch-22 in Britain protests that Greenfeld (1968.B52) didn't say the novel began to sell strongly in the United States "after its publication and enthusiastic reception in England."

Writings about Joseph Heller, 1961-1977

1968

*44   EVANS, DAVID LOUIS. "Archetypes in the Recent American War Novel." Ph.D. dissertation, University of Utah. Cited and Abstracted in <u>Dissertation Abstracts</u>, XXIX (October), 1226.

45   FELDMAN, BURTON. "Anatomy of Black Humor," <u>Dissent</u>, XV (March-April), 158-160.
        Simply lists Heller as one of a group of black humorists. Reprinted: 1969.B8.

46   FINDSEN, OWEN. "'Catch-22' on Stage," Cincinnati <u>Enquirer</u>, September 19, p. 38.
        A mixed notice, interesting in that it predicts accurately that curtain calls will have to be omitted if the audience is to be left "on the hook."

47   FINOCCHIARO, RAY. "Anti-war Play," Wilmington (Delaware) <u>Morning News</u>, September 23. (**)
        Regrets having to condemn the play for its wild ideas and jokes from <u>Catch-22</u> "weakly reincarnated amid torrents of symbolism...not enough to save this dull play."

48   FRENCH, MICHAEL R. "The American Novel in the Sixties," <u>Midwest Quarterly</u>, IX (Summer), 365-379.
        Places <u>Catch-22</u> in the modern trend toward surrealism based on psychological realism, where the general setting is a reflection of the absurdity or "disarray" in the minds of the characters.

49   FRIEDMAN, RALPH. Review of Book <u>We Bombed in New Haven</u>, <u>Oregon Features Journal</u>, October 19, p. 6.
        Sees <u>We Bombed in New Haven</u> as "'Catch-22' brought up to date, in play form, and in a more urgent setting."

50   FUNKE, LEWIS. "News of the Rialto--Robards Joins Up," New York <u>Times</u>, March 31, Sec. 2, pp. 1, 22.
        Reports Jason Robards will star in <u>We Bombed in New Haven</u> on Broadway and briefly describes the play.

51   GOTTFIRED, MARTIN. "Theatre--We Bombed in New Haven," <u>Women's Wear Daily</u>, October 17, p. 28.
        Objects to the production on Broadway of this "disaster" "a paperback <u>Catch-22</u>...[which] unlike the novel,...does not make its points in bitter humor but instead turns to preaching and sentiment."

1968

52 GREENFELD, JOSH. "22 Was Funnier than 14," <u>New York Times Book Review</u>, March 3, pp. 1, 49-51, 53.
 Briefly reviews the history of the writing, publication, and success of <u>Catch-22</u>, then goes on to consider whether it is a universal or "great" book, observing its relevance to the Vietnam War and its "robustly fresh...antic humor," but contending that Yossarian's failure to rebel forcefully and his personal, non-ideological opposition to the war "make his an example of the mentality of the 50's, not the '60's." Furthermore, showing war as a learning experience or game tends to glamorize it ("a hang-over from World War II"). Reprinted: 1973.A1.

53 HARRIS, LEONARD. Review of <u>We Bombed in New Haven</u> on Broadway, WCBS-TV2, October 16. Printed in <u>New York Theatre Critics' Review</u>, XXIX (October 21), 209.
 Says the play, though "disorderly and verbose," is "too passionate a play to be missed."

54 HATCH, ROBERT. "Theatre," <u>The Nation</u>, CCVII (November 4), 477-478.
 Praises Heller for involving the audience through the ambiguity between actors and citizens, audience and public, but sees the ending as less successful, "[falling] back on exhortation."

55 HERRIDGE, FRANCIS. "That Depressed Feeling Overtakes Jason Robards," New York <u>Post</u>, November 11, p. 26.
 Among Robards' remarks: <u>We Bombed in New Haven</u> "has something important to say about such foolishness as Vietnam."

56 HEWES, HENRY. "The Theater--A Game for our Sons," <u>Saturday Review</u>, LI (November 2), 53.
 Wishes Heller had brought "more of the special quality of his writing to the dialogue, and created a less abstract story," but still feels the play has "something to say and a few fresh insights to offer."

57 HILL, HAMLIN. "Black Humor: Its Cause and Cure," <u>Colorado Quarterly</u>, XVII (Summer), 57-64.
 An article which attempts to define "Black Humor," using <u>Catch-22</u>'s "bandaged patient" for an example.

*58 HILTON, LOYD. "The Time Haunted World of <u>Catch-22</u>," <u>Laurel Review</u>, VIII (Fall), 2743.
 Cited in <u>Annual Bibliography of English Language and Literature</u>, XLIII, 544.

1968

59 HIPP, EDWARD SOUTHERN. "New York Stage--Heller War Satire," Newark Evening News, October 17, p. 74.
Feels the play reads better than it acts and that Heller could have moved people against war more effectively if he had tried "touching hearts" from the beginning instead of "reaching for the funny bone."

60 _____. "War Dissent As a Satire," Newark Sunday News, October 27, Sec. 6, pp. E1, E3.
Alludes to a number of others writers who, like Heller, have written anti-war plays out of their own war experiences; then criticizes the form of We Bombed in New Haven and the "trowled on" satire.

61 HOBE. "Shows on Broadway," Variety, October 23, pp. 57-58.
Judges the first act "largely irrelevant and much too long" but the final scene "a stinging expression of a passionate attitude about one of the most vital issues in the world."

62 HOGAN, WILLIAM. "Joseph Heller's 'Catch-22' Cont'd.," San Francisco Chronicle, August 19, p. 41.
Rates the play as "Grade-A Heller...very good stuff."

63 HUNT, JOHN W. "Comic Escape and Anti-Vision: The Novels of Joseph Heller and Thomas Pynchon." In Nathan A. Scott, Jr., ed. Adversity and Grace: Studies in Recent American Literature. Chicago: University of Chicago Press. Pp. 87-112.
Argues that, while Heller has no quarrel with Camus' view of life's absurdity, he takes for granted its metaphysical nature, and goes on to explore "the disparity between human intention and reality within the social structure, the actual inversion of professed values, the defeat of meaning by the strategies used to protect it.... Heller shows that our experience of discontinuity, though radical, arises from the unnecessary abandonment of reason in the human enterprise." Through the comic mode he makes life meaningful again in spite of pain and death.
Article continues, describing how "Catch-22 defeats rational connections" and supporting Yossarian's desertion in the end as the choice of reason, sanity, and responsibility. Thus, Hunt shows how Heller takes the "surprise out of absurdity," and with absurdity established as a premise rather than a conclusion, he can "probe its moral implications in the belief that there must be some meaningful way whereby our fractured lives may be made whole." Reprinted: 1973.A1; 1974.A2.

1968

64 JEFFERYS, ALLAN. Review of We Bombed in New Haven on Broadway, WABC-TV7, October 16.
    Printed in New York Theatre Critics' Review, XXIX (October 21), 208.
    Summariezes the plot, notes the "same episodic, satirical anti-war approach as...Catch-22," then assesses the play as being "part profound, part sophomoric, but always emotionally charged."

*65 KENNARD, JEAN E. "Towards a Novel of the Absurd: A Study of the Relationship between the Concept of the Absurd as Defined in the Works of Sartre and Camus and Ideas and Form in the Fiction of John Barth, Samuel Beckett, Nigel Dennis, Joseph Heller, and James Purdy." Ph.D. dissertation, University of California at Berkeley. Cited and abstracted in Dissertation Abstracts, XXIX (March, 1969), 3144.

66 KERR, WALTER. "Walter Kerr vs. Joseph Heller," New York Times, October 27, Sec. II, pp. 1, 5.
    Argues that the play "doesn't work," that it doesn't make the audience feel guilty as Jack Richardson's "The Prodigal" did when an actor indicated that the audience was responsible for deaths. The reason this doesn't work is that Heller has never developed characters as believable human beings in a coherent, emotional story to make the audience care about them. He wants "not to dramatize war...but to talk about it, shout about it...."

67 KOSTELANETZ, RICHARD. "Dada and the Future of Fiction," Works, I (Spring), 58-66.
    Heller mentioned as one of a group of American writers who "have realized in extravagant prose fiction certain Dadaist inventions and biases, such as totally exterior representation, the absence of narrative resolution, unmitigated blasphermous comedy, the decomposition of traditional forms, and the rendering of worldly absurdity."

68 KROLL, JACK. "All My Sons," Newsweek, LXXII (October 28), 135.
    States We Bombed in New Haven plays "with the conventions of theater and the deeper conventions of human role-playing, to evoke in the audience a profound, decisive horror at the irrational destructive absurdity of war in the modern world." It reveals "the reductio ad absurdum of the logic of war itself."

1968

69 LEVINE, PAUL. "The Politics of Alienation," <u>Mosaic</u>, II (Fall), 3-17.
    Concentrates on <u>Catcher in the Rye</u>, <u>Catch-22</u>, and <u>Naked Lunch</u> as reflections of the change from alienation to rebellion among youth in recent years. Explores the way <u>Catch-22</u> "turns the problem of 'craziness' raised in <u>The [sic] Catcher in the Rye</u> upside down: the hero's sanity is now questioned by his society but not by his creator." Also discusses the way <u>Catch-22</u> "begins as a comedy about survival—at any cost—and ends as a melodrama about responsibility."

70 LEWIS, R. W. B. <u>The Picaresque Saint</u>. New York: J. B. Lippincott. P. 32.
    Calls Yossarian a "picaresque saint...[sharing] not only in the miseries of humanity, but in its gravest weaknesses, too, and even in its sins."

71 LEWIS, THEOPHILUS. Review of <u>We Bombed in New Haven</u>, <u>America</u>, CXIX (November 9), 447.
    Finds little to be admired in <u>We Bombed in New Haven</u>, "apparently by a member of the New Left who believes that everybody who isn't burning draft cards has to be an advocate of more and bloodier wars."

*72 LOUKIDES, PAUL. "Some Notes on the Novel of the Absurd," <u>The CEA Critic</u>, XXX, 8, 13.
    Cited by Weixlmann (1974.B213).

73 LYON, BRET and FRATKIN, RAYMOND. "Joseph Heller's <u>We Bombed in New Haven</u>: A Collection of Thoughts," <u>Yale Theater</u>, I (Spring), 106-111.
    Fratkin praises the play for alerting the audience "to the deadly interconnection between life and art." Lyon complains that the Yale production did not do justice to the "brilliant and original script" because the director missed the basic unifying metaphor of the actors becoming trapped in their roles. He also comments on Heller's involvement of the audience in responsibility for murder.

74 LYONS, LEONARD. Note on <u>We Bombed in New Haven</u>, <u>New York Post</u>, September 6, p. 47.
    Reports Heller wrote the lyrics for the theme song of <u>We Bombed in New Haven</u>, but they are unprintable.

75 MacDONALD, JAMES L. "I See Everything Twice!: The Structure of Joseph Heller's <u>Catch-22</u>," <u>University Review</u>, XXXIV (Spring), 175-180.

1968

A reaction to the popularity of Catch-22 among college students: suspects they admire it "for the wrong reasons." Proceeds to examine and admire the formal values of the book, particularly Heller's use of "Deja vu as the basis of methods by which he achieves structural unity" and his "narrative interplay between past and present, contriving elaborate parallel repetitions of and variations on his theme." Reprinted: 1973.A1.

76 McNAMARA, EUGENE. "The Absurd Style in Contemporary American Literature," The Humanities Association Bulletin, XIX, 44-49.
    Discusses Catch-22 and two novels by Thomas Pynchon as examples of the absurd movement.

77 MELLARD, JAMES M. "Catch-22: Deja vu and the Labyrinth of Memory," Bucknell Review, XVI (March), 29-44.
    An exposition of the technique of deja vu (repeated images) and its relation to the content of the novel, to Yossarian's mythical journey to "the underworld, the labyrinth, the heart of darkness" in the process of being reborn out of American culture to a sense of responsibility and life. Reprinted: 1973.A1-A2.

78 MITGANG, HERBERT. Review of Book We Bombed in New Haven, New York Times, August 30, p. 31.
    Considers We Bombed in New Haven more universal than Catch-22; and, though noting the difficulty of reviewing a play as a book, differs from many of the play reviewers in praising Ruth, the Red Cross worker, as one of the few characters who "come over naturally instead of [as] a polemicist of black antiwar humor."

79 MURRAY, JOHN J. "Opus No. 2, Catch-23," Best Sellers, XXVIII (September 1), 219.
    Contends that, given the abusrdity of the Vietnam War, Heller's writing is "not absurd enough."

80 MUSSON, KEN. "War Is Heller," Florida Accent, December 22, p. 30.
    Praises Heller for writing a tragicomedy with "the audience, the theatre, even the city [in]...his script."

81 NEWMAN, PAUL. "Self-Interest," New York Times, January 7, Sec. II, p. 6.
    Letter objecting to reviewers covering New Haven production of We Bombed in New Haven because the novice playwright deserved a chance to "see his play mounted before beginning his revisions."

1968

82   NUMASAWA, KOJI. "Black Humor: An American Aspect," Studies in English Literature, XLIV (March), 177-193.
     Counts Heller as one of the "American authors' names" which "recur whenever the subject [of black humor] is mentioned." Quotes Yossarian's speech on God in Chapter 18 to make the point that these writers make God the subject of ridicule for "creating the sorry state of the world." Also comments on the reasons Catch-22 is "perhaps the most ambitious and successful fugitive fiction of the kind so far brought out by black humorists," mainly the paradox of "Catch-22" which demands that men be "simultaneously both mad and sane" and turns everything into "one enormous force mocking the bureaucratic futility of human attempts." Interprets the ending as showing the best one can achieve in this world is "a certain comic dignity."

83   OGLESBY, CARL. "The Deserters: The Contemporary Defeat of Fiction," Motive, XXVIII (February), 14-21.
     Objects to Catch-22 because, this revolutionist-writer feels, it pictures a class war between officers and soldier-victims, symbolic of American society, but makes Yossarian's rebellion "privatistic" rather than a general and actual rebellion against Cathcart that real American-victims could be incited by.

84   OLIVER, EDITH. "The Pursuit of the Real," New Yorker, XLIV (October 26), 139.
     Complains that We Bombed in New Haven is "a better tract than it is a play," that the form is "so intricate and self-conscious that it nearly always engages our attention without engaging our minds and hearts."

85   PRIDEAUX, TOM. "Joe Heller's Peekaboo with Reality," Life, LXIV (January 12), 12.
     Names We Bombed in New Haven "the best war play of our own particular day." Feels it captures "the essence of a new American ambivalence toward war" and enhances the viewer's emotional stake by the meshing of play and reality (the play-within-a-play device).

86   PROBST, LEONARD. Review of We Bombed in New Haven on Broadway, NBC-TV4, October 16. Printed in New York Theatre Critics Review, XXIX (October 21), 209.
     Observes that some of the writing is "flowery"; but, overall, calls it "a strong and often exciting anti-war play. Bitter but funny."

1968

87 QUINN, EDWARD and PAUL J. DOLAN, eds. The Sense of the Sixties. New York: The Free Press. Pp. 435-439.
    Reprint of 1965.B12.

88 RAIDY, WILLIAM A. "Broadway On 'N' Off--Meet Joseph Heller: Man Against War," Long Island Press, October 6, p. 34.
    Interview-article mainly on Heller's play and his ideas about politics and teaching.

89 RAYMOND, ROBERT. "'New Haven' Hits Target in Portraying Militarism," Staten Island (New York) Advance, September 22, p. E6.
    Judges that in the play "war is reduced to its proper setting via comedy, satire, and tragedy. Any audience, any reader leaving this play without having suffered shock and having been moved to argument or tearful emotion, or perhaps both, must be very dull indeed."

90 ROTHBARDT, HELEN. "First Play Discussed by Author," Philadelphia Inquirer, September 11, p. 51.
    Interview-article where Heller comments on his life and writings, quipping, "I really shouldn't be against war; it's been good to me."

91 SCHULZ, MAX F. "Pop, Op, and Black Humor: The Aesthetics of Anxiety," College English, XXX (December), 230-241.
    Uses Colonel Cathcart as an example of the anxiety-ridden, self-defeating social conformist in a society with rules based on "worship of the average...which renders extremes of personality nonexistent." Also comments on Heller's fixing of time in "endless circularity," indicative of the temporality of literary form, a factor in the anxiety of the age.

92 SHAPIRO, STEPHEN. "The Ambivalent Animal: Man in the Contemporary British and American Novel," Centennial Review, XII (Winter), 1-22.
    Cites Yossarian's telling his psychoanalyst that he has an ambivalent attitude toward the fish symbol as an instance of the prevalence of ambivalent attitudes and explicit recognition of them in modern fiction. Asserts, however, that Heller fails to deal with "the terrible nature of the conflict...he does not consider the enemy as an enemy; the army itself is Yossarian's enemy." Also argues that "if an individual has the right to assert the value of his own survival against any other values...then he must earn his freedom by confronting the values that challenge it."

1968

93 SHAPIRO, WALTER. "Is Heller Playing Heller Playing Heller?" Michigan Daily, October 20, p. 5.
    Classifies We Bombed in New Haven as "a fascinating play if only for the grandeur of its ambitions," that is, its attempt to involve the audience and make them see the consequences of their apathy. Feels this attempt fails, however, because those who suffer or die are only "cardboard mock-ups masquerading as characters."

94 SHENKER, ISRAEL. "Joseph Heller Draws Dead Bead on the Politics of Gloom," New York Times, September 10, p. 49.
    Interview-article with Heller who had just watched the first Broadway run-through of We Bombed in New Haven and found it "magnificent." Rambles on with Heller's views on Vietnam, recent political campaigns, and his use of humor "to emphasize conclusions--a technique rather than an objective."

95 _____. "Did Heller Bomb on Broadway?" New York Times, December 29, Sec. II, p. 1.
    Another interview with Heller discussing the closing of his play, his political views, and, most interestingly, his distress that We Bombed in New Haven was considered an anti-war play ("I'm not that interested in the subject of war.... I was interested in personal relationships to bureaucratic authority.").

*96 SHERMAN, WILLIAM D. "The Contemporary American Novel: Beyond Comic Anarchy." Ph.D. dissertation, State University of New York at Buffalo. Cited and abstracted in Dissertation Abstracts, XXIX (August), 614.

97 SIMON, JOHN. "Dropout," New York, I, (November 4), 50.
    Assesses We Bombed in New Haven as "zesty army humor... classifiable as the intelligent writer's pratfall; it partakes of many schools, but flunks out."

98 STEELE, MIKE. "The Actors Get No Encores When Script Calls for War," Minneapolis Tribune, September 29, p. 8.
    Describes plot and structure of play briefly; adds that "Heller proves once again that he is a moral comedian, a grim humorist who can thrust a satirical blade into our psyches.... Drama is the perfect outlet for him."

99 STERN, J. P. "War and the Comic Muse: The Good Soldier Schweik and Catch-22," Comparative Literature, XX (Summer), 193-216.
    Explores the many similarities and the significant differences between these two works.

1968

100 SUTTON, HENRY. "Notes toward the Destitution of Culture," Kenyon Review, XXX (Issue 1), 108-115.
Counts Catch-22 one of a group of novels including Herzog and Giles Goat-Boy which "were paranoid simplifications of the world, and all pretended to give some suggestion about the way in which reality functions."

101 THORPE, DAY. "A Play Within a Play," Washington Star, October 13, Sec. D, p. 2.
Gives a quick sketch of the play's action, characters, and structure; then comments that while there are "sharp lines" and the subject is topical, the structure is weak, and the play is essentially static.

*102 VALANCIA, WILLA FERREE. "The Picaresque Tradition in the Contemporary English and American Novel." Ph.D. dissertation, University of Illinois. Cited and abstracted in Dissertation Abstracts, XXIX (August), 618.

103 WADE, GERALD. "Heller Play Protests War Brings It Close," Beaumont (Texas) Journal, October 4, p. 21.
Explains how the play would be performed in Beaumont, Texas. Ends with "You might come away from this play... believing you are the enemy. Well?"

*104 WALDRON, RANDALL H. "Armour's Iron Brace: The Machine in Major American Novels of World War II." Ph.D. dissertation, University of Kentucky. Cited and abstracted in Dissertation Abstracts, XXX (October, 1969), 1578-1579.

105 WATTS, RICHARD, JR. "Random Notes on This and That," New York Post, October 22, p. 68.
Calls Heller's play "completely original despite its debt to Pirandello."

106 _____. Article on We Bombed in New Haven, New York Post, November 2, p. 22.
A re-review.

107 WAY, BRIAN. "Formal Experiment and Social Discontent: Joseph Heller's Catch-22," Journal of American Studies, II (October), 253-270.
Brings out the nature of the pattern of social-protest in Catch-22, which Way sees as the beginning of a new kind of social criticism: opposed not to the wealth as earlier American social criticism had been, but to the industrial, military, and Administration bureaucracies. Heller has turned to the literature of the absurd because "its vision

1969

and logic are more in harmony with what he sees around him than naturalism would be." With "Catch-22," for example, he shows the "infinite capacity of the absurd to mask itself in reason, and to institutionalize itself in bureaucracy." The novel progresses, though not through a conventional time-sequence and plot-line, toward a deepening sense of the nature of the absurd and human commitment.

108   WEALES, GERALD. "Have Your Read Any Good Novels Lately?" The Reporter, XXXVIII (January 25), 43-44.
   An uncomplimentary review of We Bombed in New Haven which points out the "obviousness" of the material and states, "Unless one comes to the theater convinced that Heller is always funny and anti-war sentiments are inevitably moving, it is difficult to agree with him."

109   WILLERS, A. C. Review of Book We Bombed in New Haven, Library Journal, XCIII (August), 2894.
   Briefly summarizes the play, "a dramatic tragedy."

110   WINCHELL, WALTER. "'Bombed in New Haven' Bombed Here," New York Daily Column, October 17, p. 7.
   Calls the play "the latest anti-tainment...another war message from Joseph Heller...a sermon."

111   WOLFF, GEOFFREY. "Heller Stages a War," Washington Post, October 17, Sec. A, p. 23.
   Explains how the play reveals that Heller "continues to understand us better than we should want him to understand us" and how it "radically change[s] our understanding of war."

112   ZOLOTOW, SAM. "We Bombed in New Haven Bans Curtain Calls to Sustain Mood," New York Times, November 26, p. 39.
   Reports Heller's confirmation of this decision after participating in a symposium with high school students, a consensus of whom said the curtain call "broke the spell created by the play."

1969 A BOOKS

1   LUTTRELL, WILLIAM. "Tragic and Comic Modes in Twentieth Century American Literature: William Styron and Joseph Heller." Ph.D. dissertation, Bowling Green State University. Cited and abstracted in Dissertation Abstracts, XXX (December), 2537.

1969

1969 B SHORTER WRITINGS

1   ALTER, ROBERT. After the Tradition: Essays on Modern Jewish Writing. New York: E. P. Dutton. Pp. 48, 52.
    Mentions Catch-22 as one of a group of modern novels in a tradition of the "savagely comical...picaresque version of the apocalypse."

2   ANON. Excerpts of Catch-22 Reviews, A Library of Literary Criticism: Modern American Literature, 4th Enlarged Edition. New York: Frederick Ungar. Pp. 59-61, 463.
    Contains excerpts from reviews and articles by Algren (1961.B3), Hicks (1961.B41), Brustein (1961.B28), Seiden (1961.B61), Mitchell (1962.B44), and Muste (1962.B46).

3   ANON. "Lumet Dickering for 'Bombed' Film Rights," Variety, February 19, p. 69.
    Reports Lumet and Heller on the verge of a film deal to off-set the Broadway production's loss of over $100,000.

4   B. L. "Not Too Hot," Peoria, Illinois Journal-Star, December 28. (**)
    Says Heller has tried again to produce "a funny and yet powerful book about war," but "its theatrical play form weakens it," even though there are some "clever and comic passages in it."

5   CHARYN, JEROME. "Introduction," In his The Single Voice. New York: Collier Books. Pp. ix-xi.
    Says "concern with terror" is the force behind Heller and other black humorists.

6   DAVIS, ROBERT M. "The Shrinking Garden and New Exits: The Comic-Satiric Novel in the Twentieth Century," Kansas Quarterly, I (Summer), 5-16.
    Article on trends in modern comic-satire points out that readers empathize more with characters such as Yossarian in recent works, than with those in previous works of the comic-satire mode. Also, Catch-22 exemplifies a major device of this mode, frustration of conventional expectation, but in a new direction. Instead of turning the serious into farce, it turns the farcical into the grotesque and painful.

7   DeMOTT, BENJAMIN. "Dirty Words?" In Marcus Klein, ed. The American Novel Since World War II. Greenwich, Connecticut: Fawcett. Pp. 210-223.
    Reprint of 1965.B8. See also 1969.B17.

1969

8   FELDMAN, BURTON. "Anatomy of Black Humor." In Marcus Klein, ed. The American Novel Since World War II. Greenwich, Connecticut: Fawcett. P. 224.
    Reprint of 1968.B45. See also 1969.B17.

9   FISCHER, RUTH. "Books--Plays in Print," Cleveland Plain Dealer, July 6, Sec. H, p. 4.
    Describes We Bombed in New Haven as "a satire on war stories...a polemic against the Vietnam war," with a play-within-a-play structure. Judges it not as good as Catch-22 but "well worth reading."

10 FROHOCK, W. M. "Polemics--The Failing Center: Recent Fiction and the Picaresque Tradition," Novel, III (Fall), 62-69.
    Alludes to Robert Scholes' study of Catch-22 and other novels (1967.B29) as examples of recent picaresque fiction.

11 GIANAKARIS, C. J. "Tracking the Rebel in Literature," Topic, IX (Fall), 11-29.
    Surveys literature from Aeschylus to find "rebel-protagonists."

12 GOLD, DALE. "Portrait of a Man Reading," Washington Post Book World, July 20, p. 2.
    An interview in which Heller discusses the kind of reading he enjoys and admires and the literary influences on his writing.

13 GUERNSEY, OTIS L., JR. The Best Plays of 1968-1969. New York: Dodd, Mead. Pp. 8, 19-20, 155, 385.
    We Bombed in New Haven listed as a play between nominal drama and nominal comedy, "one of those plays in the newly-developing form.... [It] casts the audience in a major role...the spectators are the fall guys...the jokes...are not on the characters but on you." Says play consists of "one-joke irony," but is "one of the season's noteworthy events simply because of its contemporary style and highly relevant subject matter."

14 HARTE, BARBARA and CAROLYN RILEY, eds. 200 Contemporary Authors, V-VIII. Detroit; Michigan: Gale Research. Pp. 533-534.
    Provides biographical information on Heller and comments by a number of critics on his writing.

1969

15 HOOD, STUART. "Abstract Art," <u>Spectator</u>, CCXXIII (July 12), 46.
    Notes that <u>We Bombed in New Haven</u> is "a protest against the impersonality of war" and that Heller strives for "an effect of Brechtian alienation," but condemns the play as "a not very new thought presented in terms which are emotional to the point of sheer sentimentality."

16 JANEWAY, ELIZABETH, ed. "Fiction: The Personal Dimension." In <u>The Writer's World</u>. New York: McGraw-Hill. Pp. 137-174.
    Transcript of a discussion at the New School in New York under the sponsorship of the Authors Guild. Heller discussed his attitudes on the writing of novels, twitted Dwight MacDonald, and argued that a novel is never great just because of its social message.

17 KLEIN, MARCUS, ed. <u>The American Novel Since World War II</u>. Greenwich, Connecticut: Fawcett. P. 14.
    In making the point that war is "no longer the direct invitation to disillusion that it used to be," mentions the "distraught whimsey" of <u>Catch-22</u>. See also 1969.B7-B8.

18 KLEIN, YVONNE M. "The Politics of the American Military Novel." Ph.D. dissertation, University of Minnesota. Cited and abstracted in <u>Dissertation Abstracts</u>, XXXI (November, 1970), 2388.

19 KOSTELANETZ, RICHARD. "American Fiction of the Sixties." In <u>On Contemporary Literature</u>, Expanded edition. New York: Avon (Discus Books). Pp. 634-652.
    Places Heller in the group of modern writers whose work resembles theatre of the absurd, who "create a series of absurd events--that is, nonsensical, ridiculous events--to suggest the ultimate absurdity of human history and existence. Illustrates the point briefly with examples of Major Major Major Major, Colonel Cathcart, and Yossarian.

20 MUSTE, JOHN M., PAUL ZALL, ARTHUR EPHRON, ROBERT A. KANTRA, JOHN J. McLAUGHLIN, JEAN B. KERN, and EARL ROVIT. "Modern Satire: A Mini-Symposium," <u>Satire Newsletter</u>, VI (Spring), 1-18.
    Muste discusses Heller's use of the satiric technique of playing on "audience response through shock or reversal" to make us see that "our scorn has been directed at a human being who is not very much more ludicrous than ourselves," mentioning examples from <u>Catch-22</u> and <u>We Bombed in New Haven</u>.

21 OLDERMAN, RAYMOND. "Beyond the Wasteland: A Study of the American Novel in the Nineteen Sixties." Ph.D dissertation, Indiana University. Cited and abstracted in *Dissertation Abstracts*, XXX (May, 1970), 4998.

22 RICHARDSON, KENNETH. *Twentieth Century Writing: A Reader's Guide to Contemporary Literature*. London and New York: Newnes Books. Pp. 283-284.
    Lists Heller as an American novelist who "lept to fame" with *Catch-22* at a time when war fiction was still predominantly serious. Provides a brief description of the novel with its "lethal blend of farce and fantasy, sick humor, and icy casualness."

23 RYAN, MARJORIE. "Four Contemporary Satires and the Problems of Norms," *Satire Newsletter*, VI (Spring), 40-46.
    Disputes Peter Thorpe's contention ("Great Satire and the Fragmented Norm," *Satire Newsletter*, IV [Spring, 1967], 89-95) that all satire of the past fifteen years is "barren, superficial, and destructive" because it lacks positive norms with which to identify. Argues that *Catch-22* promotes such norms as the individual's right to follow the dictates of his own conscience.

24 SCHULZ, MAX F. *Radical Sophistication*. Athens, Ohio: Ohio University Press. Pp. vii, 12.
    Heller named as one of a group of Jewish-American novelists who "acknowledge suffering to be the modus vivendi of twentieth-century existence, [but]...refuse to believe that it is a necessary cautery for society's ills."

25 SEGAL, CLANCY. "Enemy Within," London *Sunday Times*, July 13, p. 54.
    Reports "a chilling, accurate, only slightly funny play about the irresponsibility of routine, random death."

26 SOKOLOV, RAYMOND A. "There's a Catch--*Catch-22*," *Newsweek*, LXXIII (March 3), 52-55.
    An article about the making of the movie.

27 SOLOMON, ERIC. "From *Christ in Flanders* to *Catch-22*: An Approach to War Fiction," *Texas Studies in Literature and Language*, XI (Spring), 851-866.
    Shows the similarities of several earlier war novels to *Catch-22*, then argues that Heller's book, like these, is "seriously religious," although, in a more modern mode:

1969

"his antihero is an anti-Christ figure." An ambitious, but rather questionable argument, e.g. claims Orr's name here suggests, not an alternative, but "ore" or "rock," thus Peter. Reprinted: 1973.A1.

28 WALDMEIR, JOSEPH J. *American Novels of the Second World War*. The Hague: Mouton. Pp. 39, 160-165.
   Complains that the novel lacks the consistent point of view necessary for a successful portrayal of absurdity. Heller seems opposed to war until the ending when Yossarian agrees with Danby that it has been necessary to fight this war.

29 _____. "Only an Occasional Rutabaga: American Fiction Since 1945," *Modern Fiction Studies*, XV (Winter, 1969-70), 467-481.
   A very general study of the five directions American fiction has taken since 1945, in which Heller's "far-out wackiness" in *Catch-22* is listed as one extreme type (opposite *Giles Goat-Boy*) of absurd-black humor.

30 WEALES, GERALD. *The Jumping-Off Place*. New York: Macmillan. Pp. 206-208.
   Criticizes *We Bombed in New Haven* for being "more impressive in conception than in fact"--using two levels of reality is interesting experiment, but it doesn't really work on stage.

31 WILLIS, JOHN, ed. *Theatre World*, 1968-69 Season. New York: Crown Publishers. P. 22.
   Lists cast and credits, opening and closing dates for *We Bombed in New Haven*.

32 WYLDER, DELBERT E. "Thomas Berger's *Little Big Man* as Literature," *Western American Literature*, III (Winter), 273-284.
   Compares Berger's fiction to Barth and Heller's.

1970 A BOOKS - NONE

1970 B SHORTER WRITINGS

1 ADAMS, LEE. "Movie Mailbag--The Pitch on 'Catch-22,'" New York *Times*, August 2, Sec. II, p. 10.
   Accuses Schjeldahl (1970.B47) of attacking a work of "monumental worth" to become known."

1970

2 ALPERT, HOLLIS. "The Catch," Saturday Review, LIII (June 27), 24.
   Says the novel Catch-22 "worked, held together by its style"; the movie doesn't work because the style hasn't been transferred to film.

3 ANON. "Joseph Heller." In Who's Who in America, Vol. 36. Chicago: Marquis. P. 1004.
   Same biographical details listed as in 1968 edition (1968.B2) except for the publication of We Bombed in New Haven and address now listed at Knopf.

4 ANON. Screen Listings. Who Wrote the Movie and What Else Did He Write? Los Angeles: Academy of Motion Picture Arts and Sciences and the Writers Guild of America, West. P. 77.
   Gives Heller a screen credit for writing Sex and the Single Girl.

5 ANON. "The Frantic Filming of a Crazy Classic," Life, LXVIII (June 12), 44-46, 48.
   Brief article and pictures of the filming of Catch-22. Includes Buck Henry's humorous account, "A Diary of Planes, Pilots, and Praftalls."

6 ANON. "Some are More Yossarian Than Others," Time, XCV (June 15), 66-68, 73-74.
   Primarily an article about the movie version of Catch-22, the way it was made, and Mike Nichols' career. Notes that Nichols focused on portraying the "cold rage" of the book and constructed the film verison "like a spiral staircase set with mirrors" until Yossarian "comes to a landing of understanding." Reprinted: 1973.A1.

7 BARNARD, KEN. "Interview with Joseph Heller," Detroit News Magazine, September 13, pp. 18-19, 24, 27-28, 30, 65.
   Relates a conversation with Heller where the talk turned to the naming of Catch-22, the atmosphere of the fifties that inspired the novel, the incident over Avignon that actually happened to Heller, his feeling about movies especially Catch-22, and his new novel. Reprinted: 1973.A1.

8 BARNES, HAZEL E. "Literature and the Politics of the Future," Denver Quarterly, V (Spring), 41-64.
   Names Heller as one example of "absurdist writers" who illustrate the search for a new kind of future based on values that "transcend" any we now know.

1970

9   BERGONZI, BERNARD. The Situation of the Novel. London: Mac-Millan. Pp. 82-86.
    Considers Catch-22 among other "absurdist" or "comic-apocalyptic" novels. Agrees with Podhoretz (1966.B20) that Catch-22 has a weakness in not directly saying what the book implies, that the war against Hitler was a fraud. Also agrees with Podhoretz that Heller is trying "to make credible the incredible reality of American life in the middle of the twentieth century."

10 BLEVINS, WINFRED. "Catch-22--No Cinematic Experience Equivalent to the Novel," Los Angeles Herald-Examiner, June 21, pp. F1, F7.
    Views movie as a failure because it presents man as completely degraded, not capable of preserving his humanity as Heller shows him to be in the novel. It also lacks the redeeming joyful inventiveness of Heller's language.

11 BRACKMAN, JACOB. "Review of Catch-22," Esquire, LXXIV (September), 8, 12, 14.
    Focuses almost entirely on Nichols' film-making in Catch-22 and the performances of various actors. Reprinted: 1973.A1.

12 BRYANT, JERRY H. The Open Decision--The Contemporary American Novel and Its Intellectual Background. New York: The Free Press. Pp. 149, 156-164.
    Finds in Catch-22 an excellent example of the main issue of the "open decision," i.e. an authentic choice with knowledge of all options open and what they involve as opposed to obeying a law like "Catch-22" which binds one to "only those possibilities which strengthen the society rather than the individual." Yossarian justifies his "open decision" to escape in the end; he has realized that there are more possibilities than those the system offers. The chaplain also makes an "open decision," to stay and fight the system.

13 CANBY, VINCENT. "Nicholas Captures Panic of Catch-22," New York Times, June 25, p. 54.
    Reviews the film version of Catch-22 as "the best American film I've seen this year," noting that Mike Nichols and Buck Henry "whose senses of humor coincide with Heller's fondness for manic repetition of words and phrases, have rearranged the novel without intruding on it."

1970

14   _____. "A Triumphant _Catch_," New York _Times_, June 28, Sec. II, p. 1.
      Makes similar comments to those in his earlier review (1970.B13), observing the movie may not "make complete sense, or...be fully appreciated, unless one has read or admired the book." Goes on to point out that Heller's book "is complex, but...on a horizontal plane...largely told in terms of dialogue...or exposition" and is amenable to filming and that in the movie "a flashback that keeps turning back on itself," is equivalent to Heller's "verbal humor that depends on double negatives of reasoning."

15   CAPONE, ROBERT. "Movie Mailbag--The Pitch on 'Catch-22,'" New York _Times_, August 2, Sec. II, p. 10.
      Contends that Schjeldahl (1970.B47) missed the central thesis of _Catch-22_ which gives it an "appeal for all decades," _i.e._ "man's battle against the absurd, and his struggle to maintain an identity within a massive bereaucracy."

16   CASTELLI, JIM. "_Catch-22_ and the New Hero," _Catholic World_, CCXI (August), 199-202.
      Builds on the Karl (1964.B10), Brustein (1961.B28), and Doskow (1967.B10) articles to analyze Heller's orderly questioning of "the very nature of sanity" and Yossarian's "new heroism" (refusing to obey an absurd system which acts contrary to his rationality, sense of humanity). Reprinted: 1973.A1.

17   CRIST, JUDITH. "All That Glitters Is Not Nichols," _New York_, III (June 29), 54.
      Movie review which recommends turning to the book to "appreciate its accomplishment and the difficult task that confronted its screen adapters." Notes that Heller's strengths "are literary--the long probing character study, the recording of the lunacies that are the stuff of everyday dialogue, the slow enlargement of quirk to aberration to madness to exploding insanity and always the terror of death."

18   CUSKILLY, RICHARD. "_Catch-22_--Brilliant, Contradictory," Los Angeles _Herald-Examiner_, June 21, pp. F1, F8.
      Although the film is brilliant, reviewer feels director Nichols' brilliance detracts from _Catch-22_. It catches the essence of the novel but does not "comment upon or expand the underlying life force of the novel."

1970

19 DANNENBURG, EDGAR. "Movie Mailbag--The Pitch on 'Catch-22,'" New York *Times*, August 2, Sec. II, p. 2.
    Feels Schjeldahl (1970.B47) never served in Army or large business organization, since he "believes that 'these days' one can change the world or make it hot for the forces of oppression." Sees Yossarian at the end as "a Chaplinesque figure who never made it to Sweden."

20 FLAGLER, J. M. "Mike Nichols Tries the Impossible--A Movie of *Catch-22*," *Look*, XXXIV (June 30), 55-59.
    Article about the producing and filming of "Heller's almost impossibly wild war novel." Most interesting is Nichols' comment that it is "about the specific personal fear of dying"; this perhaps explains the simplification of the novel that a number of reviewers saw in the movie.

21 GALLOWAY, DAVID D. *The Absurd Hero in American Fiction*. Austin: University of Texas Press. P. 36.
    Compares *Catch-22* to *Rabbit, Run* because of its emphasis "that man is victimized by life itself, and it remains for him to seek salvation alone."

22 GAUKROGER, DOUG. "Time Structure in *Catch-22*," *Critique*, XII (No. 2, 1970-71), 70-85.
    Presents a large body of evidence to show that Solomon's reading of the time sequence (1968.B75) was incorrect, then lays out the "proper" chronological order of events (suggests the few problem points are probably errors by Heller.) Reprinted: 1973.A1; 1974.A2.

23 GOW, GORDON. "Review of *Catch-22*," *Films and Filming*, XVII (November), 48-50.
    Provides summary of film's plot and expresses disappointment with the film: "A rambling novel has become a wayward film...the balance of satire is unsteady." Reprinted: 1973.A1.

24 GREENBERG, ALVIN. "Choice--Ironic Alternatives in the World of the Contemporary Novel." In David Madden, ed. *American Dreams, American Nightmares*. Carbondale: Southern Illinois University Press. Pp. 175-187.
    Explains how Orr in *Catch-22* embodies the alternative of withdrawal which "however ironic and ultimately impossible, serves at last--to impregnate the rapidly, disintegrating world of this novel with renewed meaning and fresh possibility."

1970

25 GROSS, BEVERLY. "Catch-22," The Nation, CCXI (July 20), 60-61.
    Film does not "achieve the accelerating absurdity upon which the novel depended." Speculates that the makers may have been "awestruck by the momentous responsibility of making a movie of the most acclaimed American novel of these times."

26 HALIO, JAY L. "The Way It Is--And Was," Southern Review, VI (Winter), 250-262.
    In reviewing thirteen new novels makes references to Heller's success in Catch-22 with picturing a real world which is so absurd as to seem fantastical and characters who can't blend into the "hypocrisy, violence, and ugliness" of their milieu and therefore feel threatened by it.

*27 HARRIS, CHARLES B. "Contemporary American Novelists of the Absurd." Ph.D. dissertation, Southern Illinois University. Cited and abstracted in Dissertation Abstracts, XXXI (February, 1971), 4162.

28 HICKS, GRANVILLE. Literary Horizons. New York: New York University Press. P. 225.
    Foreword to and reprint of his Saturday Review appraisal of Catch-22 in 1961 (See 1961.B41). Foreward observes that Catch-22 was extremely popular with college students in the late sixties, probably because, as Heller said at Notre Dame, Vietnam "is the war I was writing about all the time.'

29 HOLZSCHLAG, PHYLLIS. "Is Catch-22 Male Chauvinist?" Commonweal, XCIII (October 6), 69-70.
    Offers a number of examples to reveal that women in Catch-22 are pictured as sex objects with no intelligence.

*30 JONES, PETER G. "The Developing Voice: An Appraisal of the Modern War Novel." Ph.D. dissertation, New York University. Cited and abstracted in Dissertation Abstracts, XXXII (July, 1971), 437.

31 KALTER, MICHAEL J. "Movie Mailbag--The Pitch on 'Catch-22,'" New York Times, August 2, Sec. II, p. 2.
    Says Schjeldahl's criticism of Catch-22 (1970.B47) is "surely not a valid judgment"; moreover, "that the novel has proven such an accurate forecast of America in the '70's terrifies me." Shows what he feels is the dual climax of the novel and explains why the ending is not happy.

1970

32 KAUFFMANN, STANLEY. "Films--Catch-22," New Republic, CVXIII, (July 4), 22, 32.
   Places some of the blame for his disappointment in the movie Catch-22 on the book's having become "a historical work...supplanted [as a tonal center]--by a combination of rock and psychedelia and films and social activism...a very different world outlook. Yossarian had to fly fifty missions before he saw that 'the enemy is anybody who's going to get you killed, no matter which side he's on....' Today's young men...know before they get into a uniform what Yossarian had to learn the hard way."

33 LARDNER, SUSAN. "The Current Cinema--No Comparison," New Yorker, XLVI (June 27), 62-63.
   Movie reviewer elects not to compare the book, except to say it was considerably reduced for visual purposes.

34 LEVINE, ARVIN. "Movie Mailbag--The Pitch on 'Catch-22,' "New York Times, August 2, Sec. II, p. 2.
   Another letter objecting to Schjeldahl's article (1970.B47) claims Schjeldahl never read the book, since he objects that Yossarian's escaping to Sweden on a rubber raft was out of place in the novel and "the fact is that this does not even occur in the novel."

35 MILLER, EDWIN. "Spotlight!" Seventeen, XXIX (August), 80.
   Lauds the novel Catch-22 as "a modern classic, a novel cherished by youth everywhere for its putdown of the rigid military mind and plea for the right of human survival." Finds the movie disappointing.

36 MILLER, WAYNE CHARLES. An Armed America: Its Face in Fiction. New York: New York University Press. Pp. 8, 85, 125, 167, 175, 203, 205-243, 258, 268.
   Chapter on Catch-22 (Pp. 205-243) is an exposition of Miller's theory that the novel provides a "meeting ground, for almost all the themes and ideas...followed by novelists dealing with Americans at war and Americans within the military structure.... Like most of the World War I novelists and some from World War II, he uses his work as a vehicle for criticism of an entire culture." However, while he condemns "the concepts of honor, glory, and patriotism just as much as Hemingway and Dos Passos," he does not follow in the paths they established. He introduces satire, a "new element" in this tradition, directed even at the hopefulness and sentimentality of the earlier writers, but most forcefully at "an American life Heller clearly regards as immoral and absurd...he takes on

American business, education, medicine, organization men and religion." The ending may involve a complete shift in tone, but may also represent the kind of illusions and ideals by which men and cultures survive.

37 MILNE, VICTOR J. "Heller's 'Bologniad': A Theological Perspective on Catch-22," Critique, XII (No. 2, 1970-71), 50-69.
    Sees Catch-22 as a mock-epic dramatizing the clash between two moralities: Yossarian's humanistic Christian ethic and Cathcart and Minderbinder's competitive ethic with its repression, false patriotism, and "heroic code." Illustrates the notable parallels to the Iliad and the comedy and horror which mock its outworn values, establishing the literary form of the novel as a "'Bologniad'...in which a modern Achilles says 'baloney' to the demands of a corrupt society with its iniquitous heroic code requiring the sacrifice of human lives." Article goes on to examine the theology of the novel, arguing that Yossarian's desertion is a responsible, moral act in that he can make no totally "good choice, but must resist the greater wrongs: exploiting others and letting oneself be exploited." Reprinted: 1973.A1.

38 MORGENSTERN, JOSEPH. "Into the Mad Blue Yonder," Newsweek, LXXV (June 22), 81-82.
    Expresses disappointment in the movie but notes that the book had "defied would-be adapters for years."

*39 OLMSTEAD, ROBERT TAFT, JR. "The American Novel of World War II as Social Criticism." Ph.D. dissertation, Stanford University. Cited and abstracted in Dissertation Abstracts, XXXI (May, 1971), 6067.

40 PAUL, ART. "Movie Mailbag--The Pitch on 'Catch-22,'" New York Times, August 2, Sec. II, p. 10.
    Objects to Canby's review (1970.B13) of Catch-22: the "movie was emasculated of the humor, the warmth, and the great characters found in Joseph Heller's novel."

41 PHILLIPS, McCANDLISH. "Heller Pleased with Catch-22 Film," New York Times, June 19, p. 24.
    Mostly about the making of the film, with some comments from an interview with Heller about his views on the film and his writing: "I was very glad that he [Mike Nichols] went for the somber parts of Catch-22--My literary bent is more toward the morbid and tragic...my idea was to use humor to make ridiculous the things that are irrational and very terrible that are going on."

1970

42   ROBIN, STEVE. "Films--Catch-22," After Dark, XII (July), 66-67.
    Thinks the film is "near mastery" in its making the horrors of the book "alive and menacing." On the screen Catch-22 is "more cryable than laughable."

43   SALES, GROVER. "Catch-$22," San Francisco (October), 9, 10, 13, 86-88.
    Argues that the failure of the film Catch-22 was predetermined by the "children's pop novel" upon which it was based, "a grandiose over-sold fake." Objects to the novel's repetitions, echolalia, verbosity, silly characterizations, corny jokes--but especially to the lack of seriousness about the real World War II enemy. Feels it was a waste of Nichols' talents to "be funneled into the filming of this worthless book." Reprinted: 1973.A1.

*44 SAPORTA, MARC. Histoire du Roman Americain. Paris: Seghers. Pp. 162, 229, 236, 287, 290.
    Cited by Weixlmann (1974.B213).

45   SARRIS, ANDREW. "Films in Focus--Catch-22," (New York) The Village Voice, June 25, pp. 47, 54-55.
    Complains that the movie dispenses with many characters and almost all the "obsessional power struggles of petty bureaucrats." It strips away "every last vestige of Heller's satiric sociology."

46   SCHICKEL, RICHARD. "One of Our Novels Is Missing," Life, LXIX, (July 4), 12.
    Feels Nichols failed in trying to make the movie the visual equivalent of Heller's verbal style, but he and Buck Henry "mislaid every bit of humor that made the novel emotionally bearable and esthetically memorable," mainly because of their restructuring of the novel so that it seems all one dream sequence. It simplifies the complexity of the novel which has exercised [a powerful hold] on a generation."

47   SCHJELDAHL, PETER. "Is 'Catch' Really a Miss?" New York Times, July 19, Sec. II, p. 9.
    Argues that the film version of Catch-22, "a remarkably faithful adaptation," suffers from the same faults as the novel, "an ambitious and entertaining piece riddled with cheap preciousness and sentimentality...a specimen of a particular intellectual and moral attitude born of the '50's...paranoia of the 'them-us' variety...an ethic of impotence."

1970

48   SCHLESINGER, ARTHUR, JR. "Catch-22 'disappointment,'" Vogue, CLVI (August 1), 40.
     Expresses disappointment that the film fails to capture Heller's "wildest and most murderous of contemporary visions of war."

49   SCOTT, NATHAN A., JR. "The 'Conscience' of the New Literature." In Melvin J. Freedman and John B. Vickery, eds. The Shaken Realist: Essays in Modern Literature in Honor of Frederick J. Hoffman. Baton Rouge: Louisiana State University Press. Pp. 251-283.
     Warns against classifying the work of Heller and others as "absurdism" which perhaps associates them too closely with their European contemporaries. Finds "black humor" a more appropriate term to describe their work of "ironic preposterousness and larky, outrageous joking." Sees Heller and Barth as novelists who have little patience with the "art of the novel" and controlling forms; since the world itself is "indeterminate and astonishing and intractable," they choose a "catch-as-catch can" improvisational method in order to be "truly open to the turbulent incoherence of reality."

50   SELIGSON, MARCIA. "Hollywood's Hottest New Writer--Buck Henry," New York Times Magazine, July 19, pp. 10-11, 49-50, 52.
     Reports that Henry claims to have read Catch-22 "about 20 times" so that he feels he could "write the movie as if [he'd]...written the book." Goes into problems with chronology, shifts in tone, and characters to be left out in writing the screenplay.

51   SHABER, DAVID. "The Magical Man Behind Catch-22," True, LI (July), 39-41, 78-80.
     An article on Mike Nichols, director of the film. He mentions having wanted to do Catch-22 for a long time: "I think it's about the way a lot of us feel."

52   SHENKER, ISRAEL. "Elite Riding in Happy Confusion," New York Times, December 12, p. 33.
     Reports Heller refuses to stay in city while taxicabs are on strike, has just returned from New Orleans and is going elsewhere.

53   SIMMONS, DONALD. "Movie Mailbag--The Pitch on 'Catch-22,'" New York Times, August 2, Sec. II, pp. 2, 10.
     Argues that several comments in the Schjeldahl article (1970.B47) were "considerably wide of the mark," that

1970

Heller's description of the "them-us" paranoia of the 50's is "still timely," for "Yossarian's most important discovery about 'them' was that to a great extent they were 'us'....the machine is a formalized extension and expression of ordinary American goals, methods, and philosophies... and Yossarian eventually discovers these roots even within himself--during the numbed walk through Rome and the bargain with Colonel Cathcart." Also, comments that movie was disappointing, largely because the scenes which sought to provoke the audience's rage and indignation were not funny enough: "The reader of the book is seduced by his own laughter into a sort of complicity with the inhumanities.... that disturbing experience is simply not duplicated in the movie."

*54 SIMMONS, LYDIA. "Existentialism in the Modern Novel, 1945-1967." Ph.D. dissertation, New York University. Cited and abstracted in Dissertation Abstracts, XXXI (January, 1971), 3519-3520.

55 SIMON, JOHN. New Leader, LXXX (June 22), 27.
Mostly a review of the movie with a few comments on the book which Simon admits to having only skimmed ("not my canteen of tea"); he speaks of the book's "hallmark: its dogged, doggy worrying of every funnybone it can clamp its teeth on." Reprinted: 1971.B32.

*56 STOWELL, ROBERT. "Joseph Heller: Black Comedy," Listener, XLIV, 13-14.
Cited in Annual Bibliography of English Language and Literature, XLV, 576.

57 THOMAS, W. K. "'What Difference Does It Make?' Logic in Catch-22," Dalhousie Review, L (Winter, 1970-71), 488-495.
One of the few articles on Catch-22 which provides extensive evidence to support its conclusions. Shows how the misuse of logic in the book centers on the distinction between the form and substance of what is being said or done and how Heller employs the device of faulty logic to amuse, to force looking at ideas in a new light, and to expose the sort of irrationality which causes many of the things that happen in modern life.

58 WEINBERG, HELEN. The New Novel in America: The Kafkan Mode in Contemporary Fiction. Ithaca, New York: Cornell University Press. P. 12.
Includes Catch-22 in a list of modern "absurdist novels using surreal means to present the victim-hero's situation."

In a footnote to this, Weinberg adds that Yossarian, like Holden Caulfield, is really a victim-activist in that he is not passive, though he is trapped by his situation. He prefers his madness to the world's, but in his "comic" acting-out of what has been imposed on him, he is more "deluded...defeated, than bold in quest of a better self."

59   ZALL, P. M. "<u>Catch-22</u> Uncaught," <u>Satire News Letter</u>, VIII (Fall), 69-73.
    Draws attention to the great emphasis on language in the book to show the ambiguity of language and morals, then contrasts the movie which portrays an absurd world with Yossarian making an absurd gesture at survival in the end. Calls the book's ending more ambiguous, suggesting that values such as love, faith, and hope may balance off the evil that men do to one another.

1971 A BOOKS

*1   FRANK, MICHAEL. "Rhetoric, Theme, and Consciousness in <u>Catch-22</u>: an Essay in Critical Reading." Ph.D. dissertation, Cornell Universtity. Cited and abstracted in <u>Dissertation Abstracts International</u>, XXXIII (July, 1972), 309.

2   MILLER, WALTER JAMES and BONNIE E. NELSON. <u>Joseph Heller's 'Catch-22'</u>. New York: Monarch Press, p. 114.
    <u>Catch-22</u> synopsis, analysis, and questions are somewhat superficial but would perhaps be helpful to the novice reader of contemporary literature. The early sections, which are based on an interview with Heller, provide interesting information about his life and thinking not published elsewhere. A short, annotated bibliography is included at the end along with some remarks about Heller's critics.

1971 B SHORTER WRITINGS

1   ANON. "3 Authors to Teach in C.C.N.Y. Program," New York <u>Times</u>, April 18, p. 107.
    Reports Heller will teach in new program, master's degree in creative writing.

2   BERTHOFF, WARNER. <u>Fictions and Events: Essays in Criticism and Literary History</u>. New York: E. P. Dutton. Pp. 107, 114.
    Author lists <u>Catch-22</u> as one of several modern novels that have "moved" him. Calls Heller a "remarkably ingenious and spirited jokester."

1971

3   BLUES, THOMAS. "The Moral Structure of Catch-22," Studies in the Novel, III (Spring), 64-79.
    Studies the symbolism of seeing (e.g. imperfect vision, deja vu), the way Yossarian comes to see what life is, and how the world of Catch-22 has abandoned the principle of life. But feels that Heller abandons his technique to sentimentality in the ending "clouding our vision of the meaning of Yossarian's desertion...[failing] to make us utterly aware of the price man has to pay to make his best dreams come true." Reprinted: 1973.A1-A2; 1974.A2.

4   BRYDEN, RONALD. Review of We Bombed in New Haven at Cockpit Theatre in London, (London) Observer, April 25, p. 30.
    Asks why the British premiere of this "powerful play" with its "remorseless black logic" was left to the young Holland Park Link Group at the tiny Cockpit.

5   CLANCY, JACK. "The Film and the Book: D. H. Lawrence and Joseph Heller on the Screen," Meanjin Quarterly, XXX (Autumn), 96-97, 99-101.
    In noting differences in film and novel as art forms, finds that Mike Nichols' film of Catch-22 fails because it cannot catch Heller's humor since most of it is verbal, therefore, making the horror stronger than the humor. Since "that kind of anti-war feeling has been done before," the "peculiar strength of Heller's indignation at war is muted."

6   DRUCKER, MORT and STAN HART. "Catch-All-22," Mad, CXLI (March), 4-10.
    Cartoon feature lampoons the language and "logic" of Catch-22 and the techniques of the film. Reprinted: 1973.A1.

7   FIEDLER, LESLIE. The Collected Essays of Leslie Fiedler, Vol. II. New York: Stein and Day. Pp. 379-400.
    Reprint of 1965.B11.

8   FROST, LUCY. "Violence in the Eternal City: 'Catch-22' as a Critique of American Culture," Meanjin Quarterly, XXX (Summer), 447-453.
    Argues that Catch-22 is primarily a critique of American society. Heller sees World War II not as altering civilization but as revealing what is there. By making the enemy the Army itself, Heller "opens up new metaphoric possibilities for the war novel." The episode in Rome makes particularly clear how all of society is governed by "Catch-22," by impersonal force ungoverned by higher social

Writings about Joseph Heller, 1961-1977

1971

values; the civilian who cries ironically "Police! Help! Police!" as police arrest him points up this real danger in society. Military leaders are separated from those they send on bombing missions by impersonal language just as the bombers crews are separated from their victims by distance. Violence ensues when individuals, such as Nately's whore, are driven to strike out at anyone because their real enemy is impersonal. Thus, Frost feels, Heller exposes the horror of modern American life whose institutions use the rhetoric of humanistic values but actually put first the value of acquiring objects and treat individuals as abstractions. Frost may be a bit hard on American society, but along the way she gives a perceptive reading of the novel and makes some illuminating comparisons with Heart of Darkness and The Adventures of Huckleberry Finn.

9   GONZALES, ALEXIS. "Notes on the Next Novel, an Interview [with Joseph Heller]," New Orleans Review, II (No. 3), 216-219.
    Heller comments on writers who have influenced him, the film version of Catch-22, student protests, the effect of Catch-22 on students, the "confused" prose style at the beginning of Catch-22, and his new novel Something Happened.

10 GREINER, DON. "Strange Laughter: The Comedy of John Hawkes," Southwest Review, LVI (Autumn), 318-328.
    Mentions Hawkes' comments on Heller's violence in an interview in Massachusetts Review (1966.B13).

11 GROSS, THEODORE L. The Heroic Ideal in American Literature. New York: The Free Press. P. 288.
    In essay on Mailer, Heller is mentioned as one of a group of important contemporary writers who use wit as "a shield against the humorless authority of Americans."

12 GUSSOW, MEL. "Heller Dramatizes His 'Catch-22' on L. I.," New York Times, July 23, p. 14.
    Reviews Long Island performances of play by Heller, based on his novel, but emphasizing its comic aspects: "The military atmosphere is not stressed...and there are moments when you forget the specificality of the location and are carried away with the universality of the insane situation."

13 GUTTMANN, ALLEN. The Jewish Writer in America: Assimilation and the Crisis of Identity. New York: Oxford University Press. P. 76.
    Names Heller in a footnote as one who might be included in an extended list of "nominally Jewish Black Humorists."

1971

14   HARRIS, CHARLES B. <u>Contemporary American Novelists of the Absurd</u>. New Haven: College and University Press. Pp. 20, 32, 33-50, 72, 134.
   Considers Heller one of the contemporary American novelists who treat absurdist themes with absurdist techniques, <u>i.e.</u> employing traditional novelistic devices ironically or farcically. Classes <u>Catch-22</u> as a radical protest novel because Heller, unlike other writers who picture a cosmic absurdity, indicates there is hope for reform of or at least escape from bureaucracy and has faith in the individual: "the novel not only protests absurdity but rejects it as the ultimate reality." Goes on to examine Heller's techniques, showing how he burlesques the pseudo logic of military and business absurdity and cruelty with tautological dialogues, comic reversals, and serious descriptions ending with trivial or ludicrous details. Evaluates the Solomon (1969.B32), MacDonald (1968.B75), Mellard (1968.B77), and Way (1968.B107) articles on the time sequence of <u>Catch-22</u>, deciding Heller purposely confused the chronology of events; he was not writing a conventional stream-of-consciousness novel but ushering in "the Decade of the Absurd."

15   HAUCK, RICHARD BOYD. <u>A Cheerful Nihilism</u>. Bloomington: Indiana University Press. Pp. 12, 240.
   <u>Catch-22</u> mentioned twice in regard to absurdity in fiction: once, to point out that the seemingly incredible can happen, <u>e.g.</u> Milo Minderbinder's contract could be compared to the Japanese Zeroes made out of United States scrap metal; and second, to show that one can always run, as Yossarian does, from an absurd situation in the hope of finding a tolerable one.

*16   HAVEMANN, CAROL S. P. "The Fool as Mentor in Modern American Parables of Entrapment: Ken Kesey's <u>One Flew over the Cuckoo's Nest</u>, Joseph Heller's <u>Catch-22</u>, and Ralph Ellison's <u>Invisible Man</u>." Ph.D. dissertation, Rice University. Cited and annotated in <u>Dissertation Abstracts</u>, XXXII (October), 2091-2092.

17   KAUFMAN, DONALD L. "Catch-23: The Mystery of Fact (Norman Mailer's Final Novel?)," <u>Twentieth Century Literature</u>, XVII (October), 247-256.
   A critique of Norman Mailer's <u>Why Are We in Vietnam?</u> Comments on Mailer's view that if World War II was like <u>Catch-22</u>, this war is like <u>Naked Lunch</u>. See 1966.B18.

1971

18   KAZIN, ALFRED. "The War Novel: From Mailer to Vonnegut," *Saturday Review*, LIV (February 6), 13-15, 36.
     An article analyzing the changing literary perspectives on war from writers who made their "separate peace" with war through later writers who didn't such as Mailer, Heller, and Vonnegut. Kazin feels modern writers, having experienced the previously unimagined horrors of World War II concentration camps, fire-bombing, and the A-bomb, can no longer write about war in a logical way, for it has become an insane, omnipresent way of life. Thus, Heller pictures the "craziness" of war by juxtaposing "the pseudo-rationality of traditional Jewish humor" with the violent horror from which one cannot escape. Reprinted: 1973.A1.

19   KENNARD, JEAN. "Joseph Heller: At War with Absurdity," *Mosaic*, IV (No. 3), 75-87.
     Illustrates in considerable detail how Heller's experimental narrative techniques, characterization, and use of tone, reason, and language in *Catch-22* are an attempt to "dramatize" an Existentialist view of the human condition, i.e. "The world has no meaning....the relationship between man and his world is therefore absurd.... Reason and language are useless....when a man discovers these facts about his condition, he has an experience...which Sartre calls 'nausea.'" Argues that while the ending may be sentimental, it presents "the key to a full understanding of what Heller is saying." Reprinted: 1973.A1-A2.

*20 KILGO, JAMES P. "Five American Novels of World War II: A Critical Study." Ph.D. dissertation, Tulane University. Cited and abstracted in *Dissertation Abstracts International*, XXXII (May, 1972), 6380.

21   LUTWACK, LEONARD. *Heroic Fiction: The Epic Tradition and American Novels of the Twentieth Century*. Carbondale: Southern Illinois University Press. Pp. 147-148.
     Mentions *Catch-22* in making the point that war could no longer be considered as a subject for an epic novel; as a result novels about war became serio-comic.

22   MARCUS, FRED H. and PAUL ZALL. "Catch-22: Is Film Fidelity an Asset?" In Fred H. Marcus, ed. *Film and Literature: Contrasts in Media*. Scranton, Pennsylvania: Chandler Publishing. Pp. 127-136.
     Primarily a comparison of the film and novel which finds that the film's weakness comes of its fidelity to the novel which depends on verbal emphases and appeals more to the mind than the emotions; the film does not grip the viewer

1971

and "his mind assesses the flow of images." Also, because of the compression required in the film, there is less time for language play as comic relief "to ease the viewer's discomfort at Catch-22's dehumanizing events." Essay makes some further comments on the novel, especially in regard to the way "language structures reality," to the form of the novel, and to the relationship between Yossarian and the chaplain.

*23   NELSON, THOMAS A. "In Defense of the Grim: A Personal View of the Film Version of Catch-22." In William F. Grayburn, ed. Studies in the Humanities. Indiana, Pennsylvania: Indiana University of Pennsylvania. Pp. 10-13.
  Cited in 1971 MLA International Bibliography of Books and Articles on the Modern Languages and Literature, p. 150.

24   _____. "Theme and Structure in Catch-22," Renascence, XXIII (Summer), 173-182.
  Argues that Catch-22 is "constructed meticulously": in the first cycle people and events are treated as glimpses; in the next they are shown to be interrelated in an inescapable way (thus man's responsibility to man) though they are indifferent; and in the concluding cycle the significance of people and events shown earlier is made clear to Yossarian and the reader, and Yossarian makes his choice to flee "to responsibility" from a world of "outmoded values, moral irresponsibility and insanity."

25   ORR, REHARD W. "Flat Characters in Catch-22," Notes on Contemporary Literature, I (January), 4.
  An article which relates E. M. Forester's definition of a flat character in his Aspects of the Novel to the characters in Catch-22, calling even Yossarian a one-dimensional man.

*26   PASCU, AL. "Joseph Heller si 'Catch-22,'" [Joseph Heller and Catch-22], Cronica, VI (July), 9.
  Cited in Annual Bibliography of English Language and Literature, XLVI, 620.

27   PEARCE, RICHARD. William Styron. Minneapolis: University of Minnesota Press. Pp. 7-8.
  Draws a distinction between Mailer and Jones who view war from a prewar perspective and Heller and Styron who view it from a postwar perspective, i.e. a world "dominated by a runaway logic."

1971

28 PROTHEROUGH, ROBERT. "The Sanity of Catch-22," The Human World, III (May), 59-70.
    Illustrates four devices Heller uses for satiric effect: 1) substitution of a word, phrase, or idea that runs contrary to the sense the reader expects, "sometimes standing logic on its head to produce a new kind of truth," then using the device on attitudes toward war; 2) deflating, questioning, or reversing a familiar cliché, in the end attacking "the whole cliché of American life"; 3) deliberate conflict between tone and subject; and 4) reduction of meaningless choices to their simplest terms, thereby revealing the absurdity of official attitudes, particularly with the most "meaningless choice...Catch-22 itself." Reprinted: 1973.A1-A2.

*29 ROBINSON, DAVID E. "Unaccommodated Man: The Estranged World in Contemporary American Fiction." Ph.D. dissertation, Duke University. Cited and abstracted in Dissertation Abstracts International, XXXII (April, 1972), 5803-5804.

30 SCHOLES, ROBERT. "'Mithridates, he died old': Black Humor and Kurt Vonnegut, Jr." In The Sounder Few: Essays from the Hollins Critic. Athens: University of Georgia Press. Pp. 172-185.
    Reprint of 1966.B23.

31 SCOTT, NATHAN A., JR. Nathanael West: A Critical Essay. Grand Rapids: William B. Eerdmans. P. 8.
    Feels current interest in West is not only a result of modern black humorists' advertising his fiction, although "such books as...Catch-22 do surely belong amongst the most impressive fictions of the present time."

32 SHAPIRO, JAMES. "Work in Progress/Joseph Heller," Intellectual Digest, II (December), 6-11.
    An interview in which Heller discusses Something Happened, the novel he has been working on for five years. He also remarks that his early stories were not very good.

33 SIMON, JOHN. Movies into Film. New York: The Dial Press. Pp. 326-327.
    Reprint of 1970.B55.

34 TANNER, TONY. City of Words. New York: Harper and Row. Pp. 72-84, 121, 144, 204, 223, 233, 245, 429.
    Examines the plight of Yossarian, menaced by many kinds of death, but particularly by the Air Force's (American society's) "complete structuring of life" so that identity

1971

"is a matter of papers rather than flesh and blood" and the human being is reduced to "a manipulable and disposable thing." Notes that those not victimized by the system, e.g. Milo Minderbinder, who "responds automatically to... commercial opportunity," and Aarfy, "devoid of human responses," offer no better ways to hold on to one's individuality. Also traces Yossarian's efforts to do so, culminating in his decision to leave, a move seen as similar to the choice of many fictional American heroes "to redefine the direction in which true reality lies." Essay then goes on to analyze Heller's "own struggle with language and the existing conventions of the novel," finding that both Heller and Yossarian "keep on spinning to avoid being trapped... a mode of motion [which] turns out to be a way, perhaps the only way, of life."

35 WILLIS, JOHN, ed. Screen World. New York: Crown Publishers. Pp. 38, 75.
   Makes note of film Catch-22 based on novel by Heller and as one of writers of screenplay for Dirty Dingus Magee.

1972 A BOOKS - NONE

1972 B SHORTER WRITINGS

1 ALDRIDGE, JOHN W. "Donald Barthelme and the Doggy Life." In his The Devil in the Fire. New York: Harper's Magazine Press. P. 261.
   Mentions Heller as one of a number of Black Humorists who seem "notable more for their potential than for their clearly major distinction."

2 ANON. "Joseph Heller." In Who's Who in America, Vol. 37. Chicago: Marquis. P. 1395.
   Same information given as in 1970 edition (1970.B3).

3 ANON. "Set 'Bombed' Revival Off-B'Way for Fall," Variety, May 10, p. 79.
   A report.

4 BARNES, CLIVE. "Theater: New Haven Bombed Again," New York Times, September 25, p. 49.
   Gives a highly critical review of Peter John Bailey's "new interpretation of the play." Barnes feels this revival at Circle in the Square emphasizes the weaknesses of the play, which were overly obvious, but it did have something worthwhile to say.

1972

*5 BARTH, JOHN. "Having It Both Ways: A Conversation Between John Barth and Joe David Bellamy," New American Review, XV, 134-150.
Cited by Weixlmann (1974.B213).

6 BRUSTEIN, ROBERT. "Catch-22." In Gilbert A. Harrison, ed. The Critic as Artist. New York: Liveright. Pp. 47-54.
Reprint of 1961.B28.

7 CLARITY, JAMES F. "Notes on People," New York Times, August 15, p. 28.
Reports that Heller was one of several celebrities who played softball to benefit the McGovern campaign. Heller reportedly made a number of good catches.

8 DOWIE, WILLIAM. "Walker Percy: Sensualist-Thinker," Novel, VI (Fall), 52-65.
Quotes Karl (1964.B10) on the theme of Catch-22 ("the only sure thing in a swamp of insanity is one's own identity") to contrast the theme of The Moviegoer.

9 GREEN, ALAN. "Book Business," Saturday Review, LV (July 1), 62.
In article on "drugstore paperbacks," names Dell edition of Catch-22 as a book that sells well.

*10 JANOFF, BRUCE LEE. "Beyond Satire: Black Humor in the Novels of John Barth and Joseph Heller." Ph.D. dissertation, Ohio University. Cited and abstracted in Dissertation Abstracts International, XXIII (October), 1728.

11 _____. "Black Humor: Beyond Satire," Ohio Review, XIV (Fall), 5-20.
Heller is one of the writers included in this general analysis of black humor.

*12 KOCHANCK, PATRICIA SHARPE. "In Pursuit of Proteus: a Piagetian Approach to the Study of the Grotesque in American Fiction of the Fifties." Ph.D. dissertation, The Pennsylvania State University. Cited and abstracted in Dissertation Abstracts International, XXXIII (April, 1973), 5729-5730.

13 KORT, WESLEY A. Shriven Selves. Philadelphia: Fortress Press. Pp. 38, 61.
This discussion of Peter DeVries' work notes a consistency in method and vision among the work of Heller and others, i.e. mixing serious problems with funny material.

1972

14 LASSON, ROBERT. "Humor: Book of Job to 'Catch-22,'" Washington Post, August 25, Sec. B, p. 8.
    Reviews Treasury of Great Humor, an anthology edited by Louis Untermeyer, which includes a section from Catch-22. Notes that Heller is one of four living writers included.

15 MIZENER, ARTHUR. "The New Romance," Southern Review, VIII (Winter), 106-117.
    Contends that modern writers such as Heller can be seen in relation to older writers of romance in that they "represent as reality the images in their minds and relations among those images that satisfy them."

16 NELSON, GERALD B. Ten Versions of America. New York: Knopf. Pp. x, xiv, 163-182.
    The story of Yossarian and his friends is one of ten sad examples of the end of the American dream. Reads the message of Catch-22 as the loneliness of modern man whose only responsibility is to save himself from a power system that would destroy him. This interest in self is vastly different from the "self-interest of Cathcarts and Korns who work against their fellow man because of greed and envy." Yossarian recognizes the destructive power of their corruption of the American dream into self-aggrandizement. There is safety only in making a deal with them or escaping. Feels Americans should learn from Catch-22 by reading it as comic reality, not ironic unreality.

17 OLDERMAN, RAYMOND M. Beyond the Wasteland: A Study of the American Novel in the Nineteen-sixties. New Haven and London: Yale University Press. Pp. 28, 86, 94-114, 142, 154, 165, 197, 204, 221.
    Sees Catch-22 as a typical novel of the sixties in its rebellion against a dehumanizing institution, the military-economic establishment which, even more than the war, destroys "sanity and life and the human spirit."

18 PINSKER, SANFORD. "The Graying of Black Humor," Studies in the Twentieth Century, XVIII (April), 15-33.
    Article on Bruce Jay Friedman compares Heller's writing favorably with Friedman's later work; declaring that they shade black humor "into the larger concerns of an absurdist vision and the stakes are raised all around."

*19 PRICE, JONATHAN LEE. "Black Humor: Form as Manipulation." Ph.D. dissertation, Stanford University. Cited and abstracted in Dissertation Abstracts International, XXXIII (November), 2390.

1973

20 SALE, RICHARD B. "An Interview with Joseph Heller," <u>Studies in the Novel</u>, IV (Spring), 63-74.
    Heller's comments on the artistry, especially the "extraordinary amount of energy given to the details of structure in his work." He offers some explanation of the structure of <u>Catch-22</u>. Also discusses the early reviews of the novel, his beginnings as a writer, the lack of success of <u>We Bombed in New Haven</u>, the seriousness of <u>Something Happened</u>, writers who have influenced him, and the growth of Yossarian's moral responsibility.

*21 SCHOPF, WILLIAM. "Blindfolded and Backwards: Promethean and Bemushroomed Heroism in <u>One Flew Over the Cuckoo's Nest</u> and <u>Catch-22</u>," <u>Bulletin of the Rocky Mountain M.L.A.</u>, XXVI, 89-97.
    Cited in <u>Annual Bibliography of English Language and Literature</u>, XLVII, 602.

*22 SHARMA, D. R. "<u>Catch-22</u>: An Analysis of Personal Freedom vs. Group Loyalty," Banasthali Patrika, XIX (1972; published 1974), 20-29.
    Cited in 1971 <u>MLA International Bibliography of Books and Articles on the Modern Languages and Literature</u>, p. 177.

23 SPIEGEL, ALAN. "A Theory of the Grotesque in Southern Fiction," <u>Georgia Review</u>, XXVI (Winter), 426-437.
    This study, which contrasts the Southern "grotesque" with "classic gothic fiction" of the North, mentions Heller's writing as being of the latter type, viewing the world as "nightmare fantasy."

*24 TIMCHENKO, M. "My Bombili N'yu'Kheiven" (We Bombed in New Haven), <u>Teatr</u> (Moscow), Part II, 65-66.
    Cited in <u>Annual Bibliography of English Language and Literature</u>, XLVII, 602.

1973 A BOOKS

1   KILEY, FREDERICK and WALTER McDONALD, eds. <u>A 'Catch-22' Casebook</u>. New York: Thomas Y. Crowell.
        Contents:
    Kiley, Frederick and Walter McDonald. "Preface," pp. v-vi.
        Editors establish initially that they consider <u>Catch-22</u> a "masterpiece...about us as a nation and a people <u>now</u> as much as then during World War II." They comment on the metaphor of Yossarian's being sick with a "liver" condition and the "They" he opposes who are ultimately "us." They also explain the organization of their book: reviews,

1973

criticism centering on form, structure, theme, and "the Absurd" (in that order), interviews with Heller, two other works by Heller, commentary on the film <u>Catch-22</u>, a bibliographic note, and discussion questions.
Illustrations of the desk blotter on which Heller plotted <u>Catch-22</u> appear on pp. 1, 41, 271, 307, 333.

Algren, Nelson. "The Catch," pp. 3-5. Reprint of 1961.B3.
Murray, John J. "Review of <u>Catch-22</u>," pp. 5-6. Reprint of 1961.B51.
Brustein, Robert. "The Logic of Survival in a Lunatic World," pp. 6-11. Reprint of 1961.B28.
Toynbee, Philip. "Here's Greatness--in Satire," pp. 12-15. Reprint of 1962.B61.
Wincelberg, Shimon. "A Deadly Serious Lunacy," pp. 16-18. Reprint of 1962.B67.
Mitchell, Julian. "Under Mad Gods," pp. 19-20. Reprint of 1962.B44.
Leslie, Andrew. "A Comedy of Horrors," pp. 20-21. Reprint of 1962.B41.
Bass, Milton R. "Review of 'Catch-22,'" pp. 21-23. Reprint of 1961.B24.
Starnes, Richard. "Review of 'Catch-22,'" pp. 23-24, Reprint of 1962.B59.
"The Heller Cult," pp. 24-27. Reprint of 1962.B19.
"A Review: 'Catch-22,'" pp. 27-39. Reprint of 1963.B1.
Wain, John. "A New Novel about Old Troubles," pp. 43-49. Reprint of 1963.B25.
Scammell, W. "Letter in Reply to Mr. Wain," pp. 49-50. Reprint of 1963.B24.
Denniston, Constance. "'Catch-22': A Romance--Parody," pp. 51-57. Revised version of 1965.B9.
Milne, Victor J. "Heller's 'Bologniad': A Theological Perspective on 'Catch-22,'" pp. 58-73. Reprint of 1970.B37.
Ritter, Jesse. "Fearful Comedy: 'Catch-22' as Avatar of the Social Surrealist Novel," pp. 73-86.

Finds Denniston's view (1965.B9) of <u>Catch-22</u> as a romance-parody limited; sees it as this plus surrealism and social satire via ironic radical juxtaposition. Explains why this classification is appropriate to convey a sense of the absurd in modern life and explains the narrative method as "<u>objectified</u> stream of consciousness." Social satire gives way as the horror of war and Yossarian's growing realization of the power of "Catch-22" increase ("the absurd gives way to the Absurd"...absurd humor becomes "Absurd tragedy" through radical juxtaposition: "theme and technique unify.").

Cheuse, Alan. "Laughing on the Outside," pp. 86-93. Reprint of 1963.B12.

1973

Solomon, Eric. "From Christ in Flanders to 'Catch-22,'" pp. 94-101. Reprint of 1969.B27.

MacDonald, James L. "I See Everything Twice!: The Structure of Joseph Heller's 'Catch-22,'" pp. 102-108. Reprint of 1968.B75.

Mellard, James M. "'Catch-22': Deja vu and the Labyrinth of Memory," pp. 109-121. Reprint of 1968.B77.

Solomon, Jan. "The Structure of Joseph Heller's 'Catch-22,'" pp. 122-132. Reprint of 1967.B32.

Gaukroger, Doug. "Time Structure in 'Catch-22,'" pp. 132-144. Reprint of 1970.B22.

Stark, Howard J. "The Anatomy of 'Catch-22,'" pp. 145-158.
  Proclaims, "What makes Heller's novel unique among other contemporary novels is the extent and complexity of structure and technique." Explicates Heller's juxtaposing of incongruities and associational digressions to show the absurd condition of modern life. Focusing particularly on deja vu, presque vu and jamais vu, illustrates how, incident by incident, image by image. Heller melds isolated imagistic scenes into a "psychological continuum," and under all, however farcical or funny they seem, lies the same horror of a world governed by irrationality. Especially helpful is Stark's explanation of Lt. Fortiori in terms of the the term a fortiori in logic and its use to distort logic, climaxing with Catch-22 and its implications to the point that "the strident grotesqueness and absurdity...no longer seems illogical or abnormal" in Rome. He sees hope, however, in Yossarian's realization of this situation and his determination to "break the lousy chain of inherited habit that was imperiling them all."

Karl, Frederick. "Joseph Heller's Catch-22," pp. 159-165. Reprint of 1964.B10.

Doskow, Minna. "The Night Journey in 'Catch-22,'" pp. 166-174. Reprint of 1967.B10.

Castelli, Jim. "'Catch-22' and the New Hero," pp. 174-181. Reprint of 1970.B16.

Day, Douglas. "'Catch-22': A Manifesto for Anarchists," pp. 181-187. Reprint of 1963.B13.

Henry, G. B. McK. "Significant Corn: 'Catch-22,'" pp. 187-201. Reprint of 1966.B14.

Protherough, Robert. "The Sanity of 'Catch-22,'" pp. 201-212. Reprint of 1971.B28.

Monk, Donald. "An Experiment in Therapy: A Study of 'Catch-22,'" pp. 212-220. Reprint of 1967.B23 (slightly revised).

Ramsey, Vance. "From Here to Absurdity: Heller's 'Catch-22,'" pp. 221-236. Reprint of 1966.B21.

Podhoretz, Norman. "The Best Catch There Is," pp. 237-241. Reprint of 1962.B49.

1973

Hunt, John W. "Comic Escape and Anti-Vision: Joseph Heller's 'Catch-22,'" pp. 242-247. Reprint of 1968.B63.

Vos, Nelvin. "The Angel, the Beast, and the Machine," pp. 247-250. Reprint of 1967.B33.

Greenfeld, Josh. "22 Was Funnier than 14," pp. 250-255. Reprint of 1968.B52.

Kennard, Jean. "Joseph Heller: At War with Absurdity," pp. 255-269. Reprint of 1971.B19.

[Krassner, Paul.] "An Impolite Interview with Joseph Heller," pp. 273-293. Reprint of 1962.B40.

Barnard, Ken. "Interview with Joseph Heller," pp. 294-301. Reprint of 1970.B7.

Balch, Clayton L. "Yossarian to Cathcart and Return: A Person Cross-Country," pp. 301-306.

    Author recalls his own experiences similar to Yossarian's, as a World War II and Vietnam airman and tells of his first reading of a humorous <u>Catch-22</u> before Heller's "depth charges" hit him. In conclusion regards Heller as a "seer" who realized the "madness" of World War II before others and looked ahead to the horrors of the Vietnam experience.

Heller, Joseph. "Love, Dad," pp. 309-318. Reprint of Heller story in <u>Playboy</u>, XVI (December, 1969), 181-182, 348.

Heller, Joseph. "'Catch-22' Revisited," pp. 316-332. Reprint of Heller article in <u>Holiday</u>, XLI (April, 1967), 44-61, 130, 141-142, 145.

"Some Are More Yossarian than Others," pp. 335-345. Reprint of 1970.B6.

Heller, Joseph. "On Translating 'Catch-22' into a Movie," pp. 346-362.

    An abridgment of remarks made by Heller at the Poetry Center, Young Men's Hebrew Center, New York City, in December, 1970. Interesting, not only for Heller's typically witty description of the film's coming to be made and his own lack of concern about its being "true to" the book, but also for his illuminating remarks on the novel: most notably, his conception of Milo vs. Nichols'; his view of the book as being more about America after World War II than during it; his intention of showing Yossarian's growing sense of guilt and responsibility in "The Eternal City"; and his idea of the way Yossarian might get to Sweden.

Brackman, Jacob. "Review of 'Catch-22'" (film), pp. 363-366. Reprint of 1970.B11.

Sales, Grover. "Catch-$22," pp. 366-372. Reprint of 1970.B43.

Drucker, Mort and Stan Hart, "Catch-All-22," pp. 373-379. Reprint of 1971.B6.

Gow, Gordon. "Review of 'Catch-22,'" pp. 380-382. Reprint of 1970.B23.

Miller, Wayne Charles. "'Catch-22': Joseph Heller's Portrait of American Culture--The Missing Portrait in Mike Nichols' Movie," pp. 383-390.
 Criticizes Nichols' film for omitting the main thrust of Heller's attack on a misguided, "dangerous" American society. To back up his point, Miller explains the satiric significance of a number of characters including Col. Cathcart, Major Danby, Doc Daneeka, Major Sanderson, Corporal Whitcomb, Captain Black, and Milo.
"Bibliographical Note," pp. 391-396.
 Mentions the Special Collections Room at Brandeis University as the best single location for studies of Catch-22 and Heller's working materials for the novel and earlier writings. Also lists a number of works about Catch-22 arranged roughly the same way the Casebook collection is arranged. Three of the listings, the Mandel, Blazer, Genauer articles, seem to be incorrect.
"Discussion Questions."
 Seventy-two questions deal with structural and thematic elements, comparisons between Heller and other writers, and various critics' views.

2 SCOTTO, ROBERT M., ed. Catch-22: A Critical Edition. New York: Dell.
Critical works include:
Scotto, Robert M. "Introduction," v-ix.
 Calls Catch-22 "our contemporary classic" and notes that "over a decade after its initial publication...it has grown rather than diminished in popularity." Believes "Yossarian's escape, the ultimate act of protest, has become a metaphor for an age wherein heroism becomes ludicrous and where the only courageous act left is desertion," and contends that Yossarian's struggle makes Catch-22 "the American existentialist novel par excellence" as well as one of the "finest examples" of "black humor." Also comments on Heller's technique, mainly Yossarian's awareness and growing sense of tragedy in the novel, and defends the ending.
Krassner, Paul. "An Impolite Interview with Joseph Heller." pp. 456-478. Reprint of 1962.B40.
Karl, Frederick R. "Joseph Heller's Catch-22: Only Fools Walk in Darkness," pp. 481-488. Reprint of 1964.B10.
Kazin, Alfred. "The War Novel: From Mailer to Vonnegut," pp. 488-491. Reprint of 1971.B18.
Doskow, Minna. "The Night Journey in Catch-22," pp. 491-500. Reprint of 1967.B10.
Solomon, Jan. "The Structure of Joseph Heller's Catch-22," pp. 501-511. Reprint of 1967.B32.

1973

    Mellard, James M. "Catch-22: Deja Vu and the Labyrinth of Memory," pp. 512-525. Reprint of 1968.B77.
    Kennard, Jean. "Joseph Heller: At War with Absurdity," pp. 526-541. Reprint of 1971.B19.
    Protherough, Robert. "The Sanity of Catch-22," pp. 541-544. Reprint of 1971.B28.
    Blues, Thomas. "The Moral Structure of Catch-22," pp. 544-559. Reprint of 1971.B3.
    "A Checklist of Critical Works on Catch-22," pp. 560-561. List most important works before 1972.
    "Representative Reviews," pp. 561-562. Lists major reviews by whether they were favorable, unfavorable, or mixed.
    "The Printing History of Catch-22," p. 562. Lists various editions.

1973 B SHORTER WRITINGS

1 ANON. Note on Catch-22 Sales. Best Sellers, XXXIII (May 1), 70.
    Takes note of Dell's two new editions of Catch-22, which have already sold six million copies.

2 BURHANS, CLINTON S., JR. "Spindrift and the Sea: Structural Patterns and Unifying Elements in Catch-22," Twentieth Century Literature, XIX (October), 239-250.
    Elucidates the structural and unifying elements which "support or control" the "apparent episodic chaos" of Catch-22. Works out the elaborate and tonal changes in structure and chronology of the novel and gives particularly interesting descriptions of how Heller's flashbacks function.

*3 CAMARA, GEORGE C. "War and the Literary Extremist: The American War Novel, 1945-1970." Ph.D. dissertation, University of Massachusetts. Cited and abstracted in Dissertation Abstracts International, XXXIV (February, 1964), 5160.

4 FUSSELL, B. H. "On the Trail of the Lonesome Dramaturge," Hudson Review, XXVI (Winter, 1973-74), 753-762.
    Classes Heller as one of several commercially successful novelists who have "recycled their non-returnable fictions." Mocks Heller's intention of changing the movie Catch-22 to drama with a "narrative line accelerating toward a climactic resolution," claiming such a scheme cannot "salvage this bag of burlesque skits."

1973

5   GREINER, DONALD J. <u>Comic Terror: The Novels of John Hawkes</u>. Memphis: Memphis State University Press. Pp. xii, xiii, xvi.
    Mentions Heller and other modern American comic novelists in relation to Hawkes in making the point that communication is still possible in "a world which is fragmented and violently so"; claims they create characters who learn to live with the probability of defeat.

6   HARMON, WILLIAM. "'Anti-Fiction' in American Humor." In Louis D. Rubin, Jr., ed. <u>The Comic Imagination in American Literature</u>. New Brunswick, New Jersey: Rutgers University Press. Pp. 375-384.
    Briefly mentions <u>Catch-22</u>, "perhaps the funniest of our anti-war novels." <u>See</u> 1973.B22.

7   HASSAN, IHAB. <u>Contemporary American Literature: 1945-1972</u>. New York: Frederick Unger Publishing. Pp. 65, 81-83, 154, 171.
    Gives high praise to Heller's surreal universe of "contemporary Hell" as an example of modern absurdist writing: "Its worlds of reference within reference...collide in a disorder that only Heller's imagination can contain, only his discontinuous form can render with integrity." Also notes that Heller "despite his outrageous humor, falls short of dramatic success in his play <u>We Bombed in New Haven</u>."

*8 HEARRON, WILLIAM THOMAS. "New Approaches in the Post-Modern American Novel: Joseph Heller, Kurt Vonnegut, and Richard Brautigan." Ph.D. dissertation, State University of New York at Buffalo. Cited and abstracted in <u>Dissertation Abstracts International</u>, XXXIV (December), 3398.

9   HUGHES, CATHERINE. <u>Plays, Politics, and Polemics</u>. New York: Drama Book Specialists. Pp. 99-105.
    Describes <u>We Bombed in New Haven</u> as a play that attempts to redo <u>Catch-22</u> and Pirandello and contains some very funny "gallows humor...[but] not much else." Feels idea provided potential for a good play but Heller let it erode into an "overwritten and overwrought example of message drama."

10 KUHNEL, WALTER. "Joseph Heller." In Martin Christadler, ed. <u>Amerikanishce Literatur der Gegenwart in Einzeldarstellungen</u>. Stuttgart: Alfred Kröner. Pp. 391-407.
    This German survey of post-1945 literature considers Heller, Barth, and Vonnegut's work as post-modern fiction.

1973

11 LEHAN, RICHARD. <u>A Dangerous Crossing: French Literary Existentialism and the Modern American Novel</u>. Carbondale: Southern Illinois University Press. Pp. 162-172.
    Reprint of 1967.B18.

12 LOUKIDES, PAUL. "The Radical Vision." <u>Michigan Academician</u>, V (Spring), 497-503.
    Argues that <u>Catch-22</u>, like several other modern novels, posits a solution to the modern crisis of belief by a "radical vision," an alternative vision of reality. Provides examples to show that the world of <u>Catch-22</u> has the logic of nightmare, not of the real world; therefore, "because science and reason are inadequate to reveal the truth, orthodox morality cannot offer any hope of an orderly solution." Concludes that the novel does not absolve itself into absurdity, though it does acknowledge the threat of absurdity; through Yossarian the novel offers belief in the human spirit after the revelation by Snowden to him that only belief in man was possible.

13 McDONALD, WALTER R. "Look Back in Horror: The Functional Comedy of <u>Catch-22</u>," <u>The CEA Critic</u>, XXXV (January), 18-21.
    Describes Heller's use of comic devices such as reversals to make a "jaded audience" recoil in horror at the realistic war scenes.

14 _____. "He Took Off: Yossarian and the Different Drummer," <u>The CEA Critic</u>, XXXVI (November), 14-16.
    Describes a cultural tradition in America of heroes who "took off" like Yossarian. Then argues that Yossarian's leaving was not an escape from duty or responsibility. Most interesting is a letter McDonald quotes from Heller where he gives his reasons for ending <u>Catch-22</u> with Yossarian's departure.

*15 RUMMO, P. E. "Afterword to Estonain translation of <u>We Bombed in New Haven</u>," Tallin: Periodka. Pp. 103.
    Cited in <u>Annual Bibliography of English Language and Literature</u>, XLVIII, 665.

16 SCHULZ, MAX F. <u>Black Humor Fiction of the Sixties</u>. Athens, Ohio: Ohio University Press. Pp. 3, 6, 13, 22-23, 25, 91-92, 95, 105, 141-142.
    Mentions <u>Catch-22</u> in regard to a number of tendencies in Black Humor: plot which does not wholly encompass theme; the warrant officer's voicing "the central vision of Black Humor," the lack of logic to "this system of rewards and punishment"; the compulsive return to the same

action; and Colonel Cathcart's exemplifying the Angst of the man who tries to satisfy society's ideals but can't understand its rules.

17 SHIRZAD, NASSER. "Guilty in Iran," New York Times, December 30, Sec. IV, p. 10.
A letter from the Press Counselor of the Iranian Embassy in response to Heller's December 16th letter to the New York Times in which he protested the imprisonment of Reza Baraheni.

18 SNIDERMAN, STEPHEN L. "'It Was All Yossarian's Fault': Power and Responsibility in Catch-22," Twentieth Century Literature, XIX (October), 251-258.
Takes issue with most commentators on Catch-22 who see Yossarian as powerless by compiling long lists of examples of how Yossarian affected the lives of those around him. Admits that a number of these cases are indirect or involuntary but still insists Yossarian is responsible--even for Nately's death. Finally asserts that Yossarian is responsible for the deaths of the men in his squadron because he lent "his presence and his tacit sanction to the system perpetrated by the USAF and distorted by Cathcart and Korn." His feeble protests like wearing no uniform only make Cathcart so insecure that he raises the number of required missions. The novel places the burden of guilt more on him than on the other men because he is the only one who sees the absurdity and danger of flying more missions and because he has a charismatic effect on others. His learning to use this power to influence others, as he does with some success when he refuses to fly more missions, is highly significant: "Heller argues that the individual, not the bureaucracy or the establishment, still holds the final trump."

19 SYLVESTER, EDWARD. "Catch-22: It's Yossarian in New Play," (Tucson) Arizona Daily Citizen, March 20, p. 21.
Explains nature of dramatization and its relevance to political events of 1972 with some comments by Heller on the trials of anti-war protestors during last year and the omnipresent danger of "Catch-22."

20 THOMAS, W. K. "The Mythic Dimension of Catch-22," Texas Studies in Language and Literature, XV (Spring), 189-198.
While showing concern in a footnote about "overly ingenious scholars," writer seems to fall into this category as an "inveterate myth-seeker," but a few of the allusions he suggests are helpful.

1973

21 WARNER, JON M. <u>Library Journal</u>, XCVIII (February 15), 561.
    Review which briefly describes the substance of the play
    and says if well performed it could offer "good theater,
    if, perhaps, a bit didactic."

22 WEBER, BROM. "The Mode of 'Black Humor.'" In Louis D. Rubin, Jr., ed. <u>The Comic Imagination in American Literature</u>. New Brunswick, New Jersey: Rutgers University Press. Pp. 361-372.
    Mentions Heller as one of the "Black Humorists" whose work "startled yet pleased" the American public. See 1973.B5.

1974 A BOOKS

*1 BANNWARTH, LUTZ. <u>Joseph Heller's Catch-22: Ein Paradigma des Grotesken</u>. Inaugural-Dissertation zur Erlangung des Doktorgrades der Philosophischen Fakultät der Westfalischen Wilhelms-Universität zu Munster.
    Published in German only.

2   NAGEL, JAMES A., ed. <u>Critical Essays on Catch-22</u>. Encino and Belmont, California: Dickenson Publishing.
        Contents:
    Nagel, James A. "Introduction," pp. 1-7
        Reviews early, mixed criticism of <u>Catch-22</u> and its commercial success. Also provides brief biography of Heller and commentary on his early stories and their fore-shadowing of <u>Catch-22</u>. Outlines the different types of scholarship done by several writers on <u>Catch-22</u>: the debate about "whether war is the subject of the book or merely the setting for it," the various philosophical and ethical questions raised by the novel, and the disagreement about Heller's technique and its purpose, his characterization of Yossarian, and the ending.
    Hicks, Granville. "Medals for Madness," pp. 11-12. Reprint of 1961.B41.
    Stern, Richard G. "Bombers Away," p. 13. Reprint of 1961.B64.
    Algren, Nelson. "The Catch," pp. 14-16. Reprint of 1961.B3.
    Brustein, Robert. "The Logic of Survival in a Lunatic World," pp. 16-21. Reprint of 1961.B28.
    Smith, Roger H. "Review," pp. 21-33. Reprint of 1963.B1, published anonymously and later printed anonymously in 1973.B2, which Smith edited.
    Lehan, Richard and Jerry Patch. "<u>Catch-22</u>: The Making of a Novel," pp. 37-44. Reprint of 1967.B18.

Writings about Joseph Heller, 1961-1977

1974

Ritter, Jess. "What Manner of Men Are These," pp. 45-56.
Argues for the thesis that in Catch-22 Heller was working in the mode of Menippean satire which presents the world in a single intellectual pattern with characters stylized along "humor" lines. Illustrates the qualities many characters in the novel represent. Gives a particularly interesting explanation of Yossarian as "Adam before the Fall" whose morality must be "the morality of refusal" in response to the aggressors, the officers and Milo (government and free enterprise). Concludes that Catch-22 is "a work of art...varied and true" that shows Heller knows "unerringly where his culture is going."

Walden, Daniel. "'Therefore Choose Life': A Jewish Interpretation of Heller's Catch-22," pp. 57-63.
Argues that Catch-22 is written in the Hasidic tradition, basing his contention on Heller's past, his comments in interviews, and the "moral content" of the novel, particularly Yossarian's choice of moral position and life at the end.

Denniston, Constance. "The American Romance-Parody: A Study of Heller's Catch-22," pp. 64-77. Reprint of 1965.B9.

Solomon, Jan. "The Structure of Joseph Heller's Catch-22," pp. 78-88. Reprint of 1967.B32.

Gaukroger, Doug. "Time Structure in Catch-22," pp. 89-101. Reprint of 1970.B22.

Blues, Thomas. "The Moral Structure of Catch-22," pp. 102-116. Reprint of 1971.B3.

Gordon, Caroline and Jeanne Richardson. "Flies in Their Eyes? A Note on Joseph Heller's Catch-22," pp. 117-124. Reprint of 1967.B13.

Hunt, John W. "Comic Escape and Anti-Vision: Joseph Heller's Catch-22," pp. 125-130. Reprint of 1968.B63.

Stark, Howard. "Catch-22: The Ultimate Irony," pp. 130-141.
Provides yet another interpretation of Catch-22 in terms of existentialism and the absurd. In a carefully reasoned argument, traces Yossarian's growing awareness of his absurd situation from which there is no escape; explains Orr, Korn, and the old man in the bordello as characters who embody various kinds of surrender to the system; and points up the "disappearing" of Major de Coverly, Doc Daneeka, the old man, General Dreedle, Clevinger, Dunbar, and Dr. Stubbs. Sees Yossarian's desertion as commitment only to a dream, whereas Heller showed a rational and meaningful choice, to stay, as the chaplain did, "and persevere."

Martini, James J. "The Courage to Defy," pp. 142-149.
Essay gives attention to Heller's early stories and academic background. Sees a talent for characterization in early stories that was not manifested in Catch-22.

1974

>Traces Yossarian's coming to vision and understanding through the Snowden episode, to a sense of responsibility from Nately's whore and her sister, and a sense of direction and hope from Orr. Applauds Heller's "sense of the epic" and great theme of looking for meaning in an absurd and meaningless world and his insistence on human responsibility--even if his artistry has shortcomings.

Waldmeir, Joseph J. "Joseph Heller--a Novelist of the Absurd," pp. 150-154. Reprint of 1964.B16.

Doskow, Minna. "The Night Journey in Catch-22," pp. 155-163. Reprint of 1967.B10.

Nagel, James. "Yossarian, the Old Man, and the Ending of Catch-22," pp. 164-174.

>Outlines the similarities between Yossarian and the old man, suggesting that the old man serves as an alter-ego for Yossarian until Nately's whore ("a manifestation of part of Yossarian's mind") helps him to reject that direction and chose his "first act of positive affirmation," similar to Huck Finn's escaping to a territory "less a place than a possibility."

"Suggested Readings for Further Study," pp. 175-179.

>Lists other contemporary novels and annotates significant criticism of Catch-22.

1974 B SHORTER WRITINGS

1   ABRAHAMSON, IRVING. "A Modern American Horror Story?" Chicago Sunday Sun-Times Showcase, October 6, p. 1.
    Explains how "Slocum is a classic case of a man in the existential situation, doomed by his failure to respond to its challenge." Nonetheless, sees Something Happened as failing "to provide the rich experience of fine fiction."

2   ACKROYD, PETER. "Long Longings," Spectator, CXXXIII (October 26), 541.
    Concedes that Something Happened conveys "monumental inactivity with some panache," but is generally not enthusiastic about the book.

3   ALDRIDGE, JOHN. "Vision of a Man Raging in a Vacuum," Saturday Review World, II (October 19), 18-21.
    Notes the dangers facing the writer of a famous novel but observes that there is evidence everywhere in this new novel that Heller's originality is of the order that depends on the constant reexamination of imaginative premises and the deepening exploration of more and more complex areas of consciousness. Says he has produced a major work of fiction, an abrasively brilliant commentary on American

1974

life that must surely be recognized as the most important novel to appear in this country in at least a decade. Goes on to explain the individual's problem in dealing with the modern "collapse of moral and social structure that once helped to give purpose and continuity," the problem to which Heller has given dramatic form in Something Happened through psychological realism, and "a disquieting verisimilitude." See also 1975.B12.

4   ALEXANDER, JOHN. Charlotte News, November 3. (**)
    Recounts the moroseness of Something Happened but argues that it has redeeming value, for in Slocum, Heller has created a "character" for whom "history and culture have been internalized."

5   ALGREN, NELSON. Critic, XXXIII (October-December), 90.
    Reviewer thoroughly dislikes Slocum and feels uneasy because he is never sure if Heller rejects him. Decides there is no one to care about in Something Happened.

6   ANON. "Heller redux," Newsweek, LXXXIII (March 18), 113.
    Reports that Heller has turned new novel Something Happened over to publisher. Also gives some of Heller's comments on the nature of the book and the reason it took so long for him to write it. One notable distinction he makes is that "Catch-22 was external and this one is internal."

7   ANON. "Heller, Joseph--Something Happened," Kirkus Review, XLII (August 1), 825.
    Predicts that judging Heller's new novel will be "the hottest game of Russian roulette in town this fall" and describes the story and length of the book. Says we know Slocum "only too well and it is the recognition factor which counts, along with the book's bravura, expertise, and cumulative hook." Feels certain the book will be "read and read and read."

8   ANON. "PW Forecasts--Something Happened," Publishers' Weekly, CCVI (August 19), 75.
    Finds the book "extraordinary...a work of genuine brilliance...a true novel of our times." Reprinted July 14, 1975.

9   ANON. "New Heller Book," Richmond News Leader, August 21. (**)
    Announces publication of Something Happened to be in October and that it will be October Literary Guild selection.

1974

10 ANON. "Joseph Heller: 13 Years From 'Catch-22' To 'Something Happened,'" Harvard Crimson, October 11, pp. 3, 6.
   Excerpts from a conversation Heller had with Crimson editors Seth Kupferberg and Greg Lawless. Heller comments on style as content in Catch-22 and Something Happened, Catch-22 as depicting the military and our society after World War II, the endings of Catch-22 and Something Happened, Slocum's process of "depersonalization," and how Heller's literary goals differ from those Faulkner expressed in his Nobel speech.

11 ANON. "This Week's Arrivals," Christian Century, XCI (October 16), 970.
   Suggests that Something Happened will be "the big one" among serious novels published in the fall of 1974.

12 ANON. "New Heller Novel Is a Major Work," Jersey City Journal, October 22, p. 15.
   Advises that Something Happened is "not in any traditional way a sequel to Catch-22" but believes it is an "extraordinary revelation throughout and enriched by some of the best dialog written in English today."

13 ANON. Review of Something Happened. Little Rock Letter (A Review of Books), V (October 25), 1.
   Describes Slocum's life briefly and asserts that he has "sold his soul." Guesses that Something Happened will not be "well received."

14 ANON. "The Critics Are Saying," New York Post, October 26, p. 35.
   Summarizes Clemons (1974.B58), Vonnegut (1974.B210), Maddocks (1974.B125), and New York (1974.B81) reviews.

15 ANON. "Another U.S. View," Buffalo Courier-Express, October 27, p. 20.
   Announces that the American scene will be the material of Heller's new book.

16 ANON. "This Week's Books," Fort Worth Press, October 27, p. 4B.
   Brief review suggests that the patient reader will find much "clever" writing and many "trenchant observations on modern man" in Something Happened.
   Reprinted in Manchester (Connecticut) Herald, November 21. (**)

1974

17   ANON. "Playboy After Hours--Books," Playboy, XXI (November), 24.
     Dismisses Something Happened as "a novel in which nothing happens except that words accumulate page after page... ad nauseam." Reviewer would accept this if it had been written by Roth but by the "sole owner of the imagination that came up with Yossarian, Milo Minderbinder, Colonel Korn and all those others."

18   ANON. "Heller, in Sweden, Says Why He Likes Living in New York," New York Times, November 9, p. 22.
     Report on press conference in Sweden, where Heller is enjoying the tremendous success of Something Happened. He talks about his preference for success over failure and for New York City, in spite of its faults, over other cities. ("I can't take too much friendliness.")

19   ANON. "Brief Reviews of New Books," Charleston, (South Carolina) Evening Post, November 15, p. 9A.
     Includes Something Happened, a "well constructed" and "revealing" book about "the effects that life has on human beings."

20   ANON. "Full Fathom Five," Economist, CCLIII (November 30), 4-5.
     Judges Something Happened "a tour de force," though "it is not Catch-22." Praises the "agonizing realism" of the monologue, calling the language the "master-stroke."

21   ANON. "Christmas Books--Seven Significant Books of 1974," New York Times Book Review, December 1, p. 1.
     Commends Something Happened, "a serious painful, and important book" where Heller turned from "expansive comedy" to "claustrophobic tragedy."

22   ANON. "The First Books of Christmas," Washington Post Book World, December 8, p. 1.
     Includes Something Happened on "best books" list under heading "Once is quite enough." Describes the book briefly with complaint that the book suffers because of its imitation of Slocum's boredom.

23   ANON. Review of Something Happened. Booklist, LXXI (December 15), p. 406.
     Praises Heller's "verbal alchemy" in making Slocum's "numbing litany of self-pity and impotent humor into an arresting fabric of tensile strength."

1974

24 ANTONE, EVAN HAYWOOD. "Current Best Sellers," El Paso *Times Sundial*, December 8, p. 27.
   Uses the idea of Slocum as Everyman to suggest that Heller's theme is that man's only hope and ultimate destruction is man himself, observing that Slocum says, "Everyone seemed pleased with the way I've taken command."

25 ARTHUR, ROBERT ALAN. "Hanging Out," *Esquire*, LXXXII (September), 50, 54, 64.
   Article based on interviews with Heller and Murray Schisgal comments on the "brilliant" book Heller has written and his capacity for food. Heller talks in a leisurely way about his writing and eating habits as well as his love of teaching. He explains, also, how he came to call the narrator Bob Slocum.

26 AVANT, JOHN ALFRED. "Heller, Joseph. *Something Happened*," *Library Journal*, XCIX (October 1), 2500.
   Rejects *Something Happened* as a "dreadfully weak novel" full of "adult whining."

27 BAKER, A. T. "Czech 22," *Time*, CIII (March 25), 88.
   In this review of "The Good Soldier Svejk," its hero is compared to Yossarian. More importantly, the casual allusion to *Catch-22* in the title of this article gives an indication of how widespread knowledge of the novel is in American culture.

28 BANDLER, MICHAEL J. "For Heller's Man It's Catch-1974," *Providence Journal Arts and Leisure*, November 3, p. H-22.
   Declares that Heller has created "one of the more troubled and troubling creations of this or any other recent year."

29 BANNON, BARBARA. "PW Interviews: Joseph Heller," *Publishers' Weekly*, CCIV (September 30), 6.
   Interview-article reflects Heller's reasons for taking so long in writing *Something Happened* and his feeling about the book. Especially noteworthy are his comments on Slocum's autistic son as "a reflection of himself, symbolically."

30 BARKHAM, JOHN. Review of *Something Happened*, Cincinatti *Post*, October 12, p. 26.
   Classifies the novel as a "monument of narcissistic depression" and warns that it is a "study done in gray and black...in depth and with relentless realism."

Writings about Joseph Heller, 1961-1977

1974

This syndicated review also appeared in:
Covington (Kentucky) <u>Post</u>, October 12 (**);
Youngstown (Ohio) <u>Vindicator</u>, October 13, p. B8;
Washington (D.C.) <u>Federal Times</u>, October 23. (**)

31   BARRETT, MARY ELLIN. "Cosmo Reads the New Books," <u>Cosmopolitan</u>, CLXXVII (November), 12.
    A brief note.

32   BASS, MILTON R. "The Lively World," Berkshire (Massachusetts) <u>Eagle</u>, October 8, p. 6.
    Because of the attitude of fear so prevalent today and because Heller is such a successful novelist, reviewer feels, "This is a book you live with while you are reading it and that lives with you after you finish."

33   BAUER, MALCOLM. "Heller's Latest 'Hero' Wears Tarnish of Modern Times," (Portland, Oregon) <u>The Sunday Oregonian</u>, October 20, p. B21.
    Does not make a final judgment on <u>Something Happened</u>, simply says, "There will probably be those among 'Catch-22' fans who will be disappointed in this one, and others who will prefer Heller's second novel to his first. For the two are vastly different in form." Briefly describes the substance of <u>Something Happened</u>, observing that "The catch in <u>Something Happened</u> is that not very much happens."

34   BEAM, ALVIN. "Books--'Something Happened,'" Cleveland <u>Plain Dealer</u>, October 20, p. 8G.
    Describes the difficulties of getting through <u>Something Happened</u>, yet sees a "kind of truth" as well as "cult-minded untruth" in it. Doesn't see the characters as "wholly representative" of an American generation.

35   BECK, DAVID L. "New Heller Novel 'a Masterpiece'--but Tedious," Salt Lake City (Utah) <u>Tribune</u>, September 29. (**)
    Explains why Slocum is another Cathcart, claims a comparison of <u>Something Happened</u> with Joyce's <u>Ulysses</u> is "not frivolous," and extols Heller's perceptions and skill in writing prose.

36   BEDIENT, CALVIN. "Demons Ordered from Sears," <u>The Nation</u>, CCXIX (October 19), 377-378.
    Dismisses <u>Something Happened</u> as a "monstrous effort to make literature out of pettiness" even though it is "readable, largely because of its gritty perceptions." The review takes issue with Heller's cynicism in "accepting" self-serving behavior as "all there is."

1974

37 BELL, PEARL K. "Heller's Trial by Tedium," New Leader, LVII (October 28), 17-18.
   Finds Something Happened totally boring in spite of the promise in its beginning. Calls it "a willful, disastrous exercise in futility."

38 BENKE, RICHARD. "Teetering on Boundary Between Disaster, Farce," Pasadena Star-News, October 6, p. B10.
   An enthusiastic review which looks at Slocum as "Yossarian revisited."

39 BENNET, RAY. "Joe Heller: The Laughter's Over," Windsor (Ontario) Star, November 9, p. 50.
   Explains why Slocum's apathy makes him a Mr. Hyde as opposed to Yossarian, an optimistic Dr. Jekyll.

40 BERNARD, BINA. "The Author of 'Catch-22' Brings Fourth Another Novel," People, (October 7), 48-49. (**)
   A feature article which reports briefly on Something Happened but mostly on Heller's lifestyle. Includes pictures of Heller with wife, with writer friends, and alone in New York City bachelor apartment.

41 BERTHELSEN, JOHN. "'Something Happened'--Joseph Heller's New One Is Not Another Catch-22," Sacramento Bee, October 20, p. P8.
   Compares Slocum to a Dostoevsky hero and classifies Something Happened with French existentialism of the 1940's and 1950's "where man's only hope in an insane world is to examine himself, realize the hopelessness of his situation, and continue to exist and cope anyway." Emphasizes that this is not "standard WASP-suburban novel despair."

*42 BINNI, FRANCESCO. Narrativa americana degli anni sessanta. Torino, Italy: E.R.I.
   According to Rolando Anzilotti in the "Italian Contributions" section of American Literary Scholarship, X, 448, this book examines the trends that distinguish Heller and other modern writers, primarily their "new sociopolitical culture" and their literature's sense of "exhaustion" and "anticipation."

43 BLACKWOOD, CAROLINE. "The Horrors of Peace," The London Times Literary Supplement, October 25, p. 1183.
   Appreciates Heller's "ferocious, gory, and memorable" attacks on American companies and middle-class family life but finds Slocum unbelievable as a narrator because he

1974

seems too "commonplace and tiresome" to have the "superior insights" Heller endows him with and because he seems too flawed with fears to be as sexually competent as he claims to be.

44 BLYTHE, RONALD. "A Novel Full of Pleasure," London Sunday Times, October 27, p. 36.
Objects to Heller's "familiar targets" in American writing but finds Slocum's feelings for his son interesting. Overall, the "sight of a man in a trap emerges with intermittent forcefulness."

45 BOARDMAN, KATHRYN G. "Heller Novel Full of Hopelessness," St. Paul (Minnesota) Pioneer Press Focus, November 3, p. 10.
Calls Something Happened "a big, beautifully put together novel." Opinion is that Slocum's tragedy is not the accident with his son but that Slocum is able to go back to his job and carry on with preparations for the convention.

46 BONI, JOHN. "Analogous Form: Black Comedy and Some Jacobean Plays," Western Humanities Review, XXVIII (Summer), 201-215.
Observes similarities between Jacobean plays and contemporary writing, noting particularly Catch-22's mixture of comic and tragic elements as a way to provide the "dimensions of experience" and valuing of self-preservation.

47 BRADY, CHARLES A. "Fine Novels for Yule List," Buffalo News, December 1, p. 7.
Notes that "no serious student of the American novel should overlook Joseph Heller's Something Happened."

48 BRESLIN, JOHN B. "Autumn Book Leaves," America, CXXXI (October 5), 173-176.
Article on books to be published soon includes Heller's "long anticipated second novel Something Happened."

49 _____. "Living with Absurdity," America, CXXXI (October 26), 235-236.
Depicts Something Happened as an attempt to create a mirror-image of Catch-22 where the "complications, contradictions, and absurdities are generated from within" rather than from the army or external world. Calls it a "fascinating tour de force, but ultimately an unsatisfying one" because he eventually grew tired of Bob Slocum.

1974

50 BUNKE, JOAN. "Heller's Babbit," Des Moines Sunday Register, October 20, p. 3B.

   Compares Slocum with Sinclair Lewis' Babbit, concluding that "Where Babbit knew too little about himself and his drives, perhaps Slocum knows too much." Also compares Something Happened with Catch-22: the latter gave readers a feeling of solidarity against "them" whereas in Something Happened "we're all in the mess alone, each out to 'get' the other." Judges the book "hard medicine to swallow" because there is some of Slocum in all of us.

51 BUSS, DOUGLAS. "Doesn't Match Catch," Hamilton (Ontario) Spectator, November 2, p. 4.

   Decides Joseph Heller is a gifted writer but a poor editor: he leaves too much in the text, and his highly-touted second novel is a disappointment.

52 CADY, RICHARD. "'Something Happened' to Shake Mediocrity," Indianapolis Star, November 10, p. 14.

   Predicts long popularity for this "ponderous, incisive" examination of the "modern American psyche."

53 CECCHINI, PAT. (University of) Chicago Maroon, December 3, p. 7.

   Offers an explanation of the importance of Derek on the way to judging Something Happened "more than a statement of contemporary urban angst"...a "serious consideration of the problems of growth and knowledge."

54 CHESSLER, MICHAEL. "Something Happened," Grinnell Scarlet and Black (Grinnell College, Iowa), December 6, p. 5.

   Hails Something Happened as a classic which leaves one "breathless" because Heller captures so much of contemporary experience.

55 CHILDS, JAMES. "Frozen in Hell's Final Circle," New Haven Register, October 13, p. 5D.

   Classifies the novel as "masterful," "perhaps the most significant of the decade," and describes how it is a "pessimistic evaluation by a contemporary middle-class man of his middle-class life."

56 CLARK, JOHN. "Heller Creates Another Memorable Character," Wichita Falls Times Sunday Magazine, November 10, p. 4.

   Finds Slocum "embarrassingly real--a product of the American system that requires domination as the key to strength and success and shuns any sign of emotion as a sign of weakness."

1974

57   CLAYPOOL, BOB. "Everyman's Reality," Houston Post Spotlight, October 13, p. 18.
  Describes Something Happened as "first-rate Heller," and observes the way he has given Slocum "such convincing life and breath that even the stock situations emerge as Everyman's reality."

58   CLEMONS, WALTER. "Comedy of Fear." Newsweek, LXXXIV (October 14), 116, H8.
  A tentative review of Something Happened: "[it] will take time to digest." Sees the new novel as being "morose, slow and thoughtful" whereas Catch-22 was "morose, fast and buoyant." Reviewer does find "brilliant pages," however, in Something Happened, "an epic of the everyday." He is moved by the final catastrophe but thinks it leaves "an aftertaste of contrivance."

59   _____. "Two Critics Choose the Best of '74," Newsweek, LXXXIV (December 30), 62-63.
  Two months after his original tentative review of Something Happened (1974.B58), Clemons judges it the best book he has read during 1974 "because it interested and bothered me most; it sticks in my mind and won't be settled."

60   COLLINS, THOMAS. "'Something Happened': A Story of America," Newsday, October 16, p. 13A.
  In addition to explaining Bob Slocum as a man "who seems doubly monstrous because he contains so much that is in all of us...," Collins comments on the critics' "respectful" but "cautious" appraisals and relates some of Heller's comments in an interview, mainly that Slocum's views are not Heller's ("I'm a pretty jolly person, really, most of the time"). Reprinted in:
    Middletown (Connecticut) Press, February 11, 1975, p. 6;
    "Are Human Days Full of Trepidation?" Austin (Texas) American-Statesman, November 10. (**)

61   CONARROE, JOEL. "Heller's Tense, Wise, Second Novel is Superior to 'Catch-22,'" Philadelphia Evening Bulletin, October 6, Sec. II, p. 3.
  Doubts if Something Happened will be the popular success that Catch-22 was, but finds it "disturbing, wise, funny, and superior in every way to his first work...clearly written for grown-ups."

1974

62   _____. "Year's Top Fiction--Roth, Heller Novels the Most Impressive," Philadelphia Sunday Bulletin, December 1, Sec. II, p. 3.
       Lists Something Happened as #2, though "not recommended for potential depressives."

63   COOPER, ARTHUR. "Behind Closed Doors," (Garden City, New York) Newsday, October 13, pp. 36, 40.
       Describes Slocums' predicament and counsels the reader, "Read this book at risk to your psyche. But read it."

64   CRITTENDEN, YVONNE. Review of Something Happened, Toronto Sun, November 22. (**)
       A less than enthusiastic notice--the reviewer likened the novel to "a long visit to someone else's psychiatrist."

65   CROSS, LESLIE. "It's a Gala Season--but Not Everything is Fun," Milwaukee Journal, October 6, Part V, p. 4.
       Mentions that Heller was at a Boston book fair and that Something Happened is one of "the best promoted titles of the season."

66   DeMOTT, BENJAMIN. "The Significant Self--Bob at Forty-Five," Atlantic Monthly, CCXXXIV (October), 106-108.
       Objects to the lack of "drive" in Something Happened, to its "static and mechanical quality, dependence on a single trope (sustained unresponsiveness)."

67   DESRUISSEAUX, PAUL. "A Powerful, Tragic Novel of a Life Coming Apart," San Francisco Examiner and Chronicle, October 13, p. 30.
       Recommends Something Happened enthusiastically: "an important book, one that should make a difference in the lives of its readers...a powerful indictment of the rotten, meaningless lives so very many people let themselves live, and a daring attempt to change them."

68   DOAR, HARRIET. "New Heller Book Annoying: Message Will Not Go Away," Charlotte Observer, October 27, p. 7B.
       Even though Something Happened is depressing, one "must" read it.

69   DOBBS, KILDARE. "Success Is a Willing Victim. Peace According to Catch-22," Toronto Globe and Mail Entertainment, November 9, p. 31.
       Describes Slocum and his life, concluding that Slocum is a success by American standards: "he is gradually becoming exactly the kind of person the American way of life demands."

1974

70 DRUIAN, GREG. "Can't Happen Here," Portland Scribe, November 2-8, p. 22.
    Relates Slocum's problems and provides some thought-provoking speculation as to the reasons for his problems.

71 DUHAMEL, P. ALBERT. "'Something Happened' to Heller," Boston Sunday Herald Advertiser Book Guide, October 6, p. A6.
    Disagrees with advance publicity that suggested Slocum was Everyman. Feels most people's motives are more complicated than Slocum acknowledges and that it is not necessary "to admit to being worse than we are to avoid being hypocritical." Does praise some of the dialogue.

72 EPSTEIN, JOSEPH. "Joseph Heller's Milk Train: Nothing More to Express," Washington Post Book, October 6, p. 1.
    Describes Catch-22 as the novel which "fed the fiction" of writers of the next generation and Something Happened as "feed[ing] off their work." Finds Something Happened of "slight interest in itself" but of greater interest in "demonstrating that fiction written under the assumptions of the post-Modernist sensibility cannot sustain itself over the length of a large novel." Reprinted in "The Literary Scene," New York Post, October 23, p. 52.

73 EVETT, ROBERT. "Something Happened but Not Much," Washington Star-News Portfolio, October 13, p. 13.
    Lists a number of other American writers who have written in the "middle-aged commuter novel" genre and complains that Heller has done nothing more original in this book of "appalling length." Does acknowledge Heller's "superior language."

74 EWING, JAMES. "Book Beat," Nashville Banner, December 14, p. 5.
    Reports Heller wrote to thank Sandy Seawright for a review he wrote of Something Happened. See 1974.B178.

75 FINDSEN, OWEN. "The New 'Big' Novels," Cincinnati Enquirer, August 15, p. 44.
    Predicts Something Happened will be a best seller and that the critics will pan it and then "return to it in another year to explain why they were wrong."

*76 FINKEL, JAN M. "Techniques of Portraying the Grotesque Character in Selected Writings of Nathaniel Hawthorne, Sherwood Anderson, and Joseph Heller. Ph.D. dissertation, Indiana University. Cited and abstracted in Dissertation Abstracts International, XXXIV (June), 7750-7751.

1974

*77 FITZGERALD, SISTER ELLEN. "World War II in the American Novel: Hawkes, Heller, Kosinski, and Vonnegut." Ph.D. dissertation, University of Notre Dame. Cited and abstracted in Dissertation Abstracts International, XXXV (December), 3736-3737.

78 FORSYTH, ROBERT. "Heller's Newest," Sacramento (California) Union, September 22, p. F8.
    Regrets that Heller, who had the ability to touch people with Catch-22, has written a "mostly boring, mostly trite, mostly depressing, and mostly sad" second novel. Argues that the suburban life depicted in Something Happened is not "the American Way."

*79 FORT, DEBORAH CHARNLEY. "Contrast Epic: A Study of Joseph Heller's Catch-22 (1961), Gunter Grass's The Tin Drum, (Die Blechtrommel [1959]), John Barth's The Sot-Weed Factor (1960, revised 1967), and Vladmir Nabokov's Pale Fire (1962)." Ph.D. dissertation, University of Maryland, Cited and abstracted in Dissertation Abstracts International, XXXV (December), 3677.

80 FREMONT-SMITH, ELIOT. "'Something' Is Happening," New York, VII (September 16), 60-69.
    Preview of Something Happened with brief commentary on Heller's life, especially the preparation of this novel. Includes photograph of Heller by Jill Krementz.

81 _____. "Heller's Hell," New York, VII (September 30), 78-79.
    Praises Something Happened as a "very fine, wrenchingly depressing new novel" which "gnaws at one, slowly and almost nuzzingly at first, mercilessly toward the end."

82 FULLER, EDMUND. "Heller's How Glum Was My Valley," Wall Street Journal, November 18, p. 22.
    Reacts to Aldrich's praise of Something Happened (1974.B3) as "abrasively brilliant commentary on American Life," claiming that "We have met Slocum and his like before; we've walked this dreary route with them ad nauseam." Claims they are not the products of a rotten society but of "a worked out vein of the novel, arising in part out of a host of liberal assumptions about, and shallow conceptions of, a society whose deep ills and troubles--real enough, God knows--these novelists are unequipped to diagnose and for which they are totally unable to prescribe." Feels Something Happened ends with "no enlightenment, no new insight, and no hope." See also 1975.B12.

1974

83 GATES, JOHN D. "Masterpiece," Wilmington (Delaware) *Morning News*, November 7, p. 39.
    Calls *Something Happened* "heavy reading" but "probably something of a literary masterpiece."

84 GLEASON, RALPH J. "A 'Catch-22' Admirer on Heller's Latest," *San Francisco Sunday Examiner and Chronicle--This Week*, November 10, p. 30.
    Cautions that *Something Happened* is not an easy book to get into but urges everybody to read it and "see your life in clearer, and more devastating terms."

85 _____. "Heller's American Nightmare," *Rolling Stone*, November 21, (**)
    Extols *Something Happened* as "*the* important novel of the seventies--perhaps the great American novel." Calls it a study of the American Dream and of love "made malevolent by fear."

86 GLENDINNING, VICTORIA. "Some Extra," *New Statesman*, LXXXVIII (October 25), 591.
    Relates how Heller takes "560 pages chiefly to document" the malaise of modern America, though not in so "hellishly funny" a style as Vonnegut's. Judges *Something Happened* "ordinary."

87 GOLAY, HELEN. "Books for the Holidays," *Viva* (December), p. 37. (**)
    Short listing which contrasts *Something Happened* to *Catch-22* and finds the new novel about fear "overwritten and self-defeating."

88 GORNER, PETER. "13 Years after 'Catch-22,' Heller's Happened Again," Chicago *Tribune*, September 30, p. 14.
    A cursory review of *Something Happened*, plus notes from an interview with Heller and reports on his life-style. Interview notes include some interesting comments by Heller on his style and distortion of reality, *e.g.* "But I'm trying to write about people experiencing things that many other people will have experienced. So while Slocum (or Yossarian) isn't me or anyone else, he's also not unlike anyone else."

89 GROSSMAN, EDWARD. "Yossarian Lives," *Commentary*, LVIII (November), 78, 80, 82-84.
    Sees Slocum as Yossarian, who has survived but feels as if he is "living in hell." Contends that Yossarian's reasons for deserting did not ring true. There is more

1974

   integrity in the "dreary" vision of Something Happened, but the novel "sinks under its weight."

90 GRUMBACH, DORIS. "Fine Print," New Republic, CLXXI (December 21), 24-25.
   Agrees with Kennedy review (1974.B110) that Something Happened is "honest," "original," and "fascinating" in brief "re-review."

91 H. P. E. "Arts in Review--Something Happened," Long Island Business Review, November 6-12, p. 17.
   Explains how Slocum seems a success to the world and a failure to himself. Suggests Something Happened may turn out to be "THE quintessential American novel."

92 HALLMAN, RANDOLPH. "Heller Serves Readers Grim, Sad Fare," Richmond (Virginia) News Leader, November 20. (**)
   Feels the novel is compelling but lacking in the "final thrust of greatness," because Heller leaves it too much in the control of Slocum and because the ending is too contrived.

93 HALSEY, LOUIS. "Dramatic Tension in Catch-22," Midwest Quarterly, XV (Winter), 190-197.
   Studies the pattern of "dramatic tension between the preposterous events of the story and the built-in dimension of laughter." Points up the absurd and exaggeration, the way war makes everyone including Yossarian and the chaplain irrational, and the technique of making the responsive reader "walk a tight-rope as he leans first to riotous humor and then tips to the side of black tragedy," as the bitter humor "flaunts" a resistance to the pain of life but never ignores it.

94 HAND, JUDSON. "Heller's 'Something Happened' Finds Tragic Humor in Suburbia," New York News, September 29, p. 14.
   Says Something Happened puts Heller in a category with other of "today's writers" who "prefer to depict men who, having achieved the comfortable life, are rendered incapable of enjoying it by guilt and frustration," but judges the novel "an authentic slice of hell in suburbia, complete with well-wrought examples of Heller's particular brands of irony and absurdity and laced with telling one-liners."

95 HARRELL, DON. "We've Waited a Long Time for Joseph Heller's Second Book," Houston Chronicle, October 13, p. 8.

Writings about Joseph Heller, 1961-1977

1974

Insists that "our interest is kept" in Slocum in spite of all his "trivial viciousness," and "We come to know him as thoroughly as we're likely to know any fictional character." Characterizes the novel as "profoundly sad."

96   HASKILL, MOLLY. "Voice Books," <u>Village Voice</u>, October 24, p. 33.
Sees Heller's idealization of childhood as a flaw of the novel but praises his "uncanny ability to evoke...the child in us" and to show us the "crime of the family...to have shown us one shining glimpse of something we would later call happiness, leading us to think we could find it again. And we never do."

97   HAVELIN, JIM. "Stark Lesson in Despair," Rochester <u>Democrat and Chronicle,</u> October 13, Sec. H, p. 2.
Recounts Slocum's weaknesses and attempts to ready himself for what may happen. Predicts the book will open wounds.

98   HILLS, RUST. "Writing," <u>Esquire</u>, LXXXII (August), 20, 28.
Hills reveals his "worst mistake as an editor, not publishing parts of <u>Catch-22</u> in <u>Esquire</u> when it was offered to [him]," but goes on to argue that neither <u>Catch-22</u> nor <u>Something Happened</u> is really a "major literary novel" because of the repetitiousness and lack of compression in both. Does find good qualities, especially in dialogue, in <u>Something Happened</u>; says readers will respond personally to it as they would to a Thematic Apperception Test..

99   HOLLIDAY, BARBARA. "Footnotes--The Book Editor's Best Bets," Detroit <u>Free Press</u>, September 22, p. 5C.
Predicts <u>Something Happened</u> may disappoint Yossarian fans because it is "a middle-aged man's book" but that it "will probably be the season's most controversial and funny novel."

100   HOUSTON, GARY. "A Novelist Who Knows He Cannot Be Rushed," <u>Chicago Sunday Sun-Times Showcase</u>, October 6, pp. 1, 3.
Report of interview where Heller talked of his writing and possibilities for making <u>Something Happened</u> into a movie. Interesting particularly because of Heller's comments on the way he divorces himself from the project once he sells a book to the movies.

101   HOUSTON, LEVIN. "Best Sellers Aren't Always Best Books," Fredericksburg (Virginia) <u>Free Lance-Star</u>, November 20, p. 4.
Regrets that "Heller has never learned that brevity is the soul of wit." Adds that life has turned out as one

1974

might expect for Slocum: "...at 17, he was an uninteresting, sex-mad adolescent crud. Twenty-five years later, the same description applies to him."

102 HOWAT, MARK. "Who Is Bob Slocum?" (Bergen County, New Jersey) The Record Lifestyle, October 16, pp. 1, 12.
Another rave review: "an extraordinary novel...the literary event of the season." Sees Slocum as "an entire generation of middle-class white males, born about 1920, old enough to fight in World War II, young enough to believe in the American Dream." He says, "Between then and now, something happened, not just to Bob Slocum, but to his whole generation, and that is Heller's story." This review also includes notes from an interview with Heller in which he explained why he was deliberately repetitive and why Derek was the only member of the Slocum family mentioned by name.

103 HOWE, RAY. "'Marvelous,' 'Memorable,'" Chattanooga Times, October 27, p. B2.
Expresses some annoyance at Heller's use of parenthetic sentences but still thinks Something Happened "could be the major novel of 1974."

104 HYMAN, ANN. "What's Going to Happen? Something," Jacksonville Florida Times-Union and Journal, November 10, p. 11.
Tells enough about Something Happened to show that almost no one will "like" it but that it is "a great book and one to be taken seriously." Suggests that critics will argue for years over whether "what happens" in the end is redemptive or damning.

105 JANOFF, BRUCE. "Black Humor, Existentialism, and Absurdity: a Generic Confusion," Arizona Quarterly, XXX (Winter), 293-304.
Sees Catch-22 as absurdist black humor until "The Eternal City" chapter when Yossarian develops altruistic attitudes and takes an existential posture of commitment to more than preserving his own life. Writer feels this disrupts the novel's thematic momentum.

106 _____. "Black Humor, Absurdity and Technique," Studies in the Twentieth Century, XIII (Spring), 39-49.
Explains how Heller "integrates" his absurd content with absurd form.

107 JEWETT, DAVE. "'Something Happened' Unlike Any Other Novel," Vancouver (Washington) Columbian, November 3, p. 31.

1974

Rates <u>Something Happened</u> "for those who can stick with it...rewarding, memorable reading, with characters who are so well drawn they nearly come to life on the pages."

108 K. J. A. "Heller's 'Something Happened' Long-Winded but Worthwhile," Charleston <u>Evening News</u>, November 3, p. 20E.
    Finds much truth in <u>Something Happened</u>, even though it is "neither witty nor compassionate."

109 KAGIS, INDRA. "Where Nothing Is Not a Zero," Montreal <u>Star</u>, November 16, p. D5.
    Insists, "You have to read this book. It's not a scream, it's a wail." Calls Slocum this decade's counterpart of Prufrock, <u>Something Happened</u> "possibly the most significant novel of the decade.

110 KENNEDY, WILLIAM. "Endlessly Honest Confession," <u>New Republic</u>, CLXXI (October 19), 17-19.
    Although often "bored and exasperated" by Slocum, reviewer could not stop reading. Calling Heller "a big metaphor man," explains what he feels Slocum's speech, company, family, and lost girlfriend Virginia Markowitz stand for. Places Heller in "the first rank of American writers."

111 KEOUGH, WILLIAM T. "'Something Happened' after Catch-22," Philadelphia <u>Evening Bulletin</u>, October 3, pp. 8, 11.
    Recounts an interview where Heller discussed his career, particularly the way he conceived of <u>Something Happened</u> in 1962, how he teaches writing, his feeling about God, and life as a "celebrated author."

112 KING, FRANCIS. "Sting for a WASP," London <u>Sunday Telegraph</u>, October 27, p. 22.
    Rates <u>Something Happened</u> a "disappointment," because, though the "marvellous vivacity and vividness of style still remain" in Heller's writing, the book's theme is "too much like too many American novels...a WASP business executive, nailed to the cross of material success yet kicking in the teeth anyone who tries to help him off it." Also judges the climax where Slocum "hugs his son to death" too clumsy in its symbolism.

113 KIRSCH, ROBERT. "Heller's Catch-23: The Entrapment of Everyman," <u>Los Angeles Times Calendar</u>, October 13, pp. 1, 68.
    In spite of his feeling that Heller's choice of narrator is a mistake, this reviewer decides that the "tension between love and hate, between craftiness and faded ideals, between pretense and feeling, keeps the reader transfixed."

1974

114   KISER, THELMA SCOTT. "Book Review," Ashland (Kentucky) Daily Independent, December 29, p. 2.
      Calls Something Happened a "profound and disturbing portrait of the human condition.

115   KLINKOWITZ, JEROME. "Joseph Heller's Brilliance Is Again Apparent," Richmond (Virginia) Times-Dispatch, December 8, p. F5.
      Disagrees with readers who call Slocum cold or vicious, seeing the book as "a sensitive man's tale of a threatening and depressive world." Focuses particularly on Slocum's failure to shield his son from the torment he feels.

116   KLINKOWITZ, JOSEPH. "A Final Word for Black Humor," Contemporary Literature, XV (Spring), 271-276.
      In review of Black Humor Fiction of the Sixties, merely lists Heller as one of the writers often called "Black Humorists" who has veered off in another direction and notes the author's error in listing 1955 as the publication date of Catch-22.

117   LASSON, ROBERT. "A Surfeit of Bitches," West Side Literary Review, October 31, p. 9.
      Objects to the lack of editing in the "overindulgent, overwritten, overweight" aspect of Something Happened; nonetheless, rates it as "so incisive, so brilliant, so painful that it's a pity there isn't less of it."

118   LAWLESS, GREG. "Connive to Survive, Stay Alive Til Five," Harvard Crimson, October 11, p. 2.
      Recommends Something Happened as a study of "the American ethic...the effects of the corporate state on indivuals."

119   LeCLAIRE, THOMAS. Cincinnati Enquirer, October 3, p. 43.
      Urges reading of Something Happened, "the slow train to the interior of ordinary life" and praises Heller for bringing "the concentrated force of art" to a hackneyed situation. Longer than most reviews, gives special attention to Slocum's family, "the creative center of the book, a domestic Moby Dick" and to Heller's style, "an accomplishment of rare feeling and high art."

120   LEHMANN-HAUPT, CHRISTOPHER. "His First Book Since 'Catch-22,'" New York Times, October 1, p. 39.
      Contrasts Something Happened with Catch-22, tells about Slocum's problems (calling his head "a map of chauvinistic America"), then pronounces the new novel "a satisfying successor."

Writings about Joseph Heller, 1961-1977

1974

This syndicated review also appeared in:
St. Petersburg (Florida) Times, October 6, p. 12E;
Akron (Ohio) Beacon Journal, October 6, p. F13;
Tucson (Arizona) Star, October 6, p. H2;
Honolulu Star Bulletin, October 13, p. C13;
Omaha World-Herald, October 16, p. 4;
San Jose Mercury, November 10. (**)

121 LHAMON, W. T., JR. "Welcome Back, Joseph Heller," Miami Herald, October 13, pp. 1L, 7L.
Puts forth a warning that "while this novel is easily the best so far this year, its news is all bad..., the mood of this novel may well reflect the way we all now feel: simultaneously mellower and more bitter than a decade ago." Also speculates about the place of Heller's literature in contemporary culture and world literature.

122 LLOYD, PAT. Note on Something Happened. Pensacola News-Journal, December 15, p. 13E.
Brief listing calls Something Happened a "serious and painful" novel--"almost like sitting next to a stranger on a plane and hearing his life story."

123 LUPTON, WILLIAM L. "What Happened? 'Something' Is Answer Enough," Baltimore Sun, October 20, p. D5.
Although Heller's "stripped down, long-winded" technique in Something Happened may lose some readers, reviewer finds it worthwhile for giving "the raw feel of human life" and a "human image of the age."

124 McHUGH, ROY. "Heller Boring in New Novel," Pittsburgh Press, October 13, p. G5.
After describing Something Happened as "suspenseful and boring, artfully constructed and repetitious," concludes: "The critics say you better read it, because who knows? It's so different it might be a classic." This review is also noteworthy for its observation that Slocum goes on "like Molly Bloom...[but] in complete sentences."

125 MADDOCKS, MELVIN. "Boring from Within," Time, CIV (October 14), 87-88.
Sees Something Happened as "second installment" of Catch-22, describing Slocum as "dying" in "a vile and muddy peace." Concludes that the novel fails because it is a "tired retread of the anti-hero." Article goes on to comment on Heller's "slow" life and work style.

1974

126 MALIN, IRVING. "Something Happened," <u>Commonweal</u>, CI (December 20), 272-273.
   Analyzes Slocum's obsession with doors, his attempts to keep others and even his own past behind the "frosted glass" of metaphysical doors, his fears, and his "voice." Concludes, "I will not easily forget Slocum and his doors."

127 MANNING, MARGARET. "Litany of Doom," Boston <u>Globe</u>, October 14, p. 53.
   Praises Heller's "heart-breakingly believable dialogue" but predicts <u>Something Happened</u> will not be the success <u>Catch-22</u> was because Slocum is "a zombie, impossible to identify with" and the theme is "what difference does it make?"

128 _____. "About Books--The Confessions of a New Editor," Boston <u>Globe</u>, October 20, p. B23.
   Mentions that she is less enthusiastic than most reviewers about <u>Something Happened</u>.

129 MANO, D. KEITH. "Fine Writing That Irks," <u>National Review</u>, XXVI (November 22), 1364.
   Mainly an objection to the effusiveness and repetition of the style of <u>Something Happened</u> though does acknowledge some value in it.

130 MARCUS, ADRIANNE. "Are Men Really Like That?" Pacific <u>Sun</u>, Week of November 14-20, p. 8.
   Contrasts <u>Something Happened</u> to Doris Lessing's <u>The Golden Notebook</u> and judges the book, as well as Slocum, "second best."

131 MAYER, ALLEN J. "'Something Happened,'" <u>Riverside (California) Press-Enterprise Books</u>, November 3, p. C-6.
   Admires Heller's "brilliant achievement" in "giving frightening specificity to our social and psychological entropy," thereby writing "perhaps the most important and incisive novel of the last decade."

132 MELLORS, JOHN. "What Happened?" <u>The Listener</u>, XCII (October 24), 551.
   Admires Heller's sections on the office, which reviewer believes have much of the "nerve and sardonic humour" of <u>Catch-22</u> but finds the sections on family life "dull and lacking in incident." Concludes that "Heller's great gifts shine fitfully through <u>Something Happened</u> where they blazed from the pages of <u>Catch-22</u>."

1974

133 MICHELFELDER, DIANE. "Nothing Happens in 'Something,'" Bryn Mawr-Haverford College News, September 27. (**)
   A non-committal review which notes the difference between the "tight" prose of Catch-22 and Something Happened, which has only two events in 569 pages. Decides it might sell "among the commuter crowd."

134 MIDDLETON, ELLIOT. "Author Falls into Trap of Being Boring," (Denver) Rocky Mountain News Now, November 3, p. 29.
   Objects that Heller becomes boring when he means only to depict boredom and that he describes only "a very narrow segment of our national life."

135 MILLHAUSER, MILTON. "We All Manage Well--Until Something Happens," Bridgeport (Connecticut) Post, December 1. (**)
   Describes Heller's originality in this novel, especially its "carefully devised and meticulously controlled style."

136 MOODY, MINNIE HITE. "Hero Runs Scared in Heller Stunner," Columbus (Ohio) Dispatch, October 20, p. I8.
   Declares Something Happened "truer than life"; feels Heller has developed his "perception [of] the comical aspects of the grimmest, most tragic moments...to stunning perfection."

137 MORTON, KATHRYN. "About Books--Heller's Fumble," (Norfolk) Virginian Pilot, November 17, Sec. C, p. 6.
   Acknowledges that Something Happened is an "artful" book of "substance," but finds it boring. Accepts Slocum as a man, but not as Man.

138 MUSSON, KEN. "Even Second Best Heller Is Outstanding," Tampa Tribune-Times, November 10, p. 5C.
   Decides "Heller remains a genius.... But Heller's best remains his best." Offers a different interpretation of the ending: when the boy dies, Slocum can "shun the woes and fears of his own childhood" and become a man.

139 NAGEL, JAMES. "Two Brief Manuscript Sketches," Modern Fiction Studies, XX (Summer), 221-224.
   Reproduces two of Heller's early sketches for Catch-22. One describes the characters as different ethnic types with Yossarian as a Jew who cares only about women. Nagel notes that Heller has later commented, in the Krassner interview (1962.B40), on his decision to make Yossarian "outside culture in every way--ethnically as well as others." The other sketch also shows an ethnic concern, later to be

1974

submerged. As Nagel observes, these manuscripts reveal "the speculative nature of the possibilities which were occurring to Heller."

140 _____. "Catch-22 and Angry Humor: A Study of the Normative Values of Satire," <u>Studies in American Humor</u>, I (October), 99-106.

Attempts to codify and explain Heller's humor, demonstrating how <u>Catch-22</u> is an example of Juvenalian satire in that the comedy is not gentle entertainment but "harsh derision and directed social attack...hitting out against definable groups within American society." Also, its methods of characterization, episodic and cyclic plotting, the ubiquitous image, and a "normative base" of values by which to measure the society are typical of such satire. The conclusion moves from comic to tragic satire, in the tradition of Juvenal, as Yossarian, left alone in the role of tragic victim, escapes the mad military world "to become an agent of his own destiny."

141 NATANSOHN, DEBBIE. "Heller's Second Coming," Albany <u>Times-Union</u>, October 27. (**)

Praises <u>Something Happened</u> for being "beautifully written" because it "penetrates the consciousness of the successful American everyman."

142 NATHAN, JEFF. Los Angeles <u>Free Press</u>, December 9, pp. 31-32.

Reads <u>Something Happened</u> as a sequel to <u>Catch-22</u> with many similar qualities and believes it to be the finest novel he's read "since...well, since <u>Catch-22</u>."

143 NEWQUIST, RAY. "Books of the Week--'Something Happened' a Triumph for Heller," Chicago <u>Star</u>, October 27, p. 4.

Another rave review: Heller is "the top young novelist on the American scene"; <u>Something Happened</u> is "a solid triumph, the best single novel that agonizingly appraises life in our times." Explains the intense pain Heller makes us feel as a result of seeing much of ourselves in Slocum. Substantially the same review by Newquist appeared in "Books and Authors," <u>Palm Springs Life</u> (November), pp. 78-80. (**)

144 NORDELL, RODERICK. "Fiction--Joseph Heller's Catch-22," <u>Christian Science Monitor</u>, October 9, p. 13.

A generally favorable review with reservations about some of the "obscuring dross" in the way of its energy and originality. Says "Catch-22" is coping with existence itself.

Writings about Joseph Heller, 1961-1977

1974

This review also appeared in:
Oakland (California) Tribune, October 20 (**);
Framingham (Massachusetts) News, November 3 (**).

145   NORMAN, BETH. "Beth Looks at Books," Boston Herald-American, December 26, p. 104.
        A brief summary of Something Happened.

146   NORTH, KERRY. "Something Did Happen in Second Book," Corpus Christi Caller, October 20, p. 5C.
        Cautions readers not to expect the humor and drama of Catch-22 in Something Happened; nonetheless, feels they will discover it is a "mature work of great subtlety and feeling."

147   NUGENT, TOM. "Joseph Heller Is a Long Way From 'Catch-22'-- And Enjoying It He Says," Detroit Free Press, February. (**)
        Interview-article which gives some valuable insights into the similarity between Slocum's company and Time, Inc., the influence of other writers on Heller, and why it takes Heller so long to write a novel.

148   NYE, ROBERT. "Books of the Day," (Manchester) Guardian, November 2, p. 21.
        Declares that in the end of Something Happened "Slocum has smothered his life, as he smothers his material, as he smothers everything in sight in this long, easy, discomforting brilliant novel.

149   OLSON, CLARENCE E. "Little Boy Blue...," St. Louis Post-Dispatch, October 6, p. 4C.
        Draws a number of comparisons with Catch-22 and argues that Slocum in the end accepts the kind of "deal" Yossarian rejected. Suggests that the "gist" of the novel is "that the right part of the child must survive in order to produce a fully matured adult." Predicts that the book will be popular mostly with readers "old enough to see the full trajectory of their dreams and to mourn their lost innocence."

150   PACE, ERIC. "Fall Books: One Cat, Lots of Big Names," Minneapolis Tribune, September 8, p. 10D.
        Mentions Something Happened to be published in October.

1974

151 PARKER, ROY. "Three Giants Included in New Autumn Fiction," Fayetteville *Observer-Times*, October 6. (**)
Puts *Something Happened* "at the head of the class for trying at least for this season" with the reservation that it gives only a "new twist," not a "new dimension," to the organization man story.

152 PARRILL, WILLIAM. "New Heller May Raise a Good Many Questions," Nashville *Tennessean*, October 20, Sec. F, p. 10.
Notes the difference in tone between *Catch-22* and *Something Happened* and suggests that *Something Happened* may be "critic-proof," even "time-proof": "Bob Slocum may well turn out to be more representative of the seventies than any of us realize at present."

153 PERKINS, MICHAEL. "Fuckbooks—Pussies, Pawns, Pricks, and Pens," *Screw*, CCXCIX (November 25), 299.
Reviewed because of Slocum's concentration on sex, but reviewer found it boring and didn't finish the book.

154 PHILLIPS, JAMES A. Review of *Something Happened*. *Best Sellers*, XXXIV (November 15), 367-368.
Hopes for more books like *Something Happened* which "show us what man is like." Heller has "voiced the redundant, plaguing fears that beset modern man in near-perfect imitation of how they do it."

155 PLIMPTON, GEORGE. "How It Happened," *New York Times Book Review*, October 6, pp. 2, 3, 30.
Repeats interview with Heller in which he commented on the way his novels have begun, some ideas he has discarded, his strengths and weaknesses as a writer, his reasons for using Slocum as a person and his reactions to Slocum, the effect of others' opinions on his understanding of his work, and the extent to which his work is autobiographical. Substantially the same interview report appeared as:
"How Heller's 'Something Happened,'" Minneapolis *Tribune*, October 20, pp. 10D, 11D;
"Art of Fiction," *Paris Review*, XV (End of Winter), 126-147.
The latter reprint adds an introductory paragraph and some of Heller's notes.

156 PUTNEY, MICHAEL. "Slocum's Uptrodden, but a Downer," *National Observer*, week ending October 19, p. 27.
Emphasizes that Slocum "matters and so does this novel" but complains that it is repetitious and overwritten. Contrasts Slocum with Yossarian and Orr, who "acted," whereas "all Slocum can do is talk."

1974

157 RATCLIFFE, MICHAEL. "Dreaming Like Mad," London Times, October 28, p. 15.
Describes how Something Happened "complements Catch-22's controlled insanity of those earlier manoeuvres with desolate scenes of civilian life today," praising Heller's "fluency matched by few novelists in the office scenes," criticizes the bathetic "sententiousness and sentimentality" of the scenes in the Slocum home, and judges Heller's "territory" in the second novel unfortunate in that other American writers such as Updike, Cheever, and Vonnegut have written about it better.

*158 REILLY, CHARLES EDWARD. "The Ancient Roots of Modern Satiric Fiction: An Analysis of 'Petronian' and 'Apulcian' Elements in the Novels of John Barth, J. P. Donleavy, Joseph Heller, James Joyce, and Vladmir Nabokov." Ph.D. dissertation, University of Delaware. Cited and abstracted in Dissertation Abstracts International, XXXV (October), 2293-2294.

159 RICHTER, DAVID H. "The Achievement of Shape in the Twentieth-Century Fable: Joseph Heller's Catch-22." In his Fable's End: Completeness and Closure in Rhetorical Fiction. Chicago: University of Chicago. Pp. 5, 18-20, 74, 102-103, 135, 136-165, 167-171, 182, 200-201.
Contends that Heller purposely obscures his plot line in Catch-22 with "bits" of absurdity, employing a rhetorical structure instead of a plot to make the reader realize inductively and feel strongly his thesis, that the world is absurd and beneath that absurdity is the grim reality of death and dehumanization. Agreeing with Mellard (1968.B77) rather than MacDonald (1968.B75), Richter shows through illuminating studies of the soldier in white, Aarfy, Milo, Catch-22, and Snowden's death, how Heller's repetition of similar incidents are carefully ordered to make the reader see, then understand. Author also contends that these structured revelations, contrary to what Ramsey (1966.B21) and Lehan and Patch (1967.B18) had claimed, make the ending complete and appropriate, as Yossarian rejects physical and spiritual death and continues to strive toward an ideal.

160 RIFKIN, ROBERT. "The Great American Novel," Newsbeat, October 22, p. 7.
Classifies Something Happened as "The Great American Novel" because so many Americans will identify with Slocum and his problems.

1974

161   RILEY, MARY ANN. "Iowa Bookshelf," Creston (Iowa) News Advertiser, October 23, p. 9.
   Predicts "you won't be able to get him [Slocum in Something Happened] off your mind, [and] you won't be able to forget the society [ours] that made him the man he is."

162   ROBINSON, ROBERT. "Thirteen Years after 'Catch-22'--an Interview with Joseph Heller," The Listener, XCII (October 24), 550.
   In this transcript of an interview broadcast on BBC's "The Book Programme," Heller comments more than usual on his conception of Something Happened and particularly of Bob Slocum as "a typical human being in a typical situation...what has happened to him--and I think it's happened to me, and happens to many people as they approach middle-age--is that the good times are not as good as they used to be."

163   ROGERS, MICHAEL. "Books for Your Stocking--a Rolling Stone Guide for Holiday Reading," Rolling Stone, December 19, pp. 71-72.
   Recommends Something Happened: "the best depressing book of the decade and perhaps the century."

164   ROMANIUK, DON. "Nothing Really Happens on the Journey to Oblivion," Edmonton Journal, November 16, p. 80.
   Another review which calls Slocum "Everyman" in the absurdity of contemporary society. Similar to many other reviews except that it sees the son's death as the weakest part of the book.

165   ROSE, DON. "...And His New Novel Is Superb," Chicago Daily News Panorama, October 5-6, pp. 2-3.
   Believes Something Happened is not in any traditional way "a sequel to Catch-22" and will probably not "captivate broad sections of the public" as did the earlier work, yet it is a "superior" novel where he makes "even the far-out things work, such as naming people Black, White, Green, etc."
   This syndicated review also appeared in:
     The Chapel Hill Newspaper, October 6, p. 4C;
     Minneapolis Star, October 8, p. 2C;
     New Orleans Times-Picayune, November 7, Sec. 4, p. 10.

166   ROSENFELD, ARNOLD. "Fear Name of Game in Heller's New Novel," Dayton (Ohio) News, October 27. (**)
   Relates the anticipation with which Something Happened was awaited, then describes the novel as "rich with good writing" though "boring"--"a bona fide literary event."

1974

167   ROSS, JACKIE. "The Magic is Missing," Hartford Courant Views on Books, October 20, p. 7F.
    A negative notice. Regrets that Heller has lost his sense of humor and written an unoriginal, unsubtle and even "obscene" second novel.

168   RUDDEN, KEVIN. "Books--Something Happened," Fresh Fruit/The Brown Daily Herald, October 9, p. 2.
    Emphasizes the sexuality in suggesting that "we should read this novel, we should be terrified--and perhaps we can find our way out of the suffocation."

169   SACHS, MARTHA. "By Author of 'Catch-22,'" Worcester Sunday Telegram, October 20, p. 8E.
    Acknowledges "many valid observations" in Something Happened but says Slocum's description of a talk with his son, "one of our disorganized discussions about everything that might be on his mind," could apply to the novel as well.

170   SANDERS, LEONARD. "Joseph Heller's New Novel Depressing but Devastating," Fort Worth (Texas) Morning Star-Telegram, October 6. (**)
    Predicts that Something Happened will have a mixed reception because it is so depressing and seems in "the vein of a hundred other novels of recent years by Philip Roth, John Updike, John Cheever, John O'Hara, etc.," but this novel should not be ignored: "Heller's prose assumes the aura of pointillism gradually building tiny dots and brush strokes into a total effect illuminating a basic vision."

171   SCHAEFFER, SUSAN FROMBERG. "Heller's New 'Catch': the Man in the Gray-flannel Cubicle," Chicago Tribune Book World, October 13, Sec. 7, pp. 1, 5.
    Defines the "catch" of Something Happened: to be normal is to have control, but anyone who believes he controls the unpredictable world is insane. Slocum torments his family because they threaten his control and in the end takes control, "clearly insane." Reviewer lists some flaws in the novel but still calls it "a triumph."

172   SCHNEDLER, JACK. "Catch-22's Joe Heller: He's Back after 13 Years," Chicago Daily News Panorama, October 5-6, pp. 2, 3, 4.
    Another interview which describes Heller's lifestyle and writing habits. This one, however, contains his comments on ways of writing Something Happened which he rejected,

1974

       the reason he wrote it in the first person, and another novel he has considered writing about Dunbar. Reprinted in: Charlotte News, November 4, p. 15A; Houston Chronicle, October 27, p. 9.

173 SCHOLES, ROBERT. "Heller's World: Is It Ours?" Chronicle of Higher Education Review, IX (December 9), 9.
      Answers his title question affirmatively: Slocum is "one of us." Explains how this is true and praises Heller's "extraordinary" artistry but insists a man of "genius" like Heller has a responsibility to do more than "curse the darkness"; he must "break the circle of despair and quicken our lives with new vision."

174 SCHWARTZ, JOSEPH. "Portrait of Mr. 'Everyamerican,'" Milwaukee Journal, October 13, Sec. 5, p. 4.
      Warns that Something Happened is "a long, dull book" and questions whether dullness can work as a valid artistic strategy. Also is puzzled as to whom Heller thinks moral responsibility belongs, the individual or society.

175 SCHWARTZ, R. L. "Fiction--Something Happened," Minnesota Daily, October 21, p. 10.
      Theorizes about the circular motif in Catch-22 and Something Happened, concluding that while Yossarian "jumped out of the circle," Slocum does not; thus, "Heller's work has matured beyond myth, beyond childhood--and into truth."

176 SCOTT, JACK. "Heller's Weary Saga of a Neurotic Bore Too Much," Victoria Times, November 9. (**)
      Objects that Slocum is an "unbelievable jerk" and finds the novel "one-dimensional" though powerful in its effect on the reader.

177 SCOTT, MICHAEL MAXWELL. "Recent Fiction," London Daily Telegraph, October 24, p. 12.
      Recommends this "marvellously funny, sad, wise, and rewarding" book to "any grownup human who wishes he were more so."

178 SEAWRIGHT, SANDY. "'Something Happened' Full of Truth About Life," Nashville Banner, November 2. (**)
      Rates Heller's prose "brilliant" and urges reader to stay with the book for the "truths about life" it contains, even if it is terribly depressing.

1974

179 SHAPIRO, CHARLES. "A Tale of Failure the American Way," Louisville Courier-Journal and Times, October 27, p. E7.
Rates Something Happened a "brilliant novel for grown-ups," who will see a "good deal" of themselves in Slocum whose honesty goes from being a virtue to being a weapon.

180 SHARBUTT, EVE. Review of Something Happened, Roanoke Times, October 20, p. F4.
Calls Something Happened a book of "considerably more maturity than Catch-22" and comments briefly on Slocum's fears, isolation, and "inability to love or give of himself."
This Associated Press syndicated review also appeared in:
 Shreveport (Louisiana) Times, October 27, p. 6F;
 Dallas Times Herald, October 27, p. 6F;
 Tacoma (Washington) News-Tribune Sunday Magazine,
  November 10, p. 14;
 Allentown Sunday Call-Chronicle, November 10, p. F-6;
 Staten Island Advance, November 17 (**);
 Youngstown, Ohio Vindicator, November 17, p. B96;
 West Memphis (Arkansas) Times, November 21 (**);
 Tulsa Sunday World, November 24, p. 10;
 Baton Rouge (Louisiana) State Times, December 3 (**);
 Springfield (Massachusetts) Republican Leisure Time,
  January 12, p. 25.

181 ____. "Heller's Slow, But Many Find It Worth Wait," Columbia (South Carolina) State, October 20, p. 4E.
Briefly summarizes Something Happened but mainly reports on an interview at Knopf where Heller explained why he is such a slow writer and how he feels about teaching, his long marriage, and living in New York City.
The same Associated Press syndicated article appeared in:
 Richmond Times Dispatch, October 20, p. F5;
 Peninsula (California) Herald, October 20, p. 8C;
 San Jose Mercury, October 20, p. 10F;
 Youngstown Vindicator, October 20, p. B10;
 Corpus Christi Vindicator, October 20, p. 5C;
 Indianapolis News, October 26, p. 40;
 San Diego Union, October 27, p. E6;
 Bridgeport (Connecticut) Post, October 27, p. F4;
 Winston-Salem (North Carolina) Journal and Sentinel,
  October 27, p. C4;
 Baltimore News American, October 27 (**);
 Dayton News Leisure, October 27, p. 26;

Writings about Joseph Heller, 1961-1977

1974

>Jackson (Mississippi) Clarion Ledger-News, October 27, p. 6F;
>Louisville (Kentucky) Courier Journal and Times, October 27, p. E6.

182   SHARP, CHRISTOPHER. "Joseph Heller: Catching up on His Latest Novel," Women's Wear Daily, September 4, pp. 1, 44-45.
   Reports on interview with Heller where Heller discussed, among other things, his reasons for using a "tightly organized style in Something Happened." Most of the article however, describes Heller's lifestyle. Reprinted in Denver (Colorado) Rocky Mountain News Now, September 29, p. 31.

183   SHENKER, ISRAEL. "2nd Heller Book Due 13 Years after First," New York Times, February 18, p. 30.
   Report on meeting at which Heller and his editor, Robert Gottlieb, commented on the new novel and Heller's deliberate pace in writing. Reprinted as "Something--?" in Memphis Commercial Appeal, February 24, Sec. 6, p. 6.

184   SILVERMAN, WILLIAM A. "'Catch-22' Author Returns with a Hit," Detroit Sunday News, October 13, p. 2F.
   Summarizes, rather than judges, Something Happened, noting how it differs from Catch-22. Describes how Slocum proves, when his son is injured, that he is "tragically unable to cope."

185   SIMON, JEFF. "Thin, Reedy Jokes in Tundra of Pain," Buffalo Evening News, October 26, p. B-10.
   Recommends Something Happened strongly: "Most writers have examined the galling surfaces of middle-class angst but Heller has braved past the subcutaneous layers into the tender marrow."

186   SISSMAN, L. E. "Books--Twice-told Tales," New Yorker, L (November 25), 193.
   Rates Something Happened "a terrible mistake," not because it is badly written, but probably because Heller spent twelve years on it: "he indulges in overkill." Also objects that the "flatness, the blankness, and the non-humanity of these characters makes the book tractarian, and it is a tract for other times."

1974

187 SORENSEN, ROBERT. "In My Book," Minneapolis Tribune, October 20, p. 11D.
   Describes Slocum and his problems in detail, then concludes, "Something Happened may be the most depressing novel ever written. I couldn't put it down. Joseph Heller is a master."

188 SPARKS, EVE M. "Heller's Happening--Yossarian Gives Way to Bob Slocum in Biting Novel," Jackson (Tennessee) Sun, November 24, p. 11-B.
   Enthusiastically recommends Something Happened for its disturbing picture of Bob Slocum which will depress the reader who sees "bits" of himself. Judges it as written with more "control" than Catch-22.

189 SPEARMAN, WALTER. "Joseph Heller Moves from Black Comedy to a Dull, Gray Tragedy," Chapel Hill Newspaper, October 27, p. 4C.
   Claims the novel suffers from a similar mishap as that which befell Slocum's son: "So much unadulterated joylessness actually suffocates the reader." Also feels Heller abdicated responsibility for making life better than Slocum makes it. Reprinted in Greensboro, North Carolina Record, October 28. (**)

190 STANDIFORD, LES. "Novels into Film: Catch-22 as Watershed," Southern Humanities Review, VIII (Winter), 19-25.
   Mainly an article about Nichols' work in making the novel into a film where he "led viewers into the shocking revelation that they have been laughing at a funeral." Relates how Nichols "wisely" ignored the novel's exposition and put together instead "a tight progression of scenes which move Yossarian inexorably toward his enlightenment." Writer argues this is in keeping with the book's "illogical concept of time."

191 STARR, WILLIAM. "Heller Novel Sad, Powerfully Written," (Columbia, South Carolina) The State, October 20, p. 4E.
   A rave notice, which calls Something Happened "beautifully crafted...in its evocation of the fears and frustrations of this age...a literary classic."

192 STEGNER, WALLACE. "'Something Happened'...The Stacking Is Obvious," Rio Grande Sun, November 14, pp. 1-8.
   Feels Something Happened fails as a novel because Heller has "no capacity to make pictures," yet is a "curiously impressive performance" in its probing a "cliché-life" for the "ignored or forgotten truths that underlie all clichés."

1974

193   STELLA, CHARLES. "Heller's Catch '74: Nothing Happens," Cleveland (Ohio) Press Showtime, October 4, p. 23.
      Defends Heller's use of repetition and monotony as a device to show that "modest success has only made Slocum feel trapped and deflated." Doesn't rank Something Happened as high as Catch-22 but does call it "a painfully honest literary work."

194   SULLIVAN, SHIRLEY. "New Heller Novel Is No 'Catch-22,'" Savannah News-Press Sunday Magazine, November 10, p. 5F.
      Objects to the length and wordiness of Something Happened and refuses to accept Heller's evaluation of American life though admits it may be a valid picture of New York life. Suggests Heller leave Manhattan and observe the rest of the country.

195   SUSMAN, EDWARD. "'Something Happened' Joins 'Catch-22' as Heller Classic," Hartford Times, October 20, p. 56.
      Enthusiastic notice describes the deep involvement with Slocum that Heller creates and claims "Heller again has proven his ranking as one of the foremost literary figures of our generation and generations to follow."

196   SWEET, R. "Laughing Gas, Elephants, Comics, and Other Inspiring Holiday Gifts," Syracuse News Times, December 15, p. 9.
      Lists this with other books of 1974 because, though "dreary," it is "essential to an understanding of individual or collective failure."

197   SWINDELL, LARRY. "What Happened to Heller After 'Catch-22'? Something," Philadelphia Inquirer, September 22, pp. G1, G10.
      Relates conversations during a lunch with Heller and Joe Stein. Heller answers questions about reviews, his use of an editor, his current reading, Slocum, etc. This article also appeared in Cincinnati Enquirer, December 5, p. 43, in substantially the same form.

198   _____. Review of Something Happened, San Francisco Examiner, October 4, p. 28.
      Names Something Happened as "the novel of and for the '70s" and Slocum "less endearing than Yossarian but more complicated." Reviewer says no other novel he has read has plunged him into such depression: "This is its power."
      This Knight News service syndicated review also appeared in:
            Philadelphia Inquirer, October 6, p. 10K;
            Charlotte (North Carolina) Observer, October 13, p. 7B;

1974

Toledo (Ohio) Blade, October 13, p. G12; Florida, October 20, p. 35.

199 TERRY, MARSHALL. "Heller's Anti-Hero--You're No Good, His Mother Said," Dallas News, November 3, p. 13F.
Calls Something Happened "a brilliant story, a boring story" which makes us accept a "grisly kinship" with its "hollow and horrible" main character.

200 THOMAS, SIDNEY. "At Long Last, The Great One!" Atlanta Journal Constitution, October 13, Sec. C, p. 12.
Another delirious review that suggests Something Happened may be the Great American Novel.

201 THOMASES, MARTHA. "Reviews--Something Happened," Win (October 24), 19. (**)
Feels that through Slocum, who never realizes the absurdity of his position, Heller shows "everything that is wrong with our patriarchal, capitalist society."

202 THOMPSON, JOHN. "Caught Again," New York Review of Books, XXI (October 17), 24-26.
Believes Slocum will "not bear the burden of being everyman," but he does evoke an unpleasant personal recognition of the "elemental stink of life." Reviewer explains this point at length, making a number of comparisons to Catch-22.

203 THORNE, CREATH. "Joseph Heller: An Interview," The Chicago Literary Review (Book supplement to University of Chicago Maroon), December 3, p. 1.
Heller speaks in a leisurely way about his writing habits and his purpose. He also comments on Black Humor in general.

204 TIMNICK, LOIS. "The Joke Is on Heller's Hero," St. Louis Globe Democrat, October 5-6, p. 4B.
Reviewer wishes to praise Something Happened but finds it "overlong, intentionally repetitious, trite, and tedious." Describes the book's "dank and depressing view of life."

205 TRUEHEART, CHARLES. "Something--But What?" Greensboro (North Carolina), News, October 20, p. 3D.
Describes Heller's "knack" for painting unhappiness and absurdity with the "conviction of experience." Particularly praises the "exceptional" dialogue.

1974

206 TYNAN, KENNETH. "Heller's Happening," (London) Observer Weekend Review, October 27, p. 31.
    An enthusiastic and perceptive review which explains the way Heller forces us "into moments of self-recognition" and makes us almost admire Slocum's consciousness of the "unbridgeable gaps between what he ought to feel, what he claims to feel, and what he actually feels." Although reviewer judges Heller's attempt at "pure tragedy" in the climax a sentimental failure, he classifies Something Happened the "best second" novel of a writer in the postwar era.

207 VAN, ERIC. "Something Quite Stunning," Harvard Independent, October 17-23. (**)
    Urges readers to buy this "absolutely compelling" book.

208 VARGO, EDWARD P. Rainstorms and Fire: Ritual in the novels of John Updike. Port Washington, New York: Kennikat Press. P. 13.
    Sees hope and affirmation, like Updike's, in Heller's Catch-22.

209 VON HOFFMAN, NICHOLAS. "Human Suffering, Chinese Style," Washington Post, January 7, p. B1.
    In a review-article on Solzhenitsyn's The Gulag Archipelago, 1918-1956, von Hoffman comments on the concern in the latter half of twentieth century literature with the "destruction of human beings by their own governments." He says the "most frequently alluded to book title of our era is either '1984' or 'Catch-22.'"

210 VONNEGUT, KURT, JR. "Something Happened," New York Times Book Review, October 6, pp. 1-2.
    Collection of thoughts by Vonnegut which point up Heller's use of hackneyed themes in new ways (in this case resulting in a book "splendidly put together and hypnotic to read") and explain why Something Happened is one of the "unhappiest books ever written," why it speaks to and of Heller and Vonnegut's generation of American men, and why it will be hard for Americans to accept.

211 WALSH, ANNE C. "DeArzit Writes, Paints of DeVaca's Expedition," Phoenix Gazette, October 5, p. 21.
    Emphasizes Slocum's "feckless agreeability" and notes his "universality" in recommending Something Happened as "a comment on our times."

1975

212 WASSON, BEN. "Characters Lack Life," (Greenville, Mississippi) Delta Democrat-Times, October 20, p. 55.
    Reviewer complains that, though he loved Catch-22, Something Happened didn't "grab" him because the characters were all "great bores."

213 WEIXLMANN, JOSEPH. "A Bibliography of Joseph Heller's Catch-22," Bulletin of Bibliography, XXXI (January-March), 32-37.
    Provides extensive lists of writings about Catch-22. Not annotated. (All works in Weixlmann bibliography are included in this bibliography.)

214 WHITE, JON MANCHIP. "The Bookshelf," El Paso Herald-Post, November 23, Sec. A, p. 4.
    Finds "notable virtues" in the novel, though it is overly long. Admires Slocum, in spite of his faults, for struggling to "remain a responsible and loving human being."

*215 WILLIAMS, MELVIN G. "Catch-22: What the Movie Audiences Missed," Christianity and Literature, XXIII, 21-25.
    Cited in 1974 MLA International Bibliography of Books and Articles on the Modern Languages and Literature, p. 178.

216 WILLIAMSON, DAVID. "World Winding Down," Winnipeg Free Press New Leisure, November 23, p. 21.
    Assesses Something Happened as "mesmerizing...frightening" in its portrayal of the "absurdity and terrifying boredom of most people's everyday lives."

217 _____. "For Christmas Giving--And New Year's Reading," Winnipeg Free Press, December 20. (**)
    Counts Something Happened a book to be read even if it is "disturbing."

218 WOLFF, GEOFFREY. "Books--Ha, Ha," (New York) New Times, October 18, pp. 72, 74, 76.
    Compares Something Happened with Catch-22, explaining why newer book is "better made" in a style Heller learned from Faulkner.

1975 A BOOKS

1 PEEK, C. A. Catch-22 Notes. Lincoln, Nebraska: Cliff's Notes.
    Includes background on Heller's life, lists of characters in Catch-22, brief analysis of structure, plot summary, and

1975

>some critical commentary by chapters, a note on the traditions of the novel, sixteen review questions, and a selected bibliography (containing several errors).

1975 B SHORTER WRITINGS

1. ANON. Review of Something Happened, Colorado West, January 12, p. 13. (**)
   Short review and large picture of Heller.

2. ANON. "Notable Books of 1974," Booklist, LXXI (March 1), p. 670.
   Lists Something Happened (with one sentence description) as one of seven novels chosen by the Notable Books Council of 1974.

3. ANON. "The New Organization Man," Forbes, CXV (June 15), 57-58.
   Business magazine article explains how new management techniques would deal with Slocum's problems. Heller responds that he doesn't think they would do Slocum any good and explains why. He also comments on his business experiences and how they affected his writing.

4. ANON. "Fiction Reprints--Something Happened," Publishers' Weekly, CCVIII (July 14), 62.
   Summarizes August 19, 1974, review (1974.B8).

5. ANON. "Soft Covers, Hard Cores," Washington Post Book World, September 14, p. 2.
   Something Happened is included on list of recent quality paperbacks. Brief review and observations on original reviews are included.

6. BASILE, MARIA. "Heller Recites Word," (Fordham) Ram, February 12, p. 3.
   A brief report on Heller's reading from his works and a question and answer period which followed.

7. CERVENAK, TOM. "Study of a Pop Art Villain," Pacific Sun Books, Week of January 2-8, pp. 8, 10.
   Explains why he feels Something Happened is the "first pop art novel" and Slocum "a Polaroid snapshot of evil."

8. CURTIS, CHARLOTTE. "Cottage Cheese: It's a Very Quiet Issue," New York Times, August 6, p. 24.
   Mentions Heller as one of a group of celebrities who enjoy cottage cheese. Reports that his routine lunch in

1975

the Hamptons is cottage cheese and yogurt as a sort of sundae with fruit topping.

9   HENDRICKSON, PAUL. "Joe Heller: Something Happened," National Observer, April 19, p. 25.
    Recalls the great success of Catch-22 during the era of the Vietnam War (when the "title became an international synonym for any example of twisted logic") to make the case that Something Happened was bound to be a letdown. Although it has sold well, Hendrickson contends that the literary establishment has not been willing to admit that the book is boring. Includes Heller's comments from an interview on Something Happened six months after publication and on his idea for a new novel called Peddlers Cry.

10 HILL, WILLIAM B. "Something Happened," America, CXXXII (April 26), 320.
    Brief review notes fear, lack of communication, and meaninglessness in the world of the book which is "naggingly close to the universe of many modern men."

11 HOWARD, JANE. "Entertainments--Books," Mademoiselle, LXXX (January), 71.
    Sees Slocum as an "utterly amoral businessman, husband, philanderer, and father, [who]...wants to be a little boy when he grows up." Finds the novel "too long" but "full of chilling wit and apt passages."

12 KELLOGG, JEAN. "Something Happened," Christian Century, XCII (April 30), 448.
    Short review interesting mainly for its commentary on other reviews of Something Happened: "The Wall Street Journal predictably condemns it as untrue. Saturday Review accepts it, assesses it as 'solitary reading,' since most readers are, like Slocum, 'trapped in bureaucracy.'" See 1974.B3, B82.

13 LEONARD, JOHN. "Grow up, Oedipus!" New York Times Book Review, January 26, p. 31.
    Relates Richard Locke's theory that Something Happened and Bullet Park have the same theme, our inability to protect the ones we love. Goes on to list recent authors writing about children.

14 LOPEZ, EDDIE. "Upon Reaching Middle Age," Fresno Bee, January 5, p. K-5.
    Names Slocum "Everyman" and lists his problems, most notably that he "attempts to be funny but usually fails."

1975

  Feels we read about Slocum to discover things we may "not really want to know about ourselves."

15 LUCID, ROBERT F. "The Major Novelists View the American Businessman," New York Times, June 29, Sec. III, p. 14.
  Article traces the changing views of businessmen in the American novel. Notes that in Catch-22 Heller drew a sharp distinction between those who were simply involved in institutions because they had no choice and those who drew their vitality and identity from the institution. The latter group is seen as the destructive element.

16 McCONNELL, LEO. "Books To Read Soon," New England Business Journal, Issue No. 1 (January), 19.
  Judges Something Happened "the most brilliant book of the year."

17 MARCELL, DAVID W. "Something Happened," Deland (Florida) Sun News, January 11, p. 4.
  Fears American society may follow Heller's forecasts, as it did in Catch-22 and become as lacking in "loyalty, love, or principle" as Heller pictures it through the "representative" Slocum. Calls Something Happened an "important, if not a joyous book."

18 MERRILL, SAM. Playboy, XXII (June), 59-61, 64-66, 68, 70, 72-74, 76.
  An interview in which Heller explains autobiographical and anachronistic elements in Catch-22, his views on waiting, food, diversions, humor and death.

19 PENDLETON, ELSA. "Quest for Values," Progressive, XXXIX (May), 41.
  Tells of Slocum, his search for values, and the home and office scenes he pictures "of appalling familiarity." Finds Something Happened "an unbelievably fine book."

20 PHELAN, CHARLOTTE. "Heller--Cold and Calculating," Houston Post Spotlight, March 2, p. 16.
  A report of a "chat" with Heller, mostly about his process of writing.

24 PICKERING, WALTER J. K. "Follow-up to Heller's Catch-22: Is it the Epitaph for the '70s?" London Free Press, January 18, p. 23.
  Praises Heller's "hand on the pulse of an age" as he asks the "meaning of success" and the "price the individual and society must pay to maintain the corporate mechanism."

1975

22 PLUNG, DANIEL. "Something Happened," Idaho Statesman, February 16, p. 8D.
    Extols Heller's novel for attaining a more "sincere, defined perspective" than most other "alienation novels and for portraying Slocum's alienation as "symptomatic of the society," not just as one man's problems.

23 ROSENTHAL, MICHAEL. "America is Satirized by Heller, Barthelme," Hofstra University Chronicle, February 6, p. 16.
    Describes Something Happened as "a superbly crafted book about growing up frightened in America."

24 SALE, ROGER. "Fooling Around, and Serious Business," Hudson Review, XXVII (January), 623-635.
    Finds a great deal of the novel boring and the tone "too insistently sad and depressed" although the last fifty pages are "moving and searing and final" and, "however unsuccessful, Something Happened is serious business."

25 SHEED, WILFRID. "The Good Word: The Novel of Manners Lives," New York Times Book Review, February 2, p. 2.
    Considers Something Happened as a comedy of manners--or, at least, a "dead comedy of manners." Also speculates on the "disproportionate" criticism of the novel.

26 SHORTER, ERIC. "Plays in Performance," Drama, CXIX (Winter), 66-67.
    Objects that the idea of Heller's "semantic joke" is no longer true in We Bombed in New Haven, but finds this performance at the Leeds Playhouse "memorably funny."

27 SIEGEL, JACK. "Book Nook," Baltimore Jewish Times, January 3. (**)
    A review with a strongly Jewish point of view ("The people are supposed to be Christian but Heller isn't fooling anybody"), which finds the book has little of the real world in it (Slocum is "Portnoy without a psychiatrist") but is, nonetheless, "compelling."

28 SPACKS, PATRICIA MEYER. "New Novels: in the Dumps," Yale Review, LXIV (June), 583.
    Praises the "subtle sensibility, narrative skill, and capacity to contrive structure and evoke character" in Something Happened and several other contemporary novels but regrets the "shrunken range of human capacity and response" they tell of. More specifically, reviewer observes Slocum's "psychic maladies of our day" his use of parenthesis to qualify all affirmative statements, and his

1975

        individual sin as his own damnation. Questions whether the pathology of profound depression like Slocum's can be art.

29   SWANSON, WILLIAM. Review of Something Happened, Corporate Report, VI (January), 42.
        Relates several incidents and quotations from the book to show that Slocum's fear and "existential void" make him similar to "our real-life colleagues or...ourselves."

30   WALDRON, ANN. "Writing Technique Can Be Taught, Says Joseph Heller," Houston Chronicle, March 2. (**)
        Relates comments Heller made in a Houston interview. Although much of what he said has been reported in other earlier articles, he tells more about his various jobs and his children's writing than in other interviews.

31   WOODS, WILLIAM C. "'Kicking and Alive' in the Wake of Success," Washington Post, March 10, pp. B1, B5.
        Reports on a reading Heller gave at Johns Hopkins University and answers he gave to student questions about his writing and rewriting.

32   ZIFF, ANNE FINKELMAN. "Something Happened in Westport," Fairfield (Connecticut) Citizen News, March 5, p. 34.
        Reports that Heller's "casual" manner in reading his works bored and irritated his audience and that his efforts at wit were ineffective. Writer does praise Something Happened, insisting that Heller's "optimum forum for communication is the novel."

1976 A BOOKS - NONE

1976 B SHORTER WRITINGS

1   ANON. "U.S. Court Says School Boards Cannot Remove Library Books," New York Times, August 31, p. 24.
        Reports on legal ruling that Strongsville, Ohio, School Board could not remove Catch-22 and Cat's Cradle from school library shelves.

2   FRANK, MICHAEL. "Eros and Thanatos in Catch-22," Canadian Review of American Studies, VII (Spring), 77-87.
        Traces the theme in Catch-22 of "the enemy within," particularly through Milo's antics, to develop the thesis that Heller's point follows Freud's theory of thanatos and eros. Thus, arguing that the relationship between the American free enterprise system and the principle of death

"could hardly be more clearly...represented," seeing war as "merely another way of making money" and human life as a "commodity," author contends that Heller shows Yossarian and the old man in the brothel's glorification of sex as a positive assertion of the life force (eros) against the "thanatotic American morality" with its valuing of the Protestant Ethic and profit motive over the sacredness of human life. While admitting that this scheme oversimplifies the novel, Frank uses it to suggest several provocative readings--of Milo Minderbinder and Orr's names, of Yossarian's relationships with Nurse Duckett and Luciana, of Clevinger's trial, and of the chaplain's growth in understanding.

3   LEONARD, JOHN. "Why Is Kurt Vonnegut Smiling?" New York Times, March 25, p. 42.
    Reports Vonnegut and Heller confided at length their doubts about the propriety of even starting another book in "gloomy middle age"; nevertheless, Vonnegut wrote Slapstick and "word comes" that Heller has delivered to his publisher one third of a novel to be published in the fall of 1977.

4   MICHEL, PIERRE. "From Nightmare to Utopia: Some Aspects of Contemporary Fiction, Revue des Langues Vivantes Tijdschrift Voor Levende Talen, U.S. Bicentennial Issue, 225-234.
    Contends that the ending of Catch-22 is not a weakness but rather a return to the tradition of the dream or myth of the frontier, an idealistic vision of escape from the real world.

*5 PEARSON, CAROL. "Catch-22 and the Debasement of Language," CEA, XXXVIII, 30-35.
    Cited in unpublished files for 1976 MLA Bibliography.

6   ROCKWELL, JOHN. "Crawdaddy Party Mirrors Magazine," New York Times, June 9, p. 34.
    Heller listed as one of the "luminaries" to attend this party.

7   SWARDSON, H. R. "Sentimentality and the Academic Tradition," College English, XXXVII (April), 747-766.
    A thought-provoking exploration of the sentimentality of Catch-22. Considers whether Heller invites our unexamined emotional response with regard to "the enemy," those like Cathcart who use the system, the "wisdom" of the old man in the brothel, gory deaths, and Yossarian's

1976

feeling--or lack of feeling--for others. Suggests several reasons other critics may not have noticed the sentimentality, mainly the notion that the new absurdist genre demands different standards of judgment. Illustrates how reversals make serious philosophical questions trivial, suggests ways to counter students' absurdist relativism, suggests that "literature of the absurd" should be "literature alert to unreasonableness," contends that readers have misunderstood Camus and decided all reason is meaningless--thus, like Heller and Karl (1964.B10), they see no need to think about the hard moral questions such as what one's share is in the defeat of Nazi Germany. Concludes that Heller's whimsicality in Catch-22 is as sentimental and unworthy as MacKenzie's Man of Feeling.

*8 WHITMAN, ALDEN. "Something Always Happens on the Way to the Office: An Interview with Joseph Heller." In Matthew J. Bruccoli and C. E. Fraser Clark, eds. Pages. Detroit: Gale Research.
    Cited in unpublished files for 1976 MLA Bibliography.

1977 A BOOKS - NONE

1977 B SHORTER WRITINGS

1 KREBS, ALBIN. "Notes on People," New York Times, January 26, Sec. III, p. 2.
   Announcement of Heller's election to membership in American Academy and Institute of Arts and Letters.

2 NEVILLE, RICHARD. "Has the First Amendment Met Its Match?" New York Times, March 6, Sec. VI, p. 18.
   Heller listed as one of a group of writers who, in defense of Larry Flynt, signed an advertisement advocating closer looks at "restrictions of freedom of expression in America."

3 REUTER, MADALYNNE. "Heller Moves back to S & S for Third Novel," Publishers' Weekly, CCXI (February 7), 37.
   Relates that Heller will leave his editor, Robert Gottlieb of Knopf, and publish his next novel at Simon and Schuster. The deal has been rumored, but not confirmed, to be between $1.2 million and $2 million. Heller is quoted as saying the new novel, Good as Gold, to be published in 1978, deals with a Coney Island college professor who does a lot of intellectual hack writing and becomes the country's first Jewish Secretary of State.

1977

4   SEARLES, GEORGE J. "<u>Something Happened</u>: A New Direction for Joseph Heller," <u>Critique</u>, XVIII (Number 3), 74-81.

   Takes the position that Heller found a new, more sophisticated direction in <u>Something Happened</u>, turning from "hyperbole to implication," in limiting himself to the narration of the dull, unheroic Slocum. Author finds Slocum's psychological confusion more unsettling because it is presented as normal and, thus, inescapable. Slocum's experience has made him relinquish Yossarian's youthful idealism (even philandering has become unexciting). The two innocents, Slocum's two sons, are incapable of surviving alone in the world. Slocum attracts us because we identify with some of his complaints and faults and are lured by his promises to reveal the painful and grotesque. Nonetheless, the book is not immoral; it is clearly an indictment of Slocum's typical American life.

Index

Articles and books about Heller are indexed alphabetically by author, by title in the case of anonymous listings, and by the following general subjects: absurdity, Adventures of Huckleberry Finn (compared to Catch-22), Arfy, Ashmead (compared to Heller), Barth (compared to Heller), bibliographies, biographical information, black humor, Brautigan (compared to Heller), Bullet Park (compared to Something Happened), Catch-22 recommended, chaplain, characterization, deja vu, Derek, early writings, Ellison (compared to Heller), ending of Catch-22, "Eternal City," existentialism, film of Catch-22 (compared to book), Friedman (compared to Heller), Good Soldier Schweik (compared to Catch-22), Grass (compared to Heller), Heart of Darkness (compared to Catch-22), humor, Iliad (Catch-22 compared to), interviews with Heller, Jewish aspects of Heller's writing Kesey (in relation to Heller), logic, Milo in Catch-22, myth, old man, Orr, romance-parody, satire, sentimentality, technique in Catch-22, technique in Something Happened, technique in We Bombed in New Haven, time sequence, Vonnegut (compared to Heller), war novel, women, and Yossarian. The most significant entry numbers are underlined.

A

Abrahamsen, 1974.B1
Absurdity, 1964.B12, B17; 1965.B17, B19; 1966.B4, B21; 1968.B63, B65, B76; 1969.B19; 1970.B27, B49; 1971.B14, B15, B19, B28; 1973.A1, A2, B7, B12; 1974.A2, B105, B159; 1975.B7
Ackroyd, 1974.B2
"Action Novel...," 1961.B13
Adams, F., 1961.B1
Adams, L., 1970.B1

Adventures of Huckleberry Finn, compared to Catch-22, 1971.B8; 1974.A2
"Advertising...," 1962.B6
"After Acclaim...," 1963.B5
Aherne, 1961.B2
Aldridge, 1968.B1; 1972.B1; 1974.B3
Alexander, 1974.B4
Algren, 1961.B3; 1962.B1; 1974.B5
Alpert, 1970.B2
Alter, 1966.B1; 1969.B1
"American Fiction...," 1964.B3

Index

Angall, 1962.B2
"Another...," 1974.B15
Antone, 1974.B24
Archer, 1962.B63
Arfy in Catch-22, 1974.B159
Arnon, 1968.B23
Arthur, 1974.B25
Article on Catch-22, 1963.B1
Ashmead, John compared to Heller, 1962.B46
Avant, 1974.B26

B

B. L., 1969.B4
Baker, 1974.B27
Balliet, 1961.B23
Bandler, 1974.B28
Bannon, 1974.B29
Bannwarth, 1974.A1
Barkham, 1974.B30
Barksdale, 1966.B3
Barnard, 1970.B7
Barnes, C., 1967.B4; 1968.B24; 1972.B4
Barnes, H., 1970.B8
Barret, 1962.B24
Barrett, 1974.B31
Barth, 1972.B5
Barth, John, in relation to Heller, 1966.B24; 1972.B5, B10; 1973.B10; 1974.B79
Basile, 1975.B6
Bass, 1961.B24; 1962.B25; 1974.B32
Bauer, 1974.B33
Baumback, 1965.B4
Beam, 1974.B34
Beck, 1974.B35
Bedient, 1974.B36
Bell, 1974.B37
Benke, 1974.B38
Bennet, 1974.B39
Bergonzi, 1970.B9
Bernard, B., 1974.B40
Bernard, K., 1961.B25
Berthelson, 1974.B31
Berthoff, 1971.B2
"Best. Selling...," 1962.B17

Bibliographies, 1967.B18; 1971.A2; 1973.A1, A2; 1974.A2, B40, B213; 1975.A1
Bier, 1968.B25
Binni, 1974.B42
Biographical information, 1962.B20; 1964.B1; 1966.B2; 1967.B1, B18; 1968.B2; 1969.B14; 1970.B3; 1972.B2; 1973.A1; 1974.A2, B80, B172
Black, 1964.B2
Black humor, 1967.B25; 1968.B82; 1970.B49, B56, 1972.B10-B11, B18-B19; 1973.A1-A2, B16; 1974.A2, B105-B106, B116
"Black Humorists...," 1964.B2
Blackwood, 1974.B43
Blevins, 1970.B10
Blues, 1971.B3
Blythe, 1974.B44
Boardman, 1974.B45
Bolton, 1968.B26-B27
Boni, 1974.B46
"Book Awards...," 1962.B7
"Books & Authors," 1961.B10
Boroff, 1961.B26
Brackman, 1970.B11
Bradley, 1963.B11
Brady, C., 1974.B47
Brady, S., 1962.B26
Branche, 1961.B27
Braudy, 1968.B28
Brautigan, Richard, in relation to Heller, 1973.B8
Breslin, 1974.B48-B49
Brewer, 1967.B5
"Brief...," 1974.B19
Broberg, 1968.B29
Brown, 1968.B30
Brustein, 1961.B28; 1972.B6
Bryant, D., 1961.B29
Bryant, J., 1970.B12
Bryden, 1971.B4
Buckeye, 1967.B6
Bullet Park compared to Something Happened, 1975.B13
Bunce, 1968.B31
Bunke, 1974.B50
Burgess, 1965.B5; 1967.B7

Index

Burhans, 1973.B2
Buss, 1974.B51
Butler, 1961.B30
Byrd, 1968.B32

C

Cady, 1974.B52
Calder-Marshall, 1961.B31
Camara, 1973.B3
Canby, 1970.B13-B14
Capone, 1970.B15
Carlson, 1961.B32
Castelli, 1970.B16
"Catchall...," 1967.B3
"Catch-22," 1963.B4
Catch-22 Recommended, 1961.B19-B21
Cecchini, 1974.B53
Cervenak, 1975.B7
Chanan, 1968.B33
Chaplain in Catch-22, 1970.B12; 1973.A1-A2; 1974.A2; 1975.B2
Chapman, 1968.B34
Characterization in Catch-22, 1962.B49; 1966.B20; 1971.B25; 1973.A1-A2; 1974.A2, B76
Charyn, 1969.B5
Chessler, 1974.B54
Cheuse, 1963.B12
Childs, 1974.B55
"Chordorov...," 1962.B21
Christ, 1970.B17
"Christmas Books...," 1974.B21
"Christmas Classified," 1961.B15
Clancy, 1971.B5
Clarity, 1972.B7
Clark, 1974.B56
Claypool, 1974.B57
Clemons, 1974.B58-B59
Clurman, 1968.B35
Coffey, 1968.B36
Cohen, 1968.B37
Colby, 1968.B38
Collingwood, 1961.B33
Collins, 1974.B60
Colmer, 1966.B4
Conarroe, 1974.B61-B62
Cooke, 1968.B39
Cooper, 1974.B63
Cooperman, 1967.B8

"The Critics...," 1974.B14
Crittenden, 1974.B64
Cross, 1974.B65
"Currents," 1962.B15
"Currents-Yossarian...," 1963.B8
Curtis, 1975.B8
Cuskilly, 1970.B18

D

D. H. C., 1961.B34
Dannenburg, 1970.B19
"David...," 1962.B18
Davis, D., 1965.B6; 1967.B9
Davis, R., 1969.B6
Day, 1963.B13
Deja vu in Catch-22, 1971.B3; 1973.A1-A2; 1974.A2
DeMott, 1965.B7-B8; 1969.B7; 1974.B66
Denniston, 1965.B9
Derek in Something Happened, 1974.B53, B102
Desruisseaux, 1974.B67
Detweiler, 1964.B3
Diesel, 1968.B40
Diggins, 1966.B5
Dinhofer, 1964.B4
"The Dispatch...," 1961.B14
Doar, 1974.B68
Dobbs, 1974.B69
Dodd, 1966.B6
Dolbier, 1961.B35-B36
Donahue, 1964.B5
Doskow, 1967.B10
Dougherty, 1967.B11
Dowie, 1972.B8
Driver, 1968.B41
Drucker, 1971.B6
Druian, 1974.B70
Duhamel, 1974.B71
Duncan, 1968.B42

E

Early Writings, 1967.B18; 1973.A1; 1974.A2, B139
Earney, 1968.B43
Ellison, Ralph, in relation to Heller, 1972.B16
Enck, 1965.B10

145

Index

Ending of Catch-22, 1962.B49;
    1963.B25; 1966.B20; 1967.B23;
    1970.B12, B36-B37, B59;
    1971.B3, B14, B19, B24, B34;
    1973.A1-A2, B14; 1974.A2,
    B159; 1975.B4
Ephron, 1967.B12
Epstein, 1974.B72
"Eternal City" in Catch-22,
    1967.B10; 1973.A1; 1974.B105
Evans, 1968.B44
Evett, 1974.B73
Ewing, 1974.B74
Excerpts of..., 1969.B2
Existentialism in Catch-22,
    1970.B54; 1971.B19; 1973.A1-
    A2; 1974.A2

F

Feldman, 1968.B45; 1969.B8
"Fiction...," 1962.B11
"Fiction Reprints," 1975.B4
Fidler, 1961.B37
Fiedler, 1964.B6; 1965.B11;
    1966.B7; 1971.B7
"Fiery...," 1962.B9
Film of Catch-22, compared to
    book, 1970.B2, B7-B8, B13-
    B15, B17-B20, B23-B24, B31-
    B34, B38, B40-B43, B45-B48,
    B50, B53, B59; 1971.B5, B22;
    1973.A1; 1974.B190, B215
"Financial...," 1968.B6
Findsen, 1968.B46; 1974.B75
Finkel, 1974.B76
Finocchiaro, 1968.B47
"The First...," 1974.B22
Fischer, 1969.B9
Fitzgerald, 1974.B77
"534...," 1968.B7
Flagler, 1970.B20
Forsyth, 1974.B78
Fort, 1974.B79
Frank, 1971.A1; 1975.B2
"The Frantic...," 1970.B5
Fremont-Smith, 1974.B80-B81
French, M., 1968.B48
French, W., 1966.B8
Friedman, B., 1965.B12-B13

Friedman, Bruce Jay, in relation
    to Heller, 1972.B18
Friedman, R., 1968.B49
Frohock, 1969.B10
Frost, 1971.B8
"Full...," 1974.B20
Fuller, 1974.B82
Funke, 1968.B50
Fussell, 1973.B4

G

Galloway, 1965.B14; 1970.B21
Garrett, 1962.B27
Gascoigne, 1962.B28
Gates, 1974.B83
Gaukroger, 1970.B22
Gianakaris, 1969.B11
Gilbert, 1961.B38; 1962.B29
Glanville, 1966.B9
Gleason, 1962.B30; 1974.B84-B85
Glendinning, 1974.B86
Golay, 1974.B87
Gold, D., 1969.B12
Gonzales, 1971.B9
Good Soldier Schweik, compared to
    Catch-22, 1968.B99
"Good Soldier Yossarian,"
    1961.B12
Goodspeed, 1961.B39
Gordon, 1967.B13
Gorner, 1974.B88
Gottfried, 1968.B51
Gow, 1970.B23
Grass, Günter, in relation to
    Heller, 1967.B26; 1974.B79
Green, 1972.B9
Greenberg, 1966.B10; 1970.B24
Greene, A., 1962.B31
Greene, G., 1966.B11
Greenfeld, 1968.B52
Greenwood, 1961.B40
Greiner, 1971.B10; 1973.B5
Gross, B., 1970.B25
Gross, T., 1971.B11
Grossman, 1974.B89
Grumbach, 1974.B90
Guerard, 1963.B14; 1967.B14
Guernsey, 1969.B13
Gussow, 1971.B12
Guttmann, 1971.B13

Index

H

H. P. E., 1974.B91
Halio, 1970.B26
Hallman, 1974.B92
Halsey, 1974.B93
Hand, 1974.B94
Hardy, 1962.B32
Harmon, 1973.B6
Harrell, 1974.B94
Harris, C., 1970.B27; 1971.B14
Harris, L., 1968.B53
Hart, 1965.B15
Harte, 1969.B14
Haskill, 1974.B96
Hassan, 1962.B33-B34; 1963.B15; 1964.B7-B8; 1966.B12; 1973.B7
Hatch, 1968.B54
Hauck, 1971.B15
Havelin, 1974.B97
Havemann, 1971.B16
Hawkes, 1966.B13
Hearron, 1973.B7
Heart of Darkness compared to Catch-22, 1971.B8
"The Heller Cult," 1962.B19
"Heller in...," 1974.B18
"Heller, Joseph," 1974.B7
"Heller redux," 1974.B6
Hendrickson, 1975.B9
Henry, 1966.B14
Herridge, 1968.B55
Hewes, 1968.B56
Hicks, 1961.B41; 1970.B28
Hill, G., 1961.B42
Hill, H., 1968.B57
Hill, W., 1975.B10
Hills, 1974.B98
Hilton, 1968.B58
Hipp, 1968.B59-B60
Hirsch, 1967.B15
Hobe, 1968.B61
Hoffman, F., 1963.B16; 1964.B9
Hogan, 1962.B35; 1968.B62
Holliday, 1974.B99
Holloway, 1962.B36
Holzschlag, 1970.B29
Honicker, 1961.B43
"Honors...," 1963.B9
Hood, 1969.B15
Horan, 1962.B37

Houston, G., 1974.B100
Houston, L., 1974.B101
Howard, 1975.B11
Howat, 1974.B102
Howe, 1974.B103
Hughes, 1973.B7
Humor in Catch-22, 1964.B8; 1970.B53; 1973.A1-A2, B13; 1974.A2, B93
"Humor wins...," 1961.B17
Hunt, 1968.B63
Hyman, A., 1974.B104
Hyman, S., 1963.B17; 1966.B15
Hynes, 1961.B44

I

Iliad, Catch-22 compared to, 1962.B44; 1970.B37; 1973.A1
"Indiscriminate...," 1968.B19
Interviews with Heller, 1962.B19, B40, B66; 1963.B10; 1967.B19; 1968.B28, B88, B90, B94-B95; 1969.B12, B16; 1970.B7; 1971.A2, B9, B32; 1972.B20; 1973.A1-A2; 1974.B10, B25, B29, B60, B88, B100, B102, B111, B147, B155, B162, B172, B181-B183, B197, B203; 1975.B9, B18, B20, B30-B31; 1976.B8
"It's...," 1964.B1

J

Janeway, 1969.B16
Janoff, 1972.B10-B11; 1974.B105-B106
Jefferys, 1968.B64
Jewett, 1974.B107
Jewish aspects of Heller's writing, 1965.B16; 1966.B9, B16; 1969.B24; 1974.A2; 1975.A27
Johnson, 1961.B45
Jones, 1970.B30
"Joseph Heller," 1966.B2; 1967.B1; 1968.B2; 1970.B3; 1972.B2
"Joseph Heller: 13 Years...," 1974.B10

Index

K

K. J. A., 1974.B108
Kagis, 1974.B109
Kalter, 1970.B31
Karl, 1964.B10
Kauffmann, 1970.B32
Kaufman, 1971.B17
Kazin, 1962.B38; 1966.B16; 1971.B18
Kellogg, 1975.B12
Kempton, 1961.B46; 1962.B39
Kennard, 1968.B65; 1971.B19
Kennedy, 1974.B110
Keough, 1974.B111
Kerr, 1968.B66
Kesey, Ken, in relation to Heller, 1964.B17; 1972.B16, B21
Kiley, Frederick S., 1963.B18
Kiley, McDonald, 1973.A1
Kilgo, 1971.B20
King, 1974.B112
Kirsch, 1974.B113
Kiser, 1974.B114
Klaw, 1961.B47
Klein, M., 1969.B17
Klein, Y., 1969.B18
Klinkowitz, Jerome, 1974.B115
Klinkowitz, Joseph, 1974.B116
Kochanck, 1972.B12
Kort, 1972.B13
Kostelanetz, 1965.B16, B17-B19; 1966.B17; 1967.B16; 1968.B67; 1969.B19
Krassner, 1962.B40
Krebs, 1977.B1
Kroll, 1967.B17; 1968.B68
Kuhnel, 1973.B10

L

Lardner, 1970.B33
Lasson, 1972.B14; 1974.B117
Lawless, 1974.B118
LeClair, 1974.B119
Lehan, 1967.B18; 1973.B11
Lehman-Haupt, 1974.B120
Leonard, 1975.B13; 1976.B3
Leslie, 1962.B41
Lester, 1967.B19
"Letters...," 1963.B7
Levine, A., 1970.B34
Levine, P., 1967.B20; 1968.B69
Lewis, R. W. B., 1965.B20; 1968.B70
Lewis, T., 1968.B71
Lhamon, 1974.B121
"Life Guide," 1961.B7
Littlejohn, 1963.B19
Lloyd, 1974.B122
Logic in Catch-22, 1970.B57; 1973.A1-A2; 1974.A2
Lopez, 1975.B14
Loukides, 1968.B72; 1973.B12
Lucid, 1975.B15
Ludlow, 1961.B48
"Lumet...," 1969.B3;
"Lunacracy," 1961.B9
Lupton, 1974.B123
Luttrell, 1969.A1
Lutwack, 1971.B21
Lyon, 1968.B73
Lyons, 1968.B74

M

McConnell, 1975.B16
McDonald, D., 1967.B21
MacDonald, J., 1968.B75
MacDonald, W., 1973.B13-B14
McHugh, 1974.B124
McLaughlin, 1961.B49
McNamara, 1968.B76
Maddocks, 1974.B125
Mailer, 1963.B20; 1964.B11; 1966.B18
Malin, 1974.B126
Manning, 1962.B42; 1974.B127, B128
Mano, 1974.B129
Marcell, 1975.B17
Marcus, A., 1974.B130
Marcus, F., 1971.B22
Martin, 1962.B43
Mayer, 1974.B131
Mellard, 1968.B77
Mellors, 1974.B132
"Men Who...," 1962.B12
Merrill, 1975.B18
Michel, 1976.B4
Michelfelder, 1974.B133
Middleton, 1974.B134
Miller, E., 1970.B35
Miller, J., 1967.B22
Miller, W., 1970.B36

Index

Miller, W. & Nelson, 1975.A2
Millhouser, 1974.B135
Milne, 1970.B37
Milo in Catch-22, 1975.B2
Mitchell, 1962.B44
Mitgang, 1968.B78
"Mixed...," 1968.B15
Mizener, 1972.B15
Monk, 1967.B23
Moody, 1974.B136
Moore, H., 1961.B50; 1964.B10-B11
Morgenstern, 1970.B38
Morrissey, 1962.B45
Morten, 1974.B137
Murray, 1961.B51; 1968.B79
Musson, 1961.B52; 1968.B80; 1974.B138
Muste, 1962.B46; 1969.B20
Myth in Catch-22, 1967.B10; 1973.A1-A2, B20; 1974.A2

N

Nabokov, Vladimir, in relation to Heller, 1974.B79
Nagel, 1974.A2, B139-B140
Natansohn, 1974.B141
Nathan, 1974.B142
Nelson, G., 1972.B16
Nelson, T., 1971.B23-B24
Neville, 1977.B2
New, 1966.B19
"New Arrivals," 1968.B20
"New Heller Book," 1974.B9
"New Heller Novel," 1974.B12
"New Novels...," 1962.B10
"New Organization...," 1975.B3
"The New Veers," 1963.B3
Newberry, 1963.B21
Newman, 1968.B81
Newquist, 1961.B53; 1974.B143
Nordell, 1967.B24; 1974.B144
Norman, 1974.B145
North, 1974.B146
"Notable...," 1975.B2
Note on Catch-22, 1961.B16
Note on Catch-22 Sales, 1973.B1
Note on Heller, 1962.B5
Note on We Bombed in New Haven, 1968.B14, B21
"Notes...," 1962.B3

Nugent, 1974.B147
Numasawa, 1968.B82
Nye, 1974.B148

O

O'Brien, 1962.B47
Ogelsby, 1968.B83
Old man in Catch-22, 1974.A2; 1975.B2
Olderman, 1969.B21; 1972.B17
Oliver, 1968.B84
Olmstead, 1970.B39
Olson, 1974.B149
Orr, 1971.B25
Orr in Catch-22, 1969.B27; 1970.B24; 1973.A1-A2; 1974.A2; 1975.B2
"Outstanding...," 1961.B22

P

"PW Forecasts," 1974.B8
Pace, 1974.B150
Parker, 1974.B151
Parrill, 1974.B152
Pascu, 1971.B26
Paul, 1970.B40
Pearce, 1971.B27
Pearson, 1976.B5
Peek, 1975.A1
Pendleton, 1975.B19
Perkin, 1962.B48
Perkins, 1974.B153
Phelan, 1975.B20
Phillips, J., 1974.B154
Phillips, M., 1970.B41
Pickering, 1975.B21
Pine, 1961.B54
Pinsker, 1964.B12; 1972.B18
"Playboy...," 1974.B17
Plimpton, 1974.B155
Plung, 1975.B22
Podhoretz, 1962.B49; 1966.B20
Posten, 1961.B55
Prescott, 1961.B56
Price, J., 1972.B19
Price, R. G. G., 1962.B50
Prideaux, 1968.B85
Probst, 1968.B86
Protherough, 1971.B28

Index

Prusak, 1962.B51
Putney, 1974.B156
"PW Forecasts," 1974.B8

Q

Quinn, 1968.B87

R

R. C., 1963.B22
Raidy, 1968.B88
Ramsey, 1966.B21
Ratcliffe, 1974.B157
Raymond, 1968.B89
Reilly, 1974.B158
"Releases...," 1968.B13
Reuter, 1977.B3
"A Review: Catch-22," 1963.B2
Review of Book We Bombed in New Haven, 1968.B4-B5, B11, B16
Review of Catch-22, 1961.B4-B6, B11; 1962.B4, B14, B16
Review of Something Happened, 1974.B13, B23; 1975.B1
Rice, 1967.B25
Richardson, 1969.B22
Richter, 1974.B159
Rifkin, 1974.B160
Riley, 1974.B161
Ritter, 1967.B26
"Robards...," 1968.B3
Robin, 1970.B42
Robinson, D., 1971.B29
Robinson, R., 1974.B162
Rockwell, 1976.B6
Rogers, 1974.B163
Romance-parody, Catch-22 as, 1965.B9; 1973.A1; 1974.A2
Romaniuk, 1974.B164
Rose, 1974.B165
Rosenfeld, 1961.B57; 1974.B166
Rosenthal, 1975.B23
Ross, J., 1974.B167
Ross, T. J., 1963.B23
Rothbardt, 1968.B90
Rouby, 1962.B52
Rowe, 1961.B58
Rubin, 1966.B22; 1967.B27; 1973.B6, B22
Rudden, 1974.B168

Rumley, 1961.B59
Rummo, 1973.B15
Ryan, 1969.B23

S

Sachs, 1974.B169
Sainer, 1962.B53
Sale, Richard, 1972.B20
Sale, Roger, 1962.B54; 1975.B24
Sales, Grover, 1970.B43
Sanders, 1974.B170
Sanger, 1967.B28
Saporta, 1970.B44
Sarris, 1970.B45
Satire, Catch-22 as, 1969.B20, B23; 1970.B36; 1971.B28; 1973.A1-A2; 1974.A2, B140, B158
Scammell, 1963.B24
Scarborough, 1962.B55
Schaab, 1962.B56
Schaeffer, 1974.B171
"Scheduled...," 1968.B17
Schickel, 1970.B46
Schjeldahl, 1970.B47
Schlesinger, 1970.B48
Schnedler, 1974.B172
Scholes, 1966.B23; 1967.B29; 1971.B30; 1974.B173
Schopf, 1972.B21
Schroth, 1965.B21
Schulz, 1968.B91; 1969.B24; 1973.B16
Schwartz, J., 1974.B174
Schwartz, R., 1974.B175
Schweitz, 1961.B60
Scott, J., 1974.B176
Scott, N., 1970.B49; 1971.B31
Scotto, 1973.A2
Screen Listings, 1970.B4
Searles, 1977.B4
Seawright, 1974.B178
Segal, 1969.B25
Seiden, 1961.B61
Seligson, 1970.B50
"Sell...," 1968.B12
Sentimentality in Catch-22, 1963.B12; 1970.B47; 1971.B3; 1975.B7
"Set...," 1972.B3

150

Index

Shaber, 1970.B51
Shapiro, C., 1974.B179
Shapiro, J., 1971.B32
Shapiro, S., 1968.B92
Shapiro, W., 1968.B93
Sharbutt, 1974.B180-B181
Share, 1962.B57
Sharma, 1972.B22
Sharp, 1974.B182
Sheed, 1975.B25
Shenker, 1968.B94-B95; 1970.B52; 1974.B183
Sherman, 1968.B96
Shirzad, 1973.B17
Shorter, 1975.B26
Siegel, 1975.B27
Silverman, 1974.B184
Simmons, D., 1970.B53
Simmons, L., 1970.B54
Simon, Jeff, 1974.B185
Simon, John, 1968.B97; 1970.B55; 1971.B33
Sissman, 1974.B186
"Sked...," 1968.B10
Skerett, 1967.B30
Sklar, 1967.B31
Slater, 1961.B62
Smith, Marcus, 1964.B13
Smith, Miles, 1961.B63
Sniderman, 1973.B18
Snyder, 1962.B58
"So They Say," 1963.B10
Social Criticism, Catch-22 as, 1968.B107; 1970.B36, B39; 1971.B8; 1973.A1-A2; 1974.A2
"Soft...," 1975.B5
Sokolov, 1969.B26
Solomon, E., 1969.B27
Solomon, J., 1967.B32
"Some Are...," 1970.B6
Sorensen, 1974.B187
Sources for Catch-22, 1966.B14
Spacks, 1975.B28
Sparks, 1974.B188
Spearman, 1974.B189
Spiegel, 1972.B23
Standiford, 1974.B190
Stark, 1968.A1
Starnes, 1962.B59
Starr, 1974.B191
Steele, 1968.B98

Stegner, 1974.B192
Stella, 1974.B193
Stern, J. P., 1968.B99
Stern, R., 1961.B64
"Stock...," 1967.B2
Stowell, 1970.B56
Stubbs, 1966.B24
"Studio...," 1962.B22
Styron, compared to Heller, 1969.A1
Sullivan, 1974.B194
Summary of Reviews of Catch-22, 1962.B8
Summary of Reviews of We Bombed in New Haven, 1968.B18
Susman, 1974.B195
"Sustaining...," 1963.B5
Sutton, 1968.B100
Swanson, 1975.B29
Swardson, 1976.B7
Sweet, 1974.B196
Swindell, 1974.B197-B198
Sylvester, 1973.B19

T

Tanner, 1966.B25; 1971.B34
Taubman, 1962.B60
Technique in Catch-22, 1967.B13, B23, B32; 1968.A1, B75; 1969.B20; 1970.B49, B53; 1971.A1, B3, B14, B16, B19, B24, B28, B34; 1973.A1-A2, B2; 1974.A2, B93, B105, B159; 1975.A1
Technique in Something Happened, 1977.B4
Technique in We Bombed in New Haven, 1968.B66, B73, B84-B85, B93; 1969.B13, B20
Terkel, 1961.B65
Terry, 1974.B199
"The Critics...," 1974.B14
"The First...," 1974.B22
"The Heller Cult," 1962.B19
"The New...," 1963.B3
"They've...," 1961.B18
"This Week," 1968.B9
"This Week's Arrivals," 1974.B11
"This Week's Books," 1974.B16
Thomas, S., 1974.B200

Index

Thomas, W. K., 1970.B57; 1973.B20
Thomases, 1974.B201
Thompson, H., 1964.B14
Thompson, J., 1961.B66; 1974.B202
Thorne, 1974.B203
Thorpe, 1968.B101
"Three...," 1971.B1
Timchenko, 1972.B24
Time Sequence in Catch-22,
    1963.B25; 1966.B4, B21;
    1967.B32; 1970.B22; 1971.B14;
    1973.A1-A2, B2; 1974.A2, B159
Timnick, 1974.B204
Toynbee, 1962.B61
Trachtenberg, 1964.B15
Truehart, 1974.B205
Turner, 1961.B67
Tynan, 1961.B68; 1974.B206

U

"U. S. Court...," 1975.B1

V

Valancia, 1968.B102
Van, 1974.B207
Vargo, 1974.B208
Vincent, 1962.B62
von Hoffman, 1974.B209
Vonnegut, 1974.B210
Vonnegut, Kurt, in relation to
    Heller, 1973.B8, B10
Vos, 1967.B33
Voss, 1962.B63

W

W. H. R., 1961.B69
W. T. C., 1962.B64
Wade, 1968.B103
Wain, 1963.B25
Walcutt, 1966.B26
Waldmeir, 1964.B16; 1969.B28-B29
Waldron, A., 1975.B30
Waldron, R., 1968.B104
Walsh, 1974.B211
Walters, 1962.B65
"War Is...," 1961.B8
"War Made...," 1968.B8

War Novel, Catch-22 as, 1961.B8;
    1962.B46; 1964.B9; 1966.B7;
    1967.B7-B8, B28; 1968.B44,
    B104; 1969.B17-B18, B27-B28;
    1970.B30, B36, B39; 1971.B8,
    B18, B20, B27; 1973.A1-A2,
    B3; 1974.B77
Warner, 1973.B21
Wasson, 1974.B212
Watts, 1968.B105-B106
Way, 1968.B107
"We Bombed...," 1968.B22
Weales, 1968.B108; 1969.B30
Weatherby, 1962.B66
Weber, 1973.B22
Weinberg, 1970.B58
Weixlmann, 1974.B213
West, 1963.B26
"What...," 1962.B13
Whitbread, 1966.B27
White, 1974.B214
Whitman, 1976.B8
Willers, 1968.B109
Williams, 1974.B215
Williamson, 1974.B216-B217
Willis, 1969.B31; 1971.B35
Wincelberg, 1962.B67; 1964.B17
Winchell, 1968.B110
Witkin, 1967.B34
Wolff, 1968.B111; 1974.B218
Women in Catch-22, 1970.B29
Woodbury, 1962.B68
Woods, 1975.B31
"Writers...," 1962.B20
Wyatt, 1961.B70
Wylder, 1969.B32
Wyndham, 1962.B69

Y

Yates, 1965.B22; 1966.B28
Yorick, 1962.B70
Yossarian, 1964.B10, B12;
    1966.B21; 1970.B16, B37, B58;
    1971.B34; 1973.A1-A2, B13,
    B18; 1974.A2

Z

Zall, 1970.B59
Ziff, 1975.B32
Zolotow, 1968.B112